# God's Family, God's Earth

## Christian Ecological Ethics of Ubuntu

Kapya J. Kaoma

Foreword
by
Dr. Joyce Banda
The President of the Republic of Malawi

Afterword
by
Professor Marthinus L. Daneel

Copyright 2013 Kapya J. Kaoma

All rights reserved. No part of this publication may be reproduced, stored in a retrieval system or transmitted in any form or by any means, electronic, mechanical, photocopying, recording or otherwise, without prior permission from the publishers.

Published by
Kachere Series
P.O. Box 1037, Zomba, Malawi
ISBN: 978-99908-0-262-7

The Kachere Series is represented outside Africa by
African Books Collective, Oxford (orders@africanbookscollective.com)
Michigan State University Press, East Lansing (msupress@msu.edu)

Layout & Cover Design: Josephine Kawejere
Graphic Design: Patrick Lichakala

Printed in Malawi by Assemblies of God Press, P.O. Box 4749, Limbe

# God's Family, God's Earth

## Christian Ecological Ethics of Ubuntu

By

Kapya J. Kaoma

Kachere Books no. 65

Kachere Series
Zomba
2013

Kachere Series
P.O. Box 1037, Zomba, Malawi
Kachere@globemw.net
http://www.kachereseries.org.

This book is part of the Kachere Series, a range of books on religion, culture and society from Malawi. Other related Kachere titles so far are:

John Lloyd Lwanda, *Kamuzu Banda of Malawi: A Study in Promise, Power and Legacy, Malawi under Dr. Hastings Kamuzu Banda (1961-1994)*
Rhodian G. Munyenyembe, *Christianity and Socio-Cultural Issues: The Charismatic Movement and Contextualization in Malawi*
Andrew C. Ross, *Colonialism to Cabinet Crisis: A Political History of Malawi*
James Tengatenga, *The UMCA in Malawi: A History of the Anglican Church*
Isaac C. Lamba, *Contradictions in Post-War Education Policy Formulation and Application in Colonial Malawi 1945-1961: A History Study of the Dynamics of Colonial Survival*
Okoma-atani S.L. Aipira, *Malawi Takes Off: Priorities in Action*
Martin Ott, & Fidelis Kanyongoro, *Democracy in Progress*
Sheikh Imuran Shareef Mahomed, *Majlis Al-Shŭrá Consultative Assembly: Past and Present Application of the Principle of shûrâ in Islamic Governance*
Colin Baker, *Chipembere: The Missing Years*
John M.K.Mtitima, *Powers of Culture: Dilemma of the Black Race*

The Kachere Series is the publication arm of the Department of Theology and Religious Studies of the University of Malawi

**Series Editors**: Dr. F. Nsengiyumva; Dr. I. S. Mohammad; Dr. J. Thipa; Dr. G.M. Kayange; H. Mvula; M. Mbewe

To
My Father
Misheck Kaoma
*The Chief of the Mbeba (Rat) Royal Clan of Lubebe*
Who inspired my love for books,
and
**My lovely Sisters and Cousins**
Grace, Sylvia, Roydah, Dorothy, Gladys, Maria, Joyce,
Mrs. Annes Zvaraya and Mr. Stanley Zvaraya

*You all left without reading this book*
*You are gravely missed*
*You left this world*
*But not our Ancestors' hands*

# TABLE OF CONTENTS

| | |
|---|---|
| Preface | viii |
| Foreword | xi |
| **Chapter One** | **1** |

| | |
|---|---|
| The Plight of Earth: How We Are Exterminating Ourselves | 1 |
| Some Responses to Lynn White Jr.'s Argument | 5 |
| Significance of the Study | 10 |
| Literature Review | 12 |
| Research Methodology | 20 |
| Culture in Context | 20 |
| Ethical Analysis | 22 |
| Theological Analysis | 25 |
| Limitations | 27 |

| | |
|---|---|
| **Chapter Two** | **29** |

| | |
|---|---|
| African Cosmologies and the Environment: the Case of Simaamba Tonga | 29 |
| Our Ancestors/Elders Ought to Get Involved | 29 |
| Simaamba Ancestors as Guardians of the Land | 32 |
| Brief History of the Gwembe Tonga | 33 |
| The Simaamba Tonga Religious Worldview | 37 |
| Actors in *Lwiindi* of the *Bagande* (frog) Clan | 40 |
| Calling the Rain: *Lwiindi* Ceremony | 41 |
| Relating the *Lwiindi* to Anthropological Literature | 46 |
| Theological Discussion of the Cult of Ancestors | 51 |
| We Share One Earth with our Ancestors | 53 |
| Ecological Dimensions of the *Lwiindi* | 54 |
| Ecological Aspects of Tonga Holy Shrines | 56 |

| | |
|---|---|
| **Chapter Three** | **60** |

| | |
|---|---|
| Morality in the Face of Progress: Civilization, Christianity, and Commerce | 60 |
| Understanding African Morality | 62 |
| The Ethics of Interconnectedness | 64 |

Ecological Themes in African Worldviews 70
Land as a Commons 70
Sacred Spaces 70
Vital Force: The Spirit that Holds the Universe Together 70
Creation Myths 71
Mukowa: the Principle of Interconnectedness 73
The African Concept of Time: John Mbiti 76
Revisiting the African Concept of Time 78
The Ecological Implication of Time 81
The Interconnectedness of Morality and Religion 83
The Non-Religious Basis of Ethics 84
The Religious Basis of Ethics 87

**Chapter Four** **92**

The Ethics of *Ubuntu*: Africa in Early European Eyes 92
Civilization, Commerce and African Morality 92
Understanding *Ubuntu* 95
*Ubuntu* and the Power in Nature 99
*Ntu* as the Concept of Ecological Interconnectedness 100
Creation as the Sacred Offspring of the Supreme *Ntu* 102
Revisiting *Umuntu Ngubuntu Ngabantu* 108
Disintegration of Eco-social *Ubuntu* 111
*Ubuntu* in the Face of Corruption 114
The Roots of African Corruption 116
Impact of Corruption on the Environment 117

**Chapter Five** **119**

Christianity and Population Growth: Conservation of
Africa's Natural Goods 119
Population Growth in the Gwembe Valley 121
Neo-Malthusian and Neo-Böserupian Arguments 123
Is Africa's Population Growth Sustainable? 125
Economic Development amid Population Growth 128
Population Growth: Ancestral Blessing or Curse? 131
Impact of Overpopulation on Human Communities 134

    Arrest this Growth: Family Planning      136
    Looking Forward      143

**Chapter Six**      **145**

Capitalism: A Threat to Africa's Future      145
    The Question of Sustainable Development      145
    Land Degradation and Food Security      149
    Migration: We Don't Want Strangers in our Land      153
    Limitless Growth on a Limited Planet      159
    The Concept of Sustainable Development      162
    "Sustainable Development" or Sustainable Living?      165
    An Ethic of Sustainable Living      168

**Chapter Seven**      **171**

The Challenge of Doing Ethics: Toward the Christology of Earth      171
    Doing Christian Ethics in Africa      171
    From Cult to Christology      173
    Christ the Ecological Ancestor: a Biblical Perspective      175
    Celebrating Life: Rejecting Dominion      181
    Respecting Life      185
    The *Telos* of Creation      187
    Natural Rights to Life      189
    Replenishing the Earth      192
    Spitting Into the Well from Which We Drink      194

**Chapter Eight**      **196**

Christian Ethics of *Ubuntu*      196

**Afterword**      **205**
**Bibliography**      **207**
**Index**      **226**

# Preface

My interest in exploring ecological ethics developed during my life as an Anglican Franciscan brother of the Community of the Divine Compassion. As my admiration of St. Francis of Assisi grew, so did the awareness of the ecological devastation caused by economic exploitation, poverty, and corruption in Africa.

This book explores how the mounting ecological crisis has religious, political, and economic roots that enable and promote social and environmental harm. It presents the thesis that religious traditions, including their ethical expressions, can effectively address the crisis, ameliorate its effects, and advocate social and environmental betterment, now and in the future.

First, the book examines the ecological overtones of African traditional religions and Christianity, which together provide the basis for Christian ecological ethics. Critical examination of both religions uncovers their complementary emphases on human responsibility toward planet Earth and future generations. Second, it explores the interconnectedness of all elements of the universe in African cosmologies. Using the annual *lwiindi* (rain calling) ceremony of the Gwembe Tonga of Chief Simaamba, in Zambia, the study unearths some ecological overtones of African religions.

Third, it examines the foundation of African morality. Ancestors, the book argues, are the foundation of morality as well as the guardians of the land. A complementary teaching that Jesus Christ is the ecological ancestor of all Creation can direct ethical responses to the environmental crisis. Fourth, the eco-social implications of *ubuntu* (what it means to be fully human) are examined. Although some aspects of *ubuntu* are criticized, *ubuntu* can be transformed to advocate eco-social liberation.

Fifth, the book recognizes the conflict between ecological values and religious teachings. This conflict is examined by contrasting the awareness of socio-economic problems caused by overpopulation, on the one hand, and the advocacy of countless children, on the other hand. Since overpopulation threatens sustainable living and the future of our planet, the book advocates a change in the latter. Finally, the book concludes with the identification of Jesus Christ with our ancestors. It contends that the recognition of Jesus as the ecological ancestor, woven together with the ethics of *ubuntu* ought to characterize African Christian ecological consciousness, responsibilities, and actions.

I did not get here alone but benefitted from the support of countless individuals. That said, I am very humbled by, and highly indebted to the President of Malawi, Dr. Joyce Banda. President Banda took time to write the foreword despite her busy and demanding schedules. Special thanks to my mother, Jessie Ntalasha Mushili, who has accompanied my theological journey. I am also grateful to my beloved wife Phie, who read this book, while taking care of our lovely children: Dorothy, Natemwa, Namaka and Takudzwa. I am equally indebted to my brothers: my twin brother Chikulu, Chola, Nyembe, and my sisters, Mercy, Charity and Tracy. You are my pride, strength, and joy.

I am grateful to Professor Marthinus Daneel (Bishop Moses) and Professor Dana Robert for being there for me. I consider myself blessed to be in the presence of Bishop Moses. Dr. Elizabeth Parsons, and her husband, Linwood Parsons, deserve special mention. Dr. Parsons read this book countless times, providing critical feedbacks. To Professors, John Hart, Mary Elizabeth Moore, the Dean of Boston University School of Theology, Rodney Peterson, the Executive Director of The Boston Theological Institute, Jacob K. Olupona, Professor of African and American Studies, and African Religious Traditions, Harvard University, and John Gay, I say thank you for your endless support. Aside from providing critical feedbacks, Dr. Gay introduced me to Professor Thayer Scudder, who reviewed Chapter Two. Dr. Scudder's observations strengthened my understanding of Tonga culture.

The Most Rt. Rev. Desmond Mpilo Tutu, Archbishop Emeritus of Cape Town and Nobel Peace Prize winner; Most Rt. Rev. Albert Chama, Primate of the Church of the Province of Central Africa; Bishop Dereck Kamukwamba, Bishop of Central Zambia; Bishop

William Muchombo, Bishop of Eastern Zambia; Bishop David Ndjovu, Bishop of Lusaka; Bishop Robert Mumbi, Bishop of Luapula; Rev. John Kaoma Kafwanka and his wife Martha; Professor Joan Martin; Dr. Lazarus Phiri; Rev. Macdonald Sembereka and his wife Maggie; The Very Rev. Charlie Thomas; The Very Rev. Katherine Ragsdale; The Rev. Canon Mally Lloyd; Rev. Rogers Banda and his wife Esther, and Maria Planansky deserve special mention–you are always there when I need a hand.

I am grateful to the leadership and members of the Episcopal Parish of Christ Church and Iglesia de San Juan—Rev. Dr. Lisa Fortuna, Jack Corish, Pat Henderson, Ruldolf Amstrong, Gilbert Obiora, Barbara Nova, Mosses Torres, and Anne Gordon; Episcopal Divinity School, and the Bishops of the Episcopal Diocese of Massachusetts—Bishops Thomas Shaw SSJE, Gayle Harris and Bud Cederholm—your support and prayers made this book possible. Finally, I am grateful to Kachere Press, and highly indebted to Hermann Mvula for his support on this project.

I chose to publish this book with Kachere Press, the publication arm of the Department of Theology and Religious Studies of the University of Malawi because I consider this study as part of the wider discourse needed to ensure the future of Mother Africa. Our moral duty toward Earth and future generations demands that we uphold the ethics of *ubuntu*. Eco-social ethics of *ubuntu* ought to compel us to honor Jesus Christ, who is both the Creator, and the Ecological Ancestor of all life.

Kapya J. Kaoma
**Earth Day 2013**
**Boston University**

# Foreword

As a mother, grandmother, and President of the Great Nation of Malawi, I am highly apprehensive about the quality of the Earth my grandchildren's children will inherit long after I am gone. Soil erosion and the disappearance of wildlife is not something I read about in books anymore; these are daily realities. The beautiful trees that surrounded my childhood home are no more. Landslides, floods, water and air pollution, and land degradation are common across our motherland.

While many fellow Africans share my apprehension, we are doing very little to address the life-threatening environmental crisis. Future generations will judge our greatness by how we cared for the Earth; our home, and ultimately theirs. It is for this very reason that I agreed to add my voice to this important book. Together, we can save Mother Africa.

The 17$^{th}$ Conference of the Parties to the U.N. Framework Convention on Climate Change, in South Africa, and the Rio+20 U.N. Conference on Sustainable Development, in Brazil, revealed the urgency of addressing the mounting ecological crisis. However, these conferences provided us with new opportunities to reflect on what has gone wrong, and what we can do to address environmental degradation.

Long before these conferences, Africa's Heads of States jointly adopted the "African Convention on the Conservation of Nature and Natural Resources," in July 1968. This convention was born out of the conviction that Africa's natural resources were "capital of vital importance." Nevertheless, they also realized that most of these resources were "irreplaceable."

Since then, the African Union, the Southern Africa Development Community, and other regional bodies have constantly linked environmental wellbeing to economic and social development. All developmental goals, they insist, ought to take into consideration our needs and those of future generations.

African governments have championed various environmental initiatives, among them forestry, water and wildlife protection. In addition, African nations have Environmental Councils dedicated to monitoring Africa's ecological wellbeing. These councils are playing a critical role to protect our environment. Sadly, they are yet to find much needed spiritual support from religious leaders; thereby increasing the stereotype that care for God's creation is a secular initiative. However, as Dr. Kapya John Kaoma rightly observes, spiritual resources planted in Christian and African worldviews can arrest this plight. Time is running out; countless generations would love to see an African elephant, rhino, forests, and of course drink our lovely waters.

To my fellow African political leaders, I respectfully appeal to you to promote developmental policies geared toward the ecological wellbeing of Africa. Sustainable development should not be a mere tag to our development policies, but a reality. Our over-dependency on foreign currency has forced us to make hard choices; usually to the detriment of the land. Mining and timber harvesting are not just displacing millions of people but are also destroying our precious forests, most of which took hundreds of years to grow. Is it not time we instituted the policy of planting two trees, for every tree cut?

As Africans, we pride ourselves as the daughters and sons of the soil. Therefore, the destruction of the Earth means our own death and ultimately life, as we know it. We all need a great *indaba* about the ecological future of Africa. How are we going to confront pollution, deforestation, rapid population growth, and corruption by those entrusted with political power? The answers to these questions will determine our continent's future.

Those of us in positions to effect and affect policies must comprehensively address issues raised in this important book. It is not about how much money we make from the exploitation of natural resources, but how that money is made. We should not put profits above the ecological wellbeing of our motherland.

The issues explored in this book are critical to the future of Africa. As Africans, we consider the land as a sacred trust to hand over to future generations. African heroes like John Chilembwe, in our great nation of Malawi, and Mbuya Nehanda in Zimbabwe sought to reclaim our land from colonial exploitation. These prophets died so that we can reclaim what was legally ours—Africa. It is this conviction that inspired millions of Africans to fight for independence and to reclaim our rights to Africa's natural resources. For this reason, Africa's natural resources are our most precious possessions.

We must realize that the ecological crisis is hitting Africa the hardest. Environmental degradation is forcing millions to migrate into urban areas; making it harder for governments to meet basic services. As political and religious leaders, we ought to do what is right—heal the Earth. It is not too late to start repairing the damage we have caused. Political will alone won't resolve the occurring environmental crisis; we need the involvement of traditional and religious leaders, too.

Historically, the Church has partnered with African governments to address various challenges such as poverty and HIV/AIDS. As we face the ecological crisis, our pastors should be in the forefront of planting trees, campaigning against air and water pollution and the poaching of wildlife.

Inevitably, the environmental crisis has my fellow women's face. Today, my fellow women and our children are walking very long distances in search of firewood, drinking water, and other basic needs. During my visits to various hospitals, women are the ones who watch their children die from malnutrition and other environmental-related illnesses. We can all make a difference in their lives right now if we work to arrest this crisis.

Significantly, religious leaders have power to instill moral values in people's lives. We politicians make policies, but religious leaders bring spirituality into those policies. In the face of ecological degradation, our religious leaders should develop spiritual and theological justification for opposing deforestation, dumping of waste in our rivers and compounds, and protecting animals and other natural resources.

Kaoma lays bare the plight of the Earth but, he also provokes us to positively reflect on what needs to be done. Our plunder of the very eco-system that aids our own existence is a complete departure from African values.

In addition, Kaoma makes a compelling argument for our involvement in creation care. Aside from arguing that Jesus Christ is the origin and the ecological ancestor of all life, he maintains that the natural world is a sacrament, through which God is experienced and adored. Viewing Earth as a sacrament can aid governments' efforts to arrest the ecological crisis.

I grew up believing that we had the power to exploit nature. Today, however, I have realized that we must care for God's creation. Good Christian spirituality, I must say, involves caring for God's creation. In short, how we relate to the natural world says much about our own spirituality and values.

We Christians, I insist, are among those who need safe drinking water and productive lands to survive. As a confessing Christian and head of State, I feel it is time people of faith proactively addressed the growing and life-threatening ecological disaster. In the spirit of *ubuntu,* we need religious, traditional leaders and ordinary people's participation in resolving the current ecological crises.

The importance of this book is that it provokes and unsettles all of us; politicians, religious leaders, and all Africans. We have no time to point fingers; Mother Africa is counting on us to heal her wounds. We must form environmental protection clubs in schools, churches, cities and villages. These clubs can aid governments' efforts to protect our environment.

Dr. Kaoma dedicates a significant portion of this book to the concept of *ubuntu*. While some aspects of *ubuntu* are being lost to the effects of economic inequalities and globalization, this ethical ideal has potential to transform human relationships to the natural world and one another. But, *ubuntu* understood from the concept of Jesus Christ as an ecological ancestor can also increase our ecological spiritual sensitivity. We can only overlook the occurring environment predicament to our own harm. The Earth and the continent of Africa in particular is not, to use Dr. Kaoma's words, a "World Bank of raw materials." Africa is our home and the home to countless generations to come.

I am not a pastor, but a layperson, and I pray I am not stepping on my religious leaders' toes. I am highly honored to write this foreword to this important book by our own son of Africa. I highly recommend this book to be "a must read" by academics, religious leaders, and politicians across the world. It is my prayer that this book will initiate honest discussions and actions by all daughters and sons of Africa both at home and in the diaspora. I thank Dr. Kaoma, and our own Kachere Press, for making us aware of the spiritual and moral duty to Mother Africa and future generations of life. Please don't just read this book; act to save Mother Africa!

Joyce Banda (Dr.)
<u>The President of the Republic of Malawi</u>
Earth Day 2013
State House, Lilongwe, Malawi

# Chapter One
## The Plight of Earth:
## How We Are Exterminating Ourselves

Human attitudes toward the natural world will determine the future of planet Earth and life as a whole. The mounting crises of deforestation, climate change, air and water pollution, land degradation, uncontrolled population growth, and many other ecological predicaments are indicative of irresponsible attitudes toward our planet. Most of these attitudes are religiously conditioned, hence theological ethics developed with the Earth in mind can change people's perceptions of the natural world.[1] In African worldviews, the spiritual, the natural, and the human worlds are interconnected. Although these worldviews can inform Christian ecological responsibilities and actions, few studies are dedicated to the investigation of the same.

Christianity is one of the fastest growing religions in Africa; thus it can play a crucial role to address the resulting crisis. Since African Christians are influenced by both an African traditional worldview and Christian doctrines, their dual heritage is vital to the development of Christian ecological ethics on the continent.

As we shall see, Placide Tempels, John S. Mbiti, and Ferdinand C. Ezekwonna are among the scholars who argue that African ethics is deeply anthropocentric. However, critical examinations of African traditional beliefs and philosophies reveal that African ethics places much emphasis on human responsibility toward planet Earth. This is because in African cosmologies, humanity, nonhumans, the ancestors, and other spiritual forces are interconnected. In this worldview, the abuse of Earth threatens the interconnectedness of the universe on which life depends.

---

[1] David Korten, "The Great Turning: From Empire to Earth Community," *Yes! Magazine* (Summer 2006), 12-18.

Since the publication of Lynn White Jr.'s article, "The Historical Roots of our Ecologic Crisis," in 1967—which blamed Christianity for the mounting environmental crisis—Christian theologians and ethicists have explored ways in which Christianity can resolve the ecological crisis. For White, the separation of God and humanity from nature resulted in the desacralization and exploitation of the natural world.[2] Unless the Western Christian assumption that nature exists solely to serve humanity is rejected, he insisted, the ecological crisis is set to worsen. Ironically, he closed his article with the following words:

> Both our present science and our present technology are so tinctured with orthodox Christian arrogance toward nature that no solution for our ecologic[al] crisis can be expected from them alone. Since the roots of our trouble are so largely religious, the remedy must also be essentially religious, whether we call it that or not. We must rethink and refeel our nature and destiny. The profoundly religious, but heretical, sense of the primitive Franciscans for the spiritual autonomy of all parts of nature may point a direction. I propose Francis as a patron saint for ecologists.[3]

The belief that the natural world exists solely for human use is a recent development in Africa. The nineteenth-century mission theory of "Civilization, Christianity and Commerce," which led to the colonization (conquest) and Christianization of Africa, is behind this idea.[4] Whereas missionary movements promoted civilization as an instrument of Christianization, imperial governments promoted commerce. For them, Africa's value was in its natural resources (hereafter "natural goods"), which were awaiting extensive human exploitation for profit.[5] As Sallie McFague posits,

---

[2] Lynn White Jr., "The Historical Roots of Our Ecologic Crisis," *Science, New Series* 155, no. 3767 (Mar. 10, 1967), 1207.
[3] Ibid.
[4] Andrew Porter, "Commerce and Christianity: The Rise and Fall of a Nineteenth-Century Missionary Slogan," *The Historical Journal* 28, no.3 (Sep. 1985), 597-621.
[5] Natural goods usage follows that of John Hart, who argues that calling something a "resource" implies that it is provided for, and awaiting removal by humankind. Some of

this worldview (rooted in the Protestant Reformation, the Enlightenment, and eighteenth-century economic theory) is putting our planet in jeopardy.[6] Similarly, Leroy Vail faults this theory for undermining the balanced relationship between humanity and nature in Africa in the era prior to the mid-nineteenth century.[7] Sadly, while some negative effects of this theory are felt in the West, poor nations are hit the most due to their closeness to Earth.

There is an abundant body of compelling scholarly literature that documents the connection between contemporary policies inspired by this nineteenth-century theory and the negative ecological effects wrought on much of the planet.[8] Kirkpatrick Sale insists that dwellers on the land destroy the environments on which their livelihoods depend due to foreign capitalistic interests.[9] Paul Hawken adds that although the destructive effects of capitalism on poor nations are not visible to the West, it ecologically matters how profit is obtained. Thus, the fundamental principles of commerce should be re-examined from an ecological point of view if we are to meet the challenges of our time.[10]

---

Earth's natural benefits, however, are obviously not just for humans: they already serve an ecosystemic, geologic, or other need in place; and, they are used not just by humans, but by other members of the biotic community who depend on them being in place. John Hart, *Sacramental Commons: Christian Ecological Ethics* (Lanham, Maryland: Rowman and Littlefield, 2006), 150.

[6] Sallie McFague, *Life Abundant: Rethinking Theology and Economy for a Planet in Peril* (Minneapolis: Fortress Press, 2000), 117.

[7] Leroy Vail, "Ecology and History: The Example of Eastern Zambia," *Journal of Southern African Studies* 3, no.2 (Apr. 1977), 129-155.

[8] Séverine Deneulin and Masooda Bano, *Religion in Development: Rewriting the Secular Script* (London and New York: Zed Books, 2009); Jeffrey Haynes, *Religion and Development: Conflict or Cooperation?* (New York: Palgrave Macmillan, 2007).

[9] Kirkpatrick Sale, *Dwellers on the Land: the Bioregional Vision* (Athens, Georgia: University of Georgia Press, 2000). See also Maano Ramitsindela, *Transfrontier Conservation in Africa: At the Confluence of Capital, Politics and Nature* (Oxfordshire: Cabi, 2007).

[10] Paul Hawken, *The Ecology of Commerce: A Declaration of Sustainability* (New York: Harper Business, 1993), 6-17, 32, 72.

In Africa, one key example of the exploitation of nature for human use was the building of the Kariba Dam in Southern Africa. Elizabeth Colson, Thayer Scudder, and Lisa Cliggett have studied and highlighted the detrimental anthropological effects of the dam on human and nonhuman habitats of the valley.[11] Despite resisting relocation due to their belief that the *basangu* (ancestors) would make it impossible to close the dam, more than 57,000 Tonga people, were forcefully resettled on both sides of the Zambezi River—among them, the Tonga of Simaamba studied in this book.[12] In 1958, the dam walls were closed, creating a 5,580 square km reservoir. Unfortunately, no care was taken to address the fate of thousands of nonhumans that inhabited the area, and only a fraction of the animals was rescued through "Operation Noah." Charles Lagus, who witnessed and documented this disaster, bemoaned that:

> The damming at Kariba is a more than usually spectacular symptom of man's (sic) attitude to animals in many parts of the world, but nowhere is the prospect more alarming than in Africa. Just as Operation Noah has undertaken an imaginative programme of rescue work at Kariba, so in the wider context there is need for a great holding operation to bridge the fifty years it may take for man to acknowledge his responsibility to the natural world, and his responsibility for it to future generations of men. -- Like it or

---

[11] Elizabeth Colson, *The Social Consequences of Resettlement: The Impact of the Kariba Resettlement upon the Gwembe Tonga* (Manchester: Manchester University Press, 1971); Thayer Scudder, *The Ecology of the Gwembe Tonga* (Manchester: Manchester University Press 1962); *The Future Of Large Dams : Dealing with Social, Environmental, Institutional, and Political Costs* (London: Earthscan, 2005); *A History of Development in the Twentieth Century: The Zambian Portion of the middle Zambezi Valley and the Lake Kariba Basin* (New York: Clark University, 1985); Cliggett Lisa, *Grains from Grass: Aging, Gender, and Famine in Rural Africa* (Ithaca: Cornell University Press, 2005).

[12] According to Barrie Reynolds, the Zambezi Northbank population in 1959 was: BanaMainga 1,620, Goba 1,340, Kalanga 197, Korekore 558 and Valley Tonga 54,446. About Simaamba he writes, "The Tonga and Goba just above Kariba Gorge, have close ties with the Kalanga, who live on the opposite bank of the Zambezi."(4) Barrie Reynolds, *The Material Culture of the Gwembe Valley*, vol III, Kariba Studies Series (Manchester, Manchester University Press 1968), 5.

not, the White Man's disease (one might almost call it the "English Sickness," for it began in England), has come to Africa to stay.[13]

Sadly, this English preoccupation with exploiting the ecological landscape of the continent negatively affected the African environment and directed post-colonial attitudes toward Earth.

On the cultural front, however, Frank Clements viewed the damming of the Zambezi as illustrative of the struggle between Western civilization and traditional cosmologies. While the successful construction of the dam suggests that Western civilization triumphed over Tonga religion, Clements asserts that the traditional belief in the sepentine Spirit *Nyami-Nyami* (the river guardian) emerged victorious.[14] He insists that the number of problems and the appeasement of the spirits during the construction of the dam illustrate the power of *Nyami-Nyami* over Western civilization.[15]

## Some Responses to Lynn White Jr.'s Argument

Most theologians agree that human attitudes toward nature ought to be ecologically sensitive, but are divided on White's argument against Christianity. Some accept White's argument and dismiss Christianity as anti-nature. This group argues that Christianity is ecologically bankrupt and a solution to the ecological crisis should

---

[13] Charles Lagus, *Operation Noah* (London: William Kimber and Co., 1959), 37.
[14] The Tonga who lived around the Kariba Gorge believed that the river spirit *Nyami-Nyami* and ancestors would make it impossible to close the dam. While Scudder and Colson found no evidence that the large majority, namely the Middle and Upper River Tonga believed in *Nyami-Nyami*, Scudder observes that "one reason why the early authors dealing with Kariba mentioned Nyami-Nyami was because the river serpent was associated with the boiling waters of the Kariba Gorge which was centered in Simaamba Chieftaincy." Email Correspondence, January 09, 2013. It is important, however, to note that this belief is now common across the Gwembe valley and *Nyami-Nyami's* sightings are reported constantly; the latest was reported on December 23, 2012. Tendai Chara, "Nyami-Nyami Reappears, Disappears," Sunday, 23 December, 2012.
[15] Clements attributes the completion of the dam to the ritual appeasement of *Nyami-Nyami*. Frank Clements, *Kariba: The Struggle with the River God* (London: Methuen, 1959).

be found elsewhere.[16] Others argue that White erred elsewhere in his argument by avoiding other significant causes among them economics for the crisis. Such scholars seek to defend Christianity from some aspects of White's attack and maintain that properly understood Christianity demands justice and peace. According to positions developed by the World Council of Churches and Vatican documents on the environment, these themes should be extended to the poor and to the environment.

Some theologians have sought to revise, but not entirely reject, the major premises of Christianity through the study of classical Christian thought.[17] They object that critics of Christianity have ignored the ambiguous ecological premises represented in Christian traditions. James Nash and Paul Santmire, for example, have argued that a careful study of Christian thought suggests that Christianity is not ecologically bankrupt.[18] Finally, John Hart and Marthinus Daneel, pay attention to the role of religion in providing solutions to the crisis. They dialogue with other religious traditions and integrate them in Christian responses to the ecological crisis.

One vital question arising from this scholarly debate is whether White's observations can apply across the globe. Mutombo Mpanya, who argues that the establishment of mission stations and "Christian" villages led to environmental devastation, agrees with White. To Mpanya, Christian evangelization could have affected the place that the environment enjoyed in African cultures. "Several institutions linked to conservation of the environment and providing an opportunity for people to relate

---

[16] Matthew Fox, *Natural Grace: Dialogues on Creation, Darkness, and the Soul in Spirituality and Science* (New York: Image Books/Doubleday, 1997); *Creation Spirituality: Liberating Gifts for the Peoples of the Earth* (San Francisco: Harper San Francisco, 1991).
[17] Paul Santmire, *The Travail of Nature: The Ambiguous Ecological Promise of Christian Theology* (Philadelphia: Fortress Press, 1985); *Nature Reborn: The Ecological and Cosmic Promise of Christian Theology* (Minneapolis: Augsburg Press, 2000).
[18] James Nash, *Loving Nature: Ecological Integrity and Christian Responsibility* (Nashville: Abingdon Press, 1991).

intimately to nature lost their prestige."[19] Missionaries, he argues, dismissed nature-related rituals and beliefs as evil.[20] While his point is worth noting, Mpanya does not acknowledge some missionaries such as David Livingstone, Robert Moffat, and Albert Schweitzer, whose works show ecological sensitivity. In this respect, Mpanya oversimplified missionary activities in Africa.[21]

That said, in African worldviews life is interconnected. Hence, the destruction of traditional rituals and sacred places impacted African morality negatively. Kofi A. Opuku is correct; "humanity is part of nature and is expected to cooperate with it; and this sense of community with nature is often expressed in terms of identity, kinship, friendliness and respect. This reverence and respect control the use of nature."[22] Laurenti Magesa supports the above observation when he insists that African community includes all creatures.[23] "The unity of the community—equally the living, the living dead ... and the yet-to-be-born [one would add nonhuman] – –a unity that is community's life in its fullest sense," Magesa asserts, "is paramount good. The opposite constitutes the paramount destructiveness."[24] Thus, the ethical presupposition of this worldview maintains an active interaction between God, planet Earth, and humanity.

---

[19] Mutombo Mpanya, "The Environmental Impacts of a Church Project," in *Missionary Earthkeeping*, (ed.), Calvin DeWitt and Ghillean T. Prance (Macon: Mercer University Press, 1992), 104.

[20] Ibid., 104-106.

[21] John Kaoma, "David Livingstone's Attitude Toward Nature: A Challenge to Earthkeeping Mission," *Newsletter, Boston Theological Institute* 32, no.20 (Feb. 2003) and later published as "Earthkeeping as a Dimension of Christian Mission: David Livingstone's attitude Toward Life: A Challenge to Earthkeeping Missions," in *Tracing Contours: Reflecting on World Mission and Christianity*, (ed.), Rodney L. Petersen and Marian Gh. Simion (Newton Center: Boston Theological Institute, 2010), 74-76.

[22] Kofi Asare Opuku, "African Traditional Religion," in *Religious Plurality in Africa: Essays in Honor of John S. Mbiti*, (ed.), Jacob K. Olupona and Sulayman S. Nyang (New York: Mouton de Gruyter, 1993), 77.

[23] Laurenti Magesa, *African Religion: The Moral Traditions of Abundant Life* (New York: Orbis Books, 1997), 48, 65-71. Also John S. Mbiti, *African Religions and Philosophy* (London: Heinemann, 1969), 175.

[24] Ibid., 65.

So how is this active interaction maintained? Africans exemplify the ecological injunctions of their community cultures through rituals, totems, creation myths, taboos, and customs. Among the Bantu, *ubuntu* (to be fully human) implies vital interconnectedness. To possess *ubuntu* (to be virtuous) demands living in constant harmony with all of Earth's community. This interconnectedness regulates human relationships with the Supreme Being, ancestors, and the rest of creation. In short, African religions uphold an *eco-humano-relational* ethic or what John Hart calls a "creatiocentric consciousness"[25] through which humanity recognizes the intrinsic and spiritual value of creation. In this context, eco-humano-relational means an ethic that puts emphasis on human relatedness to other beings.

In his exploration of Bantu philosophy, Placide Tempels asserted this interconnectedness in his theory of *vital force*.[26] Tempels noted that every creature possesses the *vital force*; thus, "It is because all being is force and exists only in that it is force, that the category 'force' includes of necessity all 'beings': God, [humanity] living and departed, animals, plants, and minerals."[27] Edwin W. Smith interprets Tempels' theory to mean, "Every created thing is in rapport with every other creature according to a law of hierarchy. This world is like a spider's web of which you cannot touch one thread without disturbing the whole."[28]

Tempels' work has been influential in theological and philosophical studies across Africa. However, Mbiti argues that to call Tempels' book "Bantu Philosophy" is ambitious: "It is open to a great deal of criticism, and the theory of "vital force" cannot be

---

[25] Hart, *Sacramental Commons*, 121.
[26] Placide Tempels, *Bantu Philosophy*, Translated from *La Philosophie Bantu*, by A. Rubbens (Paris: Presence Africaine, 1952).
[27] According to Tempels, *muntu* (person) signifies the vital force endowed with intelligence and will; *bintu* are what we call "things;" forces not endowed with reason. Ibid., 36. See also Edwin W. Smith (ed.), *African Ideas of God: A Symposium* (London: Morrison and Gibbs, 1950), 17-20.
[28] Edwin W. Smith, "La Philosophie Bantoue," *Journal of the International African Institute* 16, no.3 (July, 1946), 200-201.

applied to other African people with whose life and ideas [Mbiti is] familiar (sic)."[29] Mbiti's criticisms, however, are unwarranted since Tempels was aware of such limitations.[30] Subsequently, Stephen O. Okafor instists that Tempels' analysis was right; nonetheless, his conclusion about the center of Bantu philosophy is misleading. To him, African philosophy is centered on the theory of life.[31]

Notably, Bantu philosophy does not share what Sallie McFague calls Western historical "apartheid thinking," the falsehood that we can exist "apart from nature or contrary to its own limits and health."[32] Neither does it share the concept of biota egalitarianism as proposed by Albert Schweitzer or deep ecologists. Rather, Bantu philosophy has humanity as the center, but it is "the center" that is connected to a sacred web of interacting vital forces—with God, clan founders, ancestors, humanity, animate, and inanimate forces existing in perfect harmony. As Mbiti puts it, all creation exists as a unity in African worldviews, so "to destroy one of them is to destroy them all."[33] Thus, the annihilation of any creature depends on the Creator, because "existence that comes from God cannot be taken from a creature by any created force."[34]

Magesa attests to this point when he asserts that in African religions, every creature has "its own force of life, its own power to sustain life. Because of the common origin of this power, however, all creatures are connected with each other in the sense that each

---

[29] John S. Mbiti, *African Religions and Philosophy* (London: Heinemann, 1969) 10-11.
[30] Edwin W. Smith observed that Tempels himself was aware that he presented "a hypothesis to be verified by further inquiry over the whole Bantu field." Smith, "La Philosophie Bantoue," 200.
[31] Stephen O. Okafor argues that critical examination of African cosmologies reveals that: a) the meaning and the meaningfulness of the universe is nothing else than the meaningfulness of life; b) the conviction that the goodness of life is only reflected in the philosophy of commensality; and c) the conviction that every phenomenon emits an aura particular to it. Stephen O. Okafor, "'Bantu Philosophy:' Placide Tempels Revisited," *Journal of Religion in Africa* 13 (1982), 91-92.
[32] McFague, *Life Abundant*, 117; 118.
[33] Mbiti, *African Religions and Philosophy,* 51.
[34] Tempels, *Bantu Philosophy*, 39.

one influences the other for good or for bad."[35] Since every force (being) shares the Creator's vital force, nonhumans have equal moral claims and natural rights to existence.[36] As Magesa avows:

> The world is the manifestation of God, God's power, and benevolence. Accordingly, a big rock where people go to sacrifice is not just a big rock, but it incorporates, shows, and for that reason is, in fact, some supernatural quality of the Divine. The same can be said...of practically anything, that inspires awe: mountains, trees, snakes, certain animals, and so on. While African Religion understands...that these elements are by no means God but creatures...it also recognizes that they have divinity in them because they exist by the will and through the power of the divinity. In a sense they "represent" the Divinity and surely demonstrate God's will and power to humanity.[37]

For Charles Nyamiti, the universe is an organic whole, composed of supra-sensible mystical participations.[38] These participations, I argue, affirm the intrinsic value of nature and account for the manifestations of ancestors and other spirits in nature. In fact, it is this reality that African Earthkeepers in Zimbabwe ritually affirm.[39] Because the universe is interconnected, ecological ethics can build on this reality to address the worsening crisis. Yet for it to become "Christian," it must be informed by the biblical heritage.

## Significance of the Study

Export-driven economic policies and practices have put extreme pressure on African natural goods to the detriment of the

---

[35] Ibid., 46.
[36] This understanding resembles the ideas of Saint Maximus the Confessor (ca. 5th century) cited by John Hart in *Sacramental Commons*. A revered figure in Eastern and Western Christianity, Maximus argued that sparks of the divine being are present in every created being. According to Hart, "Maximus viewed creation as the context and revelation of God, and referred to it as a cloak worn by the creating Word." Hart, *Sacramental Commons*, 9.
[37] Magesa, *African Religion*, 59.
[38] Charles Nyamiti, *The Scope of African Theology* (Kampala: Gaba Publications, 1973), 21.
[39] Marthinus Daneel, *African Earthkeepers: Wholistic Interfaith Mission* (Maryknoll, NY: Orbis Books, 2001), 114.

environment.[40] Since religion is central to African world life, religious ethics is crucial to arresting the exacerbating ecological despoliation. Moreover, ecological themes abound in African religious thought. Sadly, few studies have integrated them into the global ecological discourse.

This study examines the ethical notion of *"ubuntu"* or "interconnectedness" in Christian ecological ethics. It argues that the multi-disciplinary application of this concept makes it useful to resolving the ecological crisis across the globe. Since the concept is found in other religious traditions and the sciences, it can serve as a point of contact between African Christian ecological ethics and ethical theories and practices in the rest of the world.

Christian ecological ethics should embody the dual influence of African traditional religions and Christian theology. That there are many reasons why this dual influence is necessary is supported by the fact that African religions and Christian theology both believe that creation originates from the Creator God; both heritages suggest that the Spirit is present in creation and the abuse of nature is evil. In addition, the Christian doctrine of natural revelation, and the manifestation of the Spirit in nature in African religions, both affirm nature's sacramental value.

On a social level, both religions teach that Earth is a common trust and home that cannot be privatized or abused for individual gain. Additionally, both religions hold Earth to be a God-provided home to all creatures. On a cultic front, however, the role of saints in Christianity and ancestors in African religions can inform African ecological ethics. Since these sacred figures (living dead) occupy pivotal positions in both religions, their teachings on creation are

---

[40] Majid Rahnema and Victoria Bawtree (eds), *The Post-Development Reader* (London: Zed Books, 1997); Rist Gilbert, *The History of Development from Western Origins to Global Faith*, Translated by Patrick Camiller (London: Zed Books, 2008 edition); Wolfgang Sachs, *The Development Dictionary* (London: Zed Books, 1991).

useful to the development of ecological ethics.⁴¹ Furthermore, African and Christian ethics advocate the promotion of life.⁴²

Given that the ecological crisis threatens the future of Africa, there is an urgent need for Christian ecological ethics on the continent. This book argues that crony capitalism, corruption, uncontrolled demographic growth, and poverty are threats to our common humanity, Earth and future generations of life. It asserts that the relationship of Jesus Christ to the natural world as both an ecological ancestor and the first born of all creation should inform Christian ecological responsibilities and actions locally and globally. Finally, studies on the Gwembe Tonga abound, but the Tonga of Simaamba are understudied. In this regard, the study of the *lwiindi* of Simaamba is crucial to comprehend the diversity of the Gwembe community cultures and life.

## Literature Review

While White was critical of Christian attitudes toward nature, he presented Saint Francis of Assisi positively. Of course, Francis is among many Christians who lived a life of interconnectedness with humanity, nonhumans, and the Divine. Marion A. Habig's *Omnibus of St. Francis* presents St. Francis of Assisi's positive attitude toward nature. Francis' ideas are similar to the ways in which Africans understood life.⁴³ Like Africans, his love for nature was founded on the conviction that all creation has its origin in God. In an African context, this conviction complements the belief that

---

[41] The concept of "living dead" is usually attributed to John Mbiti. However, Mircea Eliade, used "living dead" to refer to ancestors in 1954. In his book, "*Cosmos and History: the Myth of the Eternal Return*" (New York, Harper and Row Publishers, 1959), 62, Eliade asserted that in traditional societies, the dead return as the "living dead" to commune with their people.

[42] Ferdinand C. Ezekwonna, *African Communitarian Ethic: The Basis for the Moral Conscience and Autonomy of the Individual: Igbo Culture as a Case Study* (Bern, New York: Peter Lang, 2005).

[43] Marion A. Habig (ed.), *St. Francis of Assisi Writings and Early Writings: English Omnibus of the Sources for the Life of St. Francis*, Translated by Raphael Brown and others (London: SPCK, 1973).

creation shares the same "ecological ancestor," Jesus Christ.

Rosemary R. Ruether's edited book, *Women Healing the Earth*, and the edited volume by Dieter T. Hessel and Rosemary R. Ruether, *Christianity and Ecology: Seeking the Well-Being of Earth and Humans*, reflect global perspectives of the ecological ethics of interconnectedness. Similarly, John Hart's *Sacramental Commons*, reveals that the ethics of interconnectedness exists among Native Americans. He observes that Native American and Christian heritages suggest that land is a sacred trust given by God to our care. The belief that Earth exists solely to serve humanity, he argues, is a form of idolatry, for Earth as a whole is a sacrament and a commons to all creatures. Thus,

> *A sacramental commons* is creation as a moment and locus of human participation in the interactive presence and caring compassion of the Spirit who is immanent and participates in the complex dance of energies, elements, entities, and events. It is a place in which people in historical time integrate the spiritual meaning of sacramental with the social meaning of commons, and consequently is characterized by a sacramental community consciousness that stimulates involvement in concrete efforts to restore and conserve ecosystems.[44]

To Hart, people who view Earth as a "sacramental commons," possess "a sacramental consciousness" that allows them to "care about and for creation as a whole; care about and for members of the biotic community; care about and for members of the human community who are denied needed goods of creation."[45] Thus, he invites "a relational consciousness," by which humanity treats all biokind as mutually interconnected beings.[46]

The interconnectedness of creation is widely recognized in Western theological literature. In his two books *The Travail of Nature*, and *Nature Reborn*, Paul Santmire asserts that traditional Christian thought possesses some positive themes which point to

---

[44] Hart, *Sacramental Commons*, xviii.
[45] Ibid.
[46] Ibid., 121.

the interconnectedness of creation. In *Loving Nature,* James A. Nash adds that creation is connected through the web of life and that the biblical concepts of justice, covenant, and love should be extended to the natural world. Whereas Nash contends that humanity is above other creatures, he nonetheless insists that this superiority makes us morally responsible to nature.

On the other hand, Pope Benedict XVI argues that humanity is superior to creation as a whole. In his 2009 encyclical *Caritas In Veritate* (Charity in Truth), Pope Benedict XVI cites approvingly these words from Vatican II's *Gaudium et Spes,* "'…believers and unbelievers agree almost unanimously that all things on earth should be ordered toward man as to their center and summit.'"[47]

Although Nash and Pope Benedict XVI reject the concept of biota-egalitarianism, Sallie McFague argues otherwise. In *The Body of God*, she insists that Christians should view Earth metaphorically as the body of God. Since every part of the body is equally valuable, this model should inform our understanding of creation, theology, Christology, ecology, and justice. In *Creation*, Hans Schwarz notes that comparative anatomy for most plant species, insects, and animals confirms the unity and involvement of all living species. In fact, the various life forms show a fundamental and astounding unity that suggests both a relationship of all living beings and a common evolution. He concludes that "[r]evelation and God's actions occur not in a realm removed from the natural world but in the midst of nature. Nature is fundamentally the arena and medium of God's action."[48]

Eco-feminists not only recognize the interconnectedness of creation, but add that patriarchy is behind the exploitation of both women and Earth. Some ecofeminists, among them Carol P. Christ, Naomi Goldenberg, and Mary Daly, go to an extent of demanding

---

[47] Pope Benedict XVI, *Caritas in Veritate* (Charity in Truth), Encyclical letter, 2009. http://www.vatican.va/holy_father/benedict_xvi/encyclicals/documents/hf_benedict_en c_200090629_caritas-in-veritate_en.html. Accessed 02/08/2010.

[48] Hans Schwarz, *Creation* (Grand Rapids: Eerdmans Publication, 2002), 109.

the replacement of the male God with a goddess *Gaia*, if our crisis is to be arrested.[49]

However, in *Gaia and God,* Rosemary Ruether argues that the ecological crisis is beyond the replacement of the male God or a "God" problem. She advocates new symbols that uphold the interrelatedness of all beings. To her, anything that threatens the interconnectedness of life is sinful; all symbols (theological and scientific) that encourage exploitation of, and violence on others should be resisted. "Human ethics," she argues, should uphold natural interdependency—"mandating humans to imagine and feel the suffering of others" to enhance life.[50]

Similarly, in *Mother/Nature,* Catherine Roach rejects the Gaia hypothesis: "While the planet is certainly life-giving," she observes, "it is not a person who gave birth to us and/or reared us in a one-on-one family relationship. While Earth may well function as a self-regulating organism—as the Gaia hypothesis claims—it is not our personal mother."[51] Although Roach disputes the Gaia hypothesis, she advances the argument that the interconnectedness of creation ought to be respected.

That said, the concept of Earth as mother is well respected in Africa. As Edwin W. Smith observed, many Africans honor "Mother Earth, a goddess who personifies, or symbolizes, the fertility of the soil."[52] Can such traditional beliefs influence Christian ethics?

---

[49] Carol P. Christ, *Laughter of Aphrodite: Reflection on a Journey to the Goddess* (San Francisco: Harper & Row, 1987); Naomi Goldenberg, *Changing of Gods: Feminism and the End of the Traditional Religions* (Boston: Beacon Press, 1979); Mary Daly, *Beyond God the Father* (Boston: Beacon Press, 1985); Kathleen M. Sands, *Escape from Paradise: Evil and Tragedy in Feminist Theology* (Minneapolis: Fortress Press, 1994), 115-135.
[50] Rosemary R. Ruether, *Gaia and God: An Ecofeminist Theology of Earth Healing* (New York: HarperCollins, 1992), 57; *Introducing Redemption in Christian Feminism* (Sheffield: Sheffield Academic Press, 1998), 92.
[51] Catherine M. Rouch, *Mother/Nature: Popular Culture and Environmental Ethics* (Bloomington: Indiana University Press, 2003), 35.
[52] Smith, *African Ideas of God,* 23-26; See also Edwin W. Smith, and Murray Andrew Dale, *The Ila-Speaking Peoples of Northern Rhodesia* (London: Macmillan, 1920), 124-131.

African theological discourse has experienced various paradigm shifts at different times. John Baur outlines these shifts by Francophone and Anglophone African theologians, who moved from adaptation, inculturation, contextualization, and finally to liberation. These shifts had Christology as their central theme; nevertheless, the socio-political realities of the time influenced their development.[53] The resulting crisis demands another shift in African theology and ethics, this book argues. This shift accords with what theologians concluded in *African Theology en Route* that "[t]he salvation of the human person in African Theology is the salvation of the universe. In the mystery of Incarnation Christ assumes the totality of humanity and the cosmos."[54]

Theologians in Africa have employed a variety of resources to develop theology. Mercy Amba Oduyoye identifies the Bible, Christian history, and African history as vital sources for theological reflections.[55] She observes that creation narratives and covenants show that the universe belongs to the Creator God and there is an interdependence of God's world and God's people. Oduyoye does not pay much attention to ecological issues in her earlier works. Later, however, in *Beads and Strands*, she observes that the biblical concept of "neighbor" should include "all creation, seen and unseen. Loving our neighbor has come to mean recycling, reforestation and cleaning up the waters around us."[56]

---

[53] In 1994, Baur argued that African theologians had positively re-evaluated traditional religions and culture but paid less attention to other areas of African life. John Baur, *2000 Years of Christianity in Africa: An African History, 1962-1992* (Nairobi: Pauline Publication, 1994).

[54] Kofi Appiah-Kubi and Sergio Torres, (eds), *African Theology en Route: Papers from the Pan-African Conference of Third World Theologians, December 17–23, 1977* (Maryknoll, N.Y.: Orbis, 1979), 81; See John Pobee, *Toward an African Theology* (Nashville: Abingdon, 1979), 32.

[55] Mercy Amba Oduyoye, *Hearing and Knowing: Theological Reflections on Christianity in Africa* (Maryknoll, NY: Orbis Books, 1986).

[56] Amba Mercy Oduyoye, *Beads and Strands, Reflections of an African Woman on Christianity in Africa* (Maryknoll, NY: Orbis, 2004), 26. This is the only page that discusses ecology in this book.

Kwesi Dickson maintains that scripture, experience, Church traditions, and culture are the main factors in theologizing. Generally, Dickson argues, Africans have a fellow-feeling relationship with nature, and that creation "plays a vital role in the apprehension of reality."[57] Similarly, John Pobee asserts that Christianity should take into consideration genuine African categories when addressing present challenges. Theologians, he contends, should uphold the past, present, and future when studying and practicing theology.[58] Although he does not extend this to ecological ethics, theology cannot uphold the past, present, and future without confronting the effects of the escalating environmental crises on coming generations and Earth as a whole.

Accordingly, theologians have consistently observed that African life is ontologically interconnected and at the most, ecologically expressed. Specifically, John Mbiti's *African Religions and Philosophy,* and *Concepts of God in Africa* illustrate how the concept of interconnectedness inform African life and spirituality. While Mbiti observes that in African cosmology, God, spirits and ancestors can manifest in creation, he asserts that the relationship between God and the animal world is of a mythological nature and should not be taken beyond face value.[59] He also notes that while nonhumans are "deitified" and prayers are offered to them, such prayers are offered to the deity or the spirit and not to the "object or phenomenon as such."[60] Mbiti undervalues these venerations, yet they are vital in our quest for ecological ethics and actions.

Matthew J. Schoffeleers, Thayer Scudder and Elizabeth Colson are agreed; African communities are essentially ecological in nature. According to Schoffeleers, Africans uphold the ancestors as

---

[57] Kwesi Dickson, *Theology in Africa* (Maryknoll, NY: Orbis Books, 1984), 29-49.
[58] Pobee, *Toward an African Theology,* 18.
[59] Mbiti, *Concepts of God in Africa* (London: Praeger Publishers, 1970), 91-128.
[60] Mbiti insists that such beliefs are likely to fade with the coming of science and education. Mbiti, *Concepts of God,* 233-34. This position was also advocated by Stephen N. Ezeanya in *Biblical Revelation and African Beliefs,* (ed.), Kwesi A. Dickson and Paul Ellingworth (London: Lutterworth Press, 1969), 46.

guardians of the land. In fact, territorial cults have ecological dimensions, since they "issue and enforce directives with regard to a community's use of its environment."[61] Terence O. Ranger concurs that such cultic observances guarded against ecological degradation.[62] Among the Tonga of Simaamba for example, persistent droughts in the Gwembe area are attributed to the annoyance of their gods and ancestors over their forced resettlement.[63] The Goba people of the same region blame such misfortunes on the Tonga people's failure to respect their *malende* (sacred groves).[64] While these ecological dimensions are present in African religions, Schoffeleers regrets that they are yet to be fully explored for their eco-theological overtones.[65]

For example, the concept of ancestors, which unifies African cultures has strong ecological overtones. Although scholars have developed various ancestor-related Christologies in their attempts to make Jesus real to Africans,[66] the ecological face of Jesus is lacking. Ancestors are the obligatory route to the Supreme Being, argues Francois Kabesele. By proposing the Christology of Jesus as "Elder Brother-Ancestor," he notes, "The figure of the tree... used by Jesus to represent the way in which his life passes to his disciples reminds the Bantu of the importance of the ongoing contact with the ancestors for the maintenance of life (John 15: 5ff)."[67]

---

[61] Matthew J. Schoffeleers (ed.), *Guardians of the Land: Essays on Central African Territorial Cults* (Gweru: Mambo Press, 1978), 2.
[62] Terence O. Ranger, *Voices from the Rocks: Nature, Culture and History in the Matopos Hills of Zimbabwe* (Indiana, Indiana University Press, 1999).
[63] Elisabeth Thomson, *Our Gods Never Helped Us Again—The Tonga People Describe Resettlement and its Aftermath* (Lusaka: Panos Southern Africa, 2005).
[64] Patrick Makukisi, Interview, November 2006, Lusitu, Zambia.
[65] Schoffeleers, *Guardians of the Land*, 1-8.
[66] See Donald J. Goergen, "The Quest for the Christ of Africa," *African Christian Studies: The Journal of the Faculty of Theology*, Catholic University of Eastern Africa 17, no. 1 (Mar. 2001), 6.
[67] Francois Kabesele, "Christ as Ancestor and Elder Brother," in *Faces of Jesus in Africa*, (ed.), Robert J. Schreiter (Maryknoll, NY: Orbis Book, 1998), 116.

Consequently, post-independence social realities led many theologians to understand Christ as a liberator. Kwame Bediako for example, analyzes the role of ancestors in the social-political life of the continent. He observes that African leaders are usually considered to be sitting on the stool of ancestors. As a result, criticism of their inept governance is viewed as an attack on the ancestors. If democracy is to take root, Bediako suggests that the gospel should desacralize the powers of African leaders.[68]

Likewise, Magesa argues that the socio-economic and political situations of Africa should inform how Christ is understood.[69] Yet just as socio-political realities led to the development of theologies of liberation, this book argues, the environmental crisis demands an inclusive theology of the liberation of God's Earth. Brazilian theologian Leonardo Boff's *Ecology and Liberation*, and *Cry of the Earth, Cry of the Poor*, bring a similar realization to ethics.

Some theologians have particularly highlighted ecological elements in African theologies. Tumani Mutasa Nyanjeka argues that the Shona "mutupo principle" (totem) connects humanity to the cosmos.[70] She adds that traditional African society did not promote humans over nature, because ancestors protected nature from human abuse. In *Environmental Crisis*, Samson Gitau has attempted to develop an African eco-theology, based on African cosmologies and biblical traditions. He argues that environmental degradation is rooted in biblical misinterpretation. Specifically, he notes that the biblical teaching on stewardship has much in common with African religions that understand Earth as a sacred trust.[71] In *African Earthkeepers*, Marthinus L. Daneel illustrates the

---

[68] Kwame Bediako, *African Christianity: Renewal of a Non-Western Religion* (Maryknoll, NY: Orbis Books, 1995), 234-249.
[69] Laurenti Magesa, "Christ the Liberator and Africa Today," in *Faces of Jesus in Africa*, 154; Harvey J. Sindima, *Religious and Political Ethics in Africa: A Moral Inquiry* (Westport: Greenwood Press, 1998).
[70] Tumani Mutasa Nyajeka, "Shona Women and the Mutupo Principle," in *Women Healing the Earth*, (ed.), Rosemary R. Ruether (Maryknoll, NY: Orbis Book, 1996).
[71] Samson K. Gitau, *The Environment Crisis: A Challenge for African Christianity* (Nairobi: Acton Publishers, 2000).

interconnectedness of the natural world in African worldviews. Besides noting that Earthkeepers relate to trees on family terms, he sees Jesus as an Earthkeeper, who suffers with his kin in creation.

## Research Methodology

This study is an interdisciplinary attempt to propose Christian ecological ethics of *ubuntu*. It particularly considers African and Western theologians/ethicists of the Christian tradition. However, this study is also informed by my association with the Gwembe Tonga of Simaamba who were forcefully resettled when the Kariba Dam was constructed, and subsequently includes a study of published works on the Gwembe Tonga of Zambia and Zimbabwe. Additionally, this study draws on personal experiences during my field research conducted in the Kariba region of Zambia.

## Culture in Context

Colson and Scudder have studied Gwembe Tonga's beliefs about the universe, sacred groves, and nature spirits. However, my personal experience among the Tonga of Simaamba will help interpret and confirm these observations from an ecological perspective. Whereas Scudder argued that immediately after the resettlement, the rain making rituals (*lwiindi*) were no longer popular among the valley Tonga, today these ceremonies are very common with some variations.[72] Traditionally, the *sikatongos or* the Earth priests were the officiants; today, chiefs usually perform

---

[72] Thayer Scudder, "The Human Ecology of Big Projects: River Basin Development and Resettlement," *Annual Review of Anthropology* 2 (1973), 45-55. The Lusitu relocatees of Chief Chipepo do not have the *Lwiindi*. Other Tongas have the *Lwiindi* twice a year. Dan O'Brien and Carolyn O'Brien, "The Monze Rain Festival: The History of Change in Religious Cult in Zambia," *The International Journal of African Historical Studies* 29, no.3 (1997), 519-541; Dan O'Brien, "Chiefs of Rain, Chiefs of Ruling: A Reinterpretation of Precolonial Tonga (Zambia) Social and Political Structure," *Africa: Journal of the International African Institute* 53, no.4 (1983), 23-43.

these rituals.[73] As an ecological guardian of the land among the living, the chief presents requests on behalf of his people to the *basangu* (ancestors).

Simaamba Tonga are part of the Gwembe Tonga of Zambia. They trace their origin to the Rozvi Empire in today's Zimbabwe. Although their history is complex, Simaamba Tonga's cosmology is similar to that of the Shona in many respects. Although they are matrilineal, they refer to their ancestors as *mizimu* and call their royal ancestors *mhodolo*, as opposed to *basangu*.

Scudder and Colson argue that the Tonga were an amorphous or stateless people, who were led by Earth priests. Until the coming of colonialism (when the office of the chief was instituted), Scudder and Colson maintain that Earth priests were the leaders of the Tonga people. This study concurs with these observations; however, it adds that the Tonga lived in *ecological* rather than *political* states. In ecological states, Earth priests controlled the fertility of the land.[74] Depending on their ability to call the rains, some Earth priests commanded more respect than the others. Successful rain callers controlled larger communities and upon contact with colonial rule, they were transformed into political chiefs.

As Chapter Two will reveal, Tonga community cultures believe in an interconnected ontological hierarchy of spiritual forces. *Leza* (the Supreme source of all life), the *basangu* or *baami bamfula* (lords of the rain), and family ancestors (*mizimu*) are the principal guardians of the land. The community's future is dependent on how it behaves in time and space. For example, during the *lwiindi*,

---

[73] Elizabeth Colson, *The Social Consequences of Resettlement* (Lusaka: University of Zambia, 1971), 226.
[74] Tim Mathews, "Notes on the Precolonial History of the Tonga, with Emphasis on the Upper River Gwembe and Victoria Falls Area," in *The Tonga-Speaking Peoples of Zambia and Zimbabwe*, (ed.), Chet Lancaster and Kenneth P. Vickery (New York: University Press of America, 2007), 15-21; O'Brien and O'Brien, "Religious and Group Identity of the Tonga: An Examination of the *Lwiindi* Festival," in *The Tonga-Speaking Peoples of Zambia and Zimbabwe*, (ed.), Chet Lancaster and Kenneth Vickery (New York: University Press of America, 2007), 65.

the living offer *kankata* (ritual beers) to their ancestors at the *malende* (sacred groves). Only then can they present their supplications for their ecological wellbeing to the *basangu* and ultimately to *Leza*. But such supplications are conditional; they are based on their obedience to the *basangu* the previous year.

Lisa Cliggett, another scholar on the Gwembe Tonga, argues that overpopulation and drought have had negative impact on food security in the valley. Prior to the construction of Kariba Dam, Cliggett contends, the Gwembe population was about 86,000 of which 52,000 lived on the Zambian side. Within 29 years, however, the population soared almost 140 percent; with approximately 125,000 Tongas living on the Zambian side alone. Cliggett notes that while "portions of the Gwembe remain forested and uninhabited, some areas, especially the land close to the lakeshore or tributaries, have become densely populated."[75]

Cliggett's argument, however, does little to address all the ecological inhabitants of the Gwembe. As evidenced by Operation Noah, the valley is home to millions of other biota. Ecologically, what Cliggett sees as uninhabited areas are homes to millions of nonhumans. Thus, the crisis of overpopulation in the Gwembe will have adverse effects on other biota.

## Ethical Analysis

The Christian doctrine of creation is in line with the African ontology of creation in which God, Spirits, humanity, and the natural world exist in constant harmony. Each ontological category has intrinsic value and rights; thus, to destroy one is to break the harmony of the entire universe. In this sense, to possess *ubuntu* is to respect the harmony and interaction of each ontological category. Any person who disturbs or destroys this ontological harmony is considered highly immoral for having lost *ubuntu*.

The African morality of *ubuntu* opposes extreme individualism, but favors cooperation. It protects and ensures land productivity,

---

[75] Ibid., 61.

rain, good health, many children, and other social and economic blessings. Although the Supreme Being is the ontological source and guardian of morality, Africans regard "elders" as moral guardians. Since, however, the term "elder" can apply to both ancestors and "old people" in society, African ethics is negotiated between the living and living-dead elders. As living-dead elders, ancestors are the route to abundant life.

The morality of *ubuntu* has economic, sociopolitical, ecological and spiritual implications. Africa's population will double to 2 billion by 2050, but this growth will not be matched by economic growth. Even where economic growth will take place, it will do so in large part alongside severe environmental degradation. As Chapter Five illustrates, Africa's population growth is threatening the well-being of planet Earth and future generations of life.

As in the Bible, ancestors sanctioned unlimited procreation; however, the ever increasing population numbers are putting extreme pressure on Earth's carrying capacity. Population increase is also contributing to the loss of ancestral lands due to soil erosion and land degradation, as is the case among the Tonga today. Just as tribal lands are failing to meet the needs of their communities, governments are finding it hard to address the socio-economic needs of their people. Aside from the widening gap between the rich and the poor, current economic development programs are based on irresponsible exploitation of natural goods.

One example of how economic development has come at the cost of environmental degradation is in the Gwembe valley. There, the ecological destruction wrought by the Kariba Dam project (mentioned above and further addressed in Chapter Two) far outweighs economic benefits. However, projects like the Kariba Dam have been one of the major reasons why African governments heralded the concept of "sustainable development"—advocating economic advancement while ensuring the wellbeing of Earth and future generations. Any discussion of sustainable development, I contend, should address the role played by corruption, poor governance and international forces in Africa's development.

But, there are theological and ecological limitations to the sustainable development model, the book argues. As with other modern economic theories, the goal of sustainable development is "unlimited economic growth." Moreover, Africa's economic growth is mostly dependent on the overexploitation of natural goods for global North markets. This "heavy reliance on natural capital" (which even the World Bank now acknowledges as a major obstacle to sustainable development in sub-Saharan Africa) invites severe environmental degradation.[76] Endless economic growth is simply impossible on the limited Earth.

Like Earth, the African continent has a limited carrying capacity. The looming crises noted above demand that we live within the limits of Earth's capacity. This book, however, advances an ethic of "sustainable living," whereby people across the globe live by needs as opposed to wants. The ethic of sustainable living demands both local and global responsibility and action by all Earth dwellers.

The environmental crisis in Africa, I argue, should be addressed at two fronts—local and global. The global North ought to change its consumption patterns, make its markets fair and just, while the global South should address massive corruption, employ measures that protect the poor, and ensure the wellbeing of the entire Earth community.

African nations are parties to environmental protocols, but this is not matched by how these countries view natural goods. Almost all African countries exploit natural goods with little regard for the poor, ecosystems, and future generations of life. But, as Mercy Amba Oduyoye observes, the identification "of the divine spirit in nature and the community spirit between human beings, other living creatures and natural phenomena could reinforce the Christian doctrine of Creation as well as contribute to Christian reflection on ecological problems."[77] Oduyoye is correct; Africans

---

[76] The World Bank, *Toward Environmentally Sustainable Development in sub-Saharan Africa: A World Bank Agenda* (Washington D.C: The World Bank, 1996), 11-13.
[77] Mercy Amba Oduyoye, "African Religious Beliefs," in *African Theology En Route* (1979), 110.

have traditional resources for ecological reflections and actions. However, the dilemma that Leonardo Boff points out is pertinent here. Africans, like other "human beings, especially with the advent of the industrial revolution, have proved that they are exterminating angels, veritable demons of Earth. But human beings could also become guardian angels, intent upon saving the earth, which is their fatherland and motherland."[78]

The ethics of *ubuntu*, which accepts the interconnectedness of life, can inform and direct how Christians relate to Earth and one another. Our current overexploitation of natural goods is driven by human greed and corruption, vices that are contrary to the ethics of *ubuntu*. *Ubuntu* should encourage the equitable distribution of natural goods to the entire Earth community.

But, the overexploitation of Earth's goods won't last forever. We ought to explore new ways of replenishing renewable natural goods—trees, animals, and fish stocks. This is even more pressing as populations explode and natural goods become scarce. For African Christianity to adopt the ethics of replenishing Earth, theologians should provide the spiritual and ethical basis for replanting trees and for repopulating wild-life and other species. Such an ethic should pay attention to all religious heritages that inform Africa today. This ethic can unite Christians and people of other faiths in Earthkeeping ministries or innitiatives. As Daneel has shown in his work with African Earthkeepers in Zimbabwe, capitalizing on the people's diverse historical, religious, and cultural heritages in Earthkeeping initiatives can revitalize ecological consciousness and actions.

## Theological Analysis

The concept of interconnectedness has bearing on the ancestor cult. This book investigates the ecological significance of the ancestor cult in Africa. As Chapters Two and Seven illustrate,

---

[78] Leonardo Boff, *Ecology and Liberation: A New Paradigm* (Maryknoll, NY: Orbis Books, 1995), 18-19.

traditions pertaining to ancestors vary from community to community, but ancestors are concerned with the ecological wellbeing of their descendants. Granting the multiple faces of Jesus in Africa today, this book explores the ecological face of Jesus as the Ecological Ancestor of all biokind. All beings, including African ancestors (the guardians of the land), it argues, find their origin in Christ.

Aptly stated, the face of Jesus as "our ancestor" begs an ecological Christology that addresses Christ as the guardian of the land *par-excellence*. This is in line with the biblical teaching that Jesus is the origin of all biokind "through whom all things were created" (Col 1:16; cf. John 1:3). Theologically therefore, Jesus is both the origin of our ancestors and the provider of abundant life *par-excellence*. Yet, Jesus is also the origin of all creation, and by default, the ancestor brother to every creature. As an ancestor-brother of all Creation, Jesus sacralizes the universe, thereby making creation a sacrament of divine presence in, and divine commitment to the natural world.

The above understanding is crucial to addressing the socio-economic inequalities in Africa today. The realization that Earth is a sacrament means that all natural goods are sacramental commons, and belong to all Earth community.[79] This understanding demands that we share Earth's goods fairly; this is the virtue of *ubuntu* to which humanity should aspire at all times.[80]

Further, creation ultimately belongs to the Supreme Being, and humanity is never the "ruler" of creation *per se*. This idea is in contrast with prominent and sometimes popular Christian notions of dominion, which argue that humanity has a God-given mandate to exercise unlimited control over the natural world.

Most scholars in Africa have accepted this interpretation of dominion without paying attention to traditional philosophies

---

[79] The concept of Sacramental commons originates with John Hart and it is addressed fully in his book, *Sacramental Commons*, chapter four, 61-78.
[80] Katherine Marshall and Marisa Bronwyn Van Saanen, *Development and Faith: Where Mind, Heart, and Soul Work Together* (Washington, DC: The World Bank. 2007).

which viewed humanity as part of Earth community. Sadly, theology in Africa has remained a theology without Earth and by implication, if sometimes unwittingly, promoted the domination of nature. But as Mbiti observes, among Africans,

> [humanity] lives in a religious universe, so that the natural phenomena and objects are intimately associated with God. They not only originate from him but also bear witness to him. Man's understanding of God is strongly colored by the universe of which man is himself a part. Man sees in the universe not only the imprint but also the reflection of God; and whether that image is marred or clearly focused and defined, it is nevertheless an image of God, and the only image known in traditional African Societies.[81]

The above perception confirms the sacramental nature of Earth Community. Here, the liberation of Earth (the mediation of God in African traditional religions) is central to Christian liberation theology and ethics.

Politically, the motif of land as a sacred trust provided the organizing principle during the struggle against colonialism. The liberation struggle was by default, an attempt to reclaim ancestral lands from colonial settlers. Africans hoped that the coming of independence would reverse the damage caused by colonialism. Sadly, their hopes were shattered, as the once heralded heroes became more repressive than colonial governments. Thus, most post-independence theological responses addressed the socio-political and economic woes that the continent was, and is currently facing. Consequently, the ecological crisis caught African scholars unaware in their self-ethicizing and self-theologizing.

## Limitations

An attempt to construct Christian ecological ethics in Africa has many limitations. First, Christian ecological ethics in Africa is

---

[81] Mbiti, *African Religions and Philosophy*, 48. From now on, "man" and other masculine pronouns will be retained when citing other scholars' works without qualification. In my own usage, however, I use humanity or other gender neutral terms.

understudied, and published literature is hard to obtain. Second, a fully comprehensive study would include participant observation of countless traditional rituals, particularly since a resurgence of traditional ceremonies in Africa holds potential for illustrating ecological concerns. Unfortunately, due to financial and time constraints, I limit myself to Chief Simaamba's *lwiindi* ceremony. Third, the relationship between African Christianity, development, and the environment deserves much more critical study, as do issues of religion and development generally.

Finally, an exhaustive study of this overall topic would also make use of classical Christian thought. I opted, though, to study contemporary theologians and ethicists to dialogue with them at this important moment in world history. Although St. Francis of Assisi and other mystics provide another basis for understanding the concept of interconnectedness, this study adds insight by exploring it from an African perspective. Within these limitations, however, is an attempt to develop Christian ecological ethics of *ubuntu* as well as the Christology of Christ as the "Ecological Ancestor" of all biota.

# Chapter Two
## African Cosmologies and the Environment: The Case of Simaamba Tonga

### Our Ancestors/Elders Ought to Get Involved

The Rio+20 U.N. Conference on Sustainable Development held in Rio de Janeiro, Brazil, from June 20-22, 2012, provided us with another opportunity to re-examine our attitudes to the natural world. Since the first Rio Earth summit of 1992, the calls for ecological consciousness have steadily increased—with the U.N. declaring environmental sustainability as one of the eight Millennium Development Goals in 2000. Yet, the Seventeenth Conference of the Parties (COP 17) U.N. Convention on Climate Change held in Durban, South Africa, from November 28 to December 9, 2011, failed to convince all nations to commit to reducing carbon emissions in the shortest possible time. The truth is, despite the calls for eco-sensitive economic policies, we are still unwilling to make hard choices to ensure the ecological wellbeing of Earth.

In retrospect, however, these conferences increased ecological consciousness across the globe and Africa in particular. The demonstrations organized by environmental activists from all parts of the globe revealed the urgency of the matter, especially in Africa. Although Africa is among the continents likely to suffer the most from the immediate effects of the ecological crisis, other continents are not immune. Be it America, Asia, or South America, animals, trees, water bodies, and marine species are disappearing while global temperatures are rising.

In October 2012, historic storm Sandy ravaged the U.S. East Coast—leaving tens of thousands homeless and over 8 million homes without power for weeks. Reuters estimated the death toll at 132.[1] The storm brought many cities to a complete standstill—flooding railway lines, roads, and homes, and causing infrastructure damages ranging from $50-$70 Billion. As this historic storm pounded the U.S., many Americans realized that they too were not immune from the effects of global warming. But, as Rio+20 and COP 17 revealed, if there were only the global political will and action, we could arrest these frightening crises.

The realization that humanity is the major cause of this problem, as well as a solution, has forced all fields of knowledge to stress ecological awareness and responsibilities. In Africa, for instance, the crisis has attracted the attention of traditionalists, academicians, church leaders, theologians, politicians, as well as African artists. In 2005, Oliver Mutukuzi, one of the most respected Southern African artists released the song entitled *Pindirai* (intervene):

| | |
|---|---|
| *Vakuruwe pindirai* | Elders intervene |
| *Vakuruwe pindirai* | Elders intervene |
| *Madzimambowe pindirai* | Chiefs intervene |
| *Madzimambowe pindirai* | Chiefs intervene |
| *Mhuri yenyu yapererwa neruzivo* | Your family has run out of wisdom |
| *Vana venyu kupererwa nenjere.* | Your children have run out of ideas. |

His reason for seeking the intervention of *vakuru* (elders) and *madzimambo* (chiefs) is due to the ecological crises that characterize Southern Africa. Human beings have cut trees at their own peril (*vanotema miti vasina ruzivo*), which he compares to skinning a skunk in the direction of the wind (*vagovhiya chidembo vari kumhepo*) or spitting into the well *(kusvipira mutsime)*. These crises have frightening effects on human livelihood:

| | |
|---|---|
| *Hatichina mumviri* | We have no shade from the trees |
| *Hatichina mapango* | We have no poles for building |
| *Duwinho hatichina* | We have no water pools |

---

[1] Reuters, Factbox: Storm Sandy blamed for at least 132 deaths in U.S., Canada, Nov 16, 2012.http://www.reuters.com/article/2012/11/16/us-storm-sandy-deaths-idUSBRE8AF0Z X201 21116. Accessed 12/5/2012.

| | |
|---|---|
| *Hove hatichina* | We have no fish |
| *Raiva dziva rava zambuko* | What used to be a big dam is now a road |
| *Aive madziva ave mazambuko.* | What used to be pools are now roads. |

Mutukudzi further complains about poor waste management in urban areas of Africa. People have turned rivers into dump sites (*kutsviirira munzizi segomba ramarara*), while human habitats are now landfills (*votora marara vounganidza muberere*). In the end, water and air are polluted. Finally, he bemoans that:

| | |
|---|---|
| *Tatadza kuchengeta masango* | We have failed to care for the forests |
| *Kutadza kuchengeta nzizi* | We have failed to care for the rivers |
| *Mhepo yekufema yangova utsi* | The air we breath is now smoke |
| *Kusvipira mutsime* | Spitting into the well |
| *Vakuruwe pindirai!* | Elders intervene! |

Mutukuzi's message is clear. The impending ecological disaster is a result of human arrogance toward the interconnected ecosphere. To resolve this crisis, he calls on *vakuru* or *madzimambo* to intervene, too. Because the Bantu uphold the hierarchical ontology of beings, seeking the intervention of elders in times of crisis is within the framework of African traditional religious thought.

Mutukudzi also illustrates the interconnectedness of the ongoing ecological crisis. For instance, deforestation has negative consequences on humanity, water, and the ecosphere as a whole. In a rural context where the majority depends on the natural world for survival, the impact is visible at many levels. Deforestation deprives humans of the comfort of *mumvuri* (the shade from the trees), under which they sit during hot seasons. It also robs the poor of much needed *mapango* (poles) for building their homes.

The felling of trees negatively effects water supplies: *duwinho* (pools), *madziva* (dams), and *nzizi* (rivers) are now dying due to human negligence. Apart from being sources of drinking water, these water bodies have spiritual significance among the Bantu. They are homes to sacred spirits (*njuzu*) as well as to fish (*hove*)—a vital source of protein for river communities. By destroying Earth, he warns, "we are spitting into the well;" thus poisoning ourselves to death. Here the moral guidance of the elders (*vakuru*) becomes imperative.

The Shona words *vakuru* or *madzimambo* could mean "living elders" or "ancestors," hence it is unclear as to whom Mutukuzi is appealing. This unclear differentiation between the authority of the "living elders" and "ancestors" has been at the center of theological and anthropological contention when attempting to understand the power of ancestors in Africa.[2] Nonetheless, the ancestors' lasting relationship with the lands they founded made them standards of morality. They are therefore obliged to intervene in any crisis that threatens their lands.[3] Among the Tonga of chief Simaamba in Zambia, the intervention of ancestors/elders is sought through the *lwiindi* ceremony (rain-calling ritual).

## Simaamba Ancestors as Guardians of the Land

The people of Simaamba are among the valley Tonga of the lower Zambezi, resettled on the Zambian side of the dam after the construction of the Kariba Dam in 1958. Today's Simaamba area includes the Kariba town of Siavonga, though the palace is located about 30 miles from the town. The chiefdom is made up of two senior *Sikatongos* (ecological guardians) or what Colson translates as "Earth prophet/priest:" *Sikatongo* Nambwele (who according to Charles Halubanje, the reigning Nambwele, is traditionally the correct person to perform the *lwiindi*), and *Sikatongo* Hakuyu. Simaamba borders with the Tonga of Chief Chipepo who were resettled around Lusitu, and the Goba (Shona) community culture of chief Sikongo, in whose land the Tonga of Chipepo and Simaamba were resettled.

---

[2] Although it is held that only those who lived morally upright lives can become ancestors, usually founding ancestors were community misfits. Thomas Q. Reefe, "Traditions of Genesis and the Luba Diaspora," *History in Africa* 4 (1977), 183-206; William Govan Robertson, "Kasembe and the Bemba (Awemba) Nation," *Journal of the Royal African Society* 3, no.10 (Jan., 1904), 183-193.

[3] Matthew Schoffeleers (ed), *Guardians of the Land: Essays on Central African Territorial Cults* (Gweru: Mambo Press, 1978).

Inheritance to the throne of Simaamba is from the matrilineal side. While the chiefs' sons are considered princes, only the chief's nephews from his matrilineal line are legitimate heirs to the throne. As mothers of chiefs, royal women and deceased chiefs are usually buried in the *malende,* where the *lwiindi* is also held.

## Brief History of the Gwembe Tonga

The history of the Gwembe Tonga is highly complex. The word "Gwembe," for example, was a Ndebele word for the Zambezi. Today, however, it applies to all the tribes (community cultures) of the Zambezi valley.[4] As for the term "Tonga," Colson argues that the meaning of the word is unknown and probably is of foreign origin.[5] In 1927, however, F.M.T. Posselt argued that the word Tonga referred to "those who do not recognize a paramount chief, or fault-finders or grumblers."[6] Likewise, in 1938, F.B. Macrae concluded that the inhabitants of the Gwembe valley:

> Appear to have come into the area about a hundred years ago, according to their own tradition. At this time they say that the valley was uninhabited. They also say they came from a country called Bunyai [today's Mashonaland] further down the river; this name is still to be found on the maps as Banyai, a tribe who were at one time prominent on the lower reaches of the Zambezi. The Banyai were also associated with the Makalanga, a number of whom live with the Batonga in the Gwembe valley at the present day.[7]

Although these scholars did not consider the Shona word, *"kutonga"* (to rule/judge), it is probable that the word *Tonga*

---

[4] In this book, I retain "tribe" when citing others, but use community culture instead of "tribe" in my work. Tribe suggests that such communities are inferior.
[5] Elizabeth Colson, *Marriage and the Family Among the Plateau Tonga of Northern Rhodesia* (Manchester: Manchester University Press for the Rhodes-Livingstone Institute, 1958), 1.
[6] In Chet S. Lancaster, "Ethnic Identity, History, and 'Tribe' in the Zambezi Valley," *American Ethnologist* 1, no.4 (Nov 1974), 724.
[7] F. B. Macrae, "Some Notes on Part of the Gwembe Valley in Northern Rhodesia," *The Geographical Journal* 91, no.5 (May, 1938), 446-449.

referred to groups who sought to rule (the verb *kutonga*) themselves. The Shona origin of this group can also be adduced from the name *Banyai* which once referred to the Shona community culture around the Zambezi river. This assertion is complemented by Lancaster's oral evidence that suggests that the Tonga "never had any real chiefs or paramounts except Mambo [a Rozvi King] south of the Zambezi whom they ran from so that they could be free people. So they were called Tongas, which means grunters, dissatisfied people who complained and rebelled against their chief."[8] Thus, the word Tonga seems to be a "descriptive term that refers to a cultural status deriving from Southern Rhodesian history as Shona speakers see it."[9]

Unlike the term "Gwembe" which refers to all valley Tongas, the word "Tonga" has now been applied to different ethnic groups in Malawi, Mozambique, Zambia, and Zimbabwe. In Zambia for example, "Tonga" describes both Plateau and Gwembe Tongas. However, some of these groups are historically and linguistically unrelated—adding to the complexities of their history. For instance, while the Gwembe Tonga of Chief Mukuni in the valley trace their origin from the Luba-Lunda Empire on the Congo basin, those of Simaamba maintain that they originated from the Rozvi Empire in present day Zimbabwe.[10] Despite lacking a common history and linguistic differences, however, valley Tongas have been incorrectly studied as a social and cultural unit.

The ecology of the Gwembe valley has always been challenging. Aside from the geographical hardships, rainfall in the area has been sporadic. In 1938, Macrae observed that the vegetation in the

---

[8] Lancaster, "Ethnic Identity, History, and 'Tribe,'" 724.
[9] Ibid. Also Tim Matthews, "Notes on the Precolonial History of the Tonga, with Emphasis on the Upper River Gwembe and Victoria Falls Area," in Chet Lancaster and Kenneth P. Vickery (eds.), *The Tonga-Speaking Peoples of Zambia and Zimbabwe* (New York: University Press of America, 2007), 13-33.
[10] While all valley Tongas are Bantu speaking, those of the Middle and Upper Zambezi belong to the Bantu-Botatwe (three people) languages (Ila, Lenje and Tonga). The earlier languages of the Sikongo and Simaamba's peoples, however, were of Southern Bantu linguistic origin.

valley is much more tropical than the rest of the country. While big trees abounded, the area had a great deal of thorn bush and a fair number of euphorbia trees. He further noted that the area "receives about 10 to 12 inches of rainfall during the rain season, while the rest of the country to the north gets anything from 25 inches upwards."[11] The Tongas' vunerability to lack of rainfall was, however, compensated by two farming seasons—one during the rain season and another after the floods. Notwithstanding, these two farming seasons depended on balanced rainfall. Too much or too little rainfall led to severe famines and hunger in the valley.

The preeminence of the rain-calling rituals and the belief among the Tonga of Simaamba and the Goba of Sikongo that *Nyami-Nyami* provided his body as meat to his people during times of famine suggest the harsh ecological conditions of valley life.[12] However, the ecology of the valley also provided the Tonga with edible flora and fauna which supplemented their diet in the years of hunger. Sadly, their displacement from the valley robbed them of traditional survival skills they had gathered over the centuries. Whereas starvation in the valley could be attributed to many factors as Lisa Cliggett has rightly demonstrated, the forced resettlement worsened it.[13]

Demographically, however, the fertility and twice-annual cultivation of alluvial soils made the valley attractive to human settlement. Because the Zambezi was the trade route to slave-traders, however, the Tonga people experienced constant attacks.

---

[11] Macrae, "Some Notes on Part of the Gwembe," 447.

[12] Simaamba Tonga religious beliefs seem to point to these existential realities. It is said that the snake-like *Nyami-Nyami* only became visible during the time of famine. The serpentine spirit would slowly move from village to village along the Zambezi valley, exposing its own body and allowing people to cut portions of meat from it. *Nyami-Nyami's* body would heal instantly. This made it possible for the people to survive the famines that characterized the valley.

[13] Lisa Cliggett, *Grains From Grass: Aging, Gender, and Famine in Rural Africa* (Ithaca: Cornell University Press, 2005); Elizabeth Colson, "Converts and Tradition: The Impact of Christianity on Valley Tonga Religion," *Southwestern Journal of Anthropology* 26, no.2 (Summer, 1970), 143-156.

Worse still, the valley faced other environmental challenges. First, the valley was a home to big animals which threatened human livelihoods. Second, it was disease-infested due to the high population of wildlife. These factors meant that the Zambezi valley always controlled its population and somehow handicapped the residents' political organization.

Politically, the Tonga did not have centralized leadership. Even the word *mwami,* which today is rendered as chief, originally applied to the royal spirits (*basangu*), mediums (persons possessed with *basangu* spirits), and occasionally to the *sikatongos*. Although *mwami* was later adopted to denote chieftainship in the colonial sense, organized chieftainships were absent in Tonga life; hence they were an amorphous or stateless people.

This pre-colonial political disorganization somehow made them easy targets to slave-raiding cultures—the Nguni, the Arabs, and the Portuguese. To protect themselves against such threats, they gathered around certain charismatic Earth priests (*sikatongos*). Using the *lwiindi* as an organizing tool, charismatic *sikatongos* managed to build a sizable following, and counter-organized against raiding community cultures and colonialism. Despite lacking hierarchical or hereditary structures of political authority, certain Tonga groups adapted new forms of governance that did not only address the exigencies of the nineteenth century, but also strengthened leadership positions of Earth priests. *Sikatongo* Monze, for example, used his rain-calling powers to negotiate the new social and political challenges of the nineteenth and early twentieth century in which his neighborhood found itself.

There is, however, another way to understand the sociological organization of traditional Tonga life. The power of the Earth priest suggests that the ecology of the valley was at the center of Tonga life. The Tonga lived in what I term "ecological states" as opposed to "political" states. Ecological states gathered around an Earth priest rather than a political King or Chief. Political leadership as practiced in the $21^{st}$ century would have been unknown among the Tonga. But, the ecological leadership of a *sikatongo* as an official representative of ancestors and the *basangu* provided the basis for the office of today's political chief. During colonialism, this ecological leadership turned political, as Tim Matthews and the O'Briens have independently confirmed.[14]

## The Simaamba Tonga Religious Worldview[15]

Like all Bantu cultures, the Simaamba Tonga believe in an interconnected ontological hierarchy of spiritual forces. *Leza* (God) is the Supreme Vital force and the source of life who is concerned with community welfare. The *basangu* or *baami bamfula* (chiefs of rain) are second in this hierarchy. They include royal ancestors and other spirits associated with natural phenomena like trees, mountains, pools, and sacred creatures residing in the *malende*.

The *malende* occupy an important place in Simaamba Tonga cosmology—they are homes to unseen powers associated with nature. The *malende* sites are usually natural objects—rocks, forests, springs, and even mountains. At these sites, the *sikatongo,* and now chiefs, supplicate the *basangu* in hard times, especially in times of drought and famine. In addition to natural sites, royal burial spaces are called *malende*. Such *malende,* however, are marked by one or several tiny huts (*kaanda).*[16] Like *Leza,* the *basangu* are concerned with community welfare. Individuals known as *basangu* (mediums) warn against drought and famines, which are mostly attributed to human infringement of social and moral order. They also determine the time for holding the *lwiindi.*

The *basangu* spirits are ontologically close to *Leza*, so it is easy to confuse them with the Supreme Being. Major A. H. Gibbons,

---

[14] Elizabeth Colson, *Tonga Religious Life in the Twentieth Century* (Lusaka, Bookworld Publishers, 2006); Dan O'Brien, "Chief of Rain—Chief of Ruling: A Reinterpretation of Pre-Colonial Tonga (Zambia) Social and Political Structure," *Journal of the International African Institute* 53, no.4 (1983), 23-42; Matthews, "Notes on the Precolonial History of the Tonga," 21; O'Brien and O'Brien, "Religious and Group Identity of the Tonga," 65.
[15] Due to the variability and diversity of the Gwembe Tongas, unless otherwise stated, the word "Tonga" is used to refer to those of Chief Simaamba.
[16] Reynolds, *The Material Cultures*, 23.

who took the expedition on the Zambezi from 1895-1900, did exactly that. He confusedly took the *malende* of *Nyami-Nyami* at Kariba Gorge as the headquarters of the Tonga deity. "This," he argued, "the boys assured me to be the headquarters of the great river god; and although many boats have gone down within these sacred precincts, neither boat, nor goods nor bodies have ever been recovered. The Portuguese...always throw in wine and calico to propitiate the deity."[17]

Frank Clements followed Gibbons to associate this river spirit with *Leza*. To him, the problems that characterized the building of the Kariba Dam were due to the struggle of this river deity, which he identifies as *Nyami-Nyami*—"the all-powerful god of the river."[18] Yet he contradicts himself when he asserts, "it is not clear what status Nyami-Nyami had as an ancestral shade, but it caused those foolish enough to shoot the Kariba Gorge to disappear from the face of Earth, and its tail was blamed for the destruction of bridges and coffer dams."[19] The people interviewed in Simaamba, Sikongo and Chipepo areas attributed the destruction of the coffers to *Nyami-Nyami*, but like Chief Simaamba, they argued that "*Nyami-Nyami* is a creature of God (Leza) and one of the most powerful spirits of the Zambezi."[20]

In Simaamba Tonga cosmology, family matters are the prerogative of family ancestors (*mizimu*). As guardians of the family line, *mizimu* demand continuity of approved behavior and customs from their descendants. In most cases, they consider attempts to reform such traditions as insubordination. But, they are open to change once the *basangu* approve such traditions.

Both the *basangu* and *mizimu* can possess individuals (*ngangas*) with healing powers. While such individuals can occasionally call the *lwiindi*, *nganga* activities are tailored to individual and family

---

[17] Major A.S.H. Gibbons, *Africa from South to North through Marotseland*, vol. 1 (London: J. Lane, 1904), 45-46.
[18] Frank Clements, *Kariba: The Struggle with the River God* (London: Methuen, 1959), 88.
[19] Ibid., 12.
[20] Chief Simaamba, Interview, October, 2006.

needs. Importantly, such diviners control evil forces—witches (*balozi*), community illnesses (*zelo*), dangerous ghosts (*zilube*), and alien spirits (*masabe*).

The relationship between the *basangu* and *mizimu* is equally complex. During the *lwiindi*, for instance, the *basangu* and *mizimu* are invoked interchangeably. Likewise, the individuals who are possessed by either the *muzimo* (singular) ancestral spirit or the *musangu* (singular) spirit can claim to be prophets or mediums of these spirits interchangeably. Since the *basangu* intermediaries are usually held in higher esteem than the *mizimu* mediums, most prophets associate their authority with the *basangu* when addressing community issues. Nonetheless, they revert to the *mizimu* when addressing individual matters.

The complex relationship between the *basangu* and *mizimu* for example, surfaced during the construction of the Kariba Dam. Despite the threats posed by the dam, most people resisted resettlement for various reasons. The report of the Commission on the violence that characterized the building of the dam noted that people believed that the construction of the dam would not be possible, and that Europeans could not close the dam.[21] The report did not provide the basis for such beliefs, but the Tonga point to religious beliefs. Some believed that the river spirits (chiefly *Nyami-Nyami*) would defend their ancestral land from western encroachment. Others, however, hoped that their *basangu* would punish the Europeans for obliterating the *malende*. A number also feared the wrath of ancestors, if they abandoned ancestral graves.

To calm these fears, the *basangu* played a vital role. Although they previously warned people not to move, they later declared that the spirits had agreed to move after the people had performed certain traditional rituals. They also encouraged people to carry soil and branches from their sacred groves as a way of

---

[21] Northern Rhodesia, *Report of the Commission Appointed to Inquire into the Circumstances Leading up to and Surrounding the Recent Deaths and Injuries Caused by the Use of Firearms in the Gwembe District and Matters Relating Thereto* (Lusaka: Government Printers, 1958), 9.

taking their ancestors with them. Mr. Patrick Makukisi, a resident of Chipepo area who was 11 at the time of the resettlement and a survivor of the Lusitu condition—the illness that led to the death of many relocatees—explained, "I remember what my father did. He followed the instructions of the *basangu* and carried the soil with him. When we got to Lusitu, he mixed it with water and gave us to drink. That is why we survived."[22]

Such innovation convinced many Tongas to move, but others ignored the rulings of the mediums and vowed to defend their land. This situation led to violent clashes between colonial authorities and Tonga groups. The violent clashes, the defeat, the forceful removal, and finally the closing of the dam walls led some Tongas to question the powers of *basangu* to protect their descendants from Western forces.[23] However, the deaths and the droughts that followed the resettlements somehow confirmed their original reservations—their ancestors were upset.

The Kariba case illustrates the influence of the *basangu* medium not only over the *lwiindi* but also over new socio-economic and political changes in Tonga life. However, this was not the first time when such negotiations took place. The solidification of the authority of Monze, and Mweemba, were due to their roles as *basangu* prophets. Just as Mbuya Nehanda and Sekuru Kagubi of Mashonaland used their prophetic powers to resist colonial rule in colonial Zimbabwe, Monze employed his ritual authority to resist Lewanika and later colonialism in Northern Rhodesia/Zambia. Dan O'Brien alludes to this when he asserts that Monze's leadership was religiously sanctioned.[24]

## Actors in *Lwiindi* of the *Bagande* (frog) Clan

The *lwiindi* ceremony illustrates the ecological significance of the *basangu* in Tonga religions. While the *sikatongo* (Earth priest) is

---

[22] Patrick Makukisi, Interview, Lusitu, Zambia, October, 2006.
[23] Clements, *Kariba*, 1959; Northern Rhodesia, *Report of the Commission*, 1958.
[24] O'Brien, "Chief of Rain—Chief of Ruling," 21, 23-42.

the rightful person to perform the *lwiindi*, today the chief is the ritual officiant. Equally important is a woman known as *mulela* (from the verb *kulela,* "to care"). Aside from being the official keeper of the *ganda* (sacred hut where the chief spends special nights and traditional artifacts are kept), a *mulela* is also the keeper of the royal artifacts. Selected among the virgins from the line of *mulela*, she is given to the ancestors as a ritual wife and takes care of all the needs of the chief while in the *ganda*.[25]

In addition to a *mulela*, there is a *muzambi*—the person who acts as a spiritual bodyguard to the chief, because of his knowledge of preventative traditional medicine.[26] During the *lwiindi*, a *muzambi* consults with the chief and protects him against the evil powers of his enemies. Traditionally, however, his other duties included sampling foods, especially in times of famine. A *muzambi* would sample wild roots first; if he dies, the chief would not eat it.

## Calling the Rain: *Lwiindi* Ceremony

The *lwiindi* usually takes place around October or November when people are preparing their fields for planting.[27] Since traditional ritual beer (*kankata*) is essential to the *lwiindi*, each household contributes grain for brewing it. The *sikatongos* and other elders collect grain from each household. The grain (sorghum, millet, or maize) is then given to old women who brew the ritual beers.

---

[25] Unlike the wives of the reigning chief whose status change with the death of their husbands, a *mulela* remains in the *ganda* until she is too old to perform ritual duties. Only then can she be replaced.
[26] According to Nambwele, traditionally a *muzambi* was picked among slaves. In November, 2006, the senior *muzambi* was Peter Hamunteka.
[27] The Tongas celebrate various *lwiindis* based on the ecological calendar. Among the plateau Tonga, *lwiindi lwa kulyata mukuba* is held during the clearing of the fields prior to planting; *lwiindi lwa mwaka* is held during the planting season; *lwiindi lwa kuyamina* is held during the weeding and scaring of birds season; *lwiindi lwakuloka* is celebrated during the eating of the first fruits; while *lwiindi lwakutebula* takes place during the celebration of the harvest and the calling of rains. *Sikatongo* Nambwele and Siakuyu celebrate all the *lwiindis*. Nambwele, Interview, Simaamba School, Feb. 27, 2009.

Seven days before the ceremony, the chief and *mulela* enter the sacred hut (*ganda*). During this period, they are excluded from all social activities. Likewise, the community is expected to do the same. No marriage ceremony, mourning or burial of the dead is allowed during this period. Around the same time, the elders and the *muzambi* go to the royal graves to clean and rebuild the sacred huts (*nsaka*), believed to be the dwelling place of the *basangu*. The gender of a specific ancestor is symbolized by the way the hut is thatched. Males have their huts thatched with the roof having grass shaped like horns, while female huts are identified by a cone.

A night before the ceremony, the royal party takes the *kankata* to the *malende*. Unlike other African *cultures* that pour the beer on the ground as libation, Simaamba Tonga pour it into clay pots. These pots are later placed in each hut as gifts to the ancestors. After invoking the ancestors to accept their people's offerings, the party leaves the shrine for their respective homes.

The following day, the people gather around the *ganda* at the chief's palace to await his coming-out ceremony. However, the two *sikatongos* and their people await the chief's party in the *malende*. The *sikatongos* position themselves at specific places resembling the directions of their villages. They will join the procession at two different intervals during the ceremony.[28] At the palace, however, invited guests, and local people are entertained to various rain-calling songs by drummers and dancers. At the appointed time, a *muzambi* enters the *ganda* to alert the chief to come out.

The *mulela* confers power on the chief by handing him traditional spears and a *bukanu* (axe) used by the founding ancestor. She also gives spears to the *muzambi*. After this, the *muzambi* emerges holding spears, and the *mudima* or *budima* (special beat) is played on drums. At this moment, the people stop singing and the chief finally emerges from the *ganda*, dressed in his royal black gown and hat. The people make loud sounds and

---

[28] According to my Tonga informants, the joining of the *sikatongos* at different times symbolizes how the three groups became part of the Simaamba royal establishment.

gesticulations. Thereafter, the chief leads an adult-only procession to the *malende*.[29]

As the parade makes its way into the *malende*, men and women separate. Women continue toward the place called *nakalindi* or *cihiba* (pool) while men go hunting in the sacred grove. (In the past, I am told, the ancestors would provide them with meat for the sacred feast. Due to the overexploitation of animals, however, no animals were found during the 2006 *lwiindi*; another indication of the current ecological disturbance in the valley). As people are hunting, the chief and his *muzambi* await the hunting party under a special tree.

Just as the hunting party rejoins the chief, the people of *sikatongo* Nambwele emerge from their hiding place to confront Simaamba with spears in an enacted war. Simaamba's people fight back until Nambwele recognizes his authority. After making peace, they together proceed toward *nakalindi*, where they are met by dancing women.[30] As the chief's party approaches *nakalindi*, Hakuyu's people confront them with spears. Again, after this enacted battle, Hakuyu accepts the authority of Simaamba and joins the party.

Then the people celebrate the unity with dancing for several minutes while the three traditional leaders are standing-by until Simaamba calls for order by raising his axe. After everybody is quiet, a ritual of water-drinking is performed with the Chief being served first by his first wife (the Tonga usually marry more than one wife). Likewise, his *muzambi* and *sikatongos* are served by their first wives. While traditionally the water for this ritual came from the *nakalindi*, today tap water is used.

---

[29] This is in contrast to Colson's findings among the Plateau Tonga where no one is excluded from the *lwiindis*, though she also notes that the Luanga Tonga exclude women. See Colson, "Rain Shrines," 280.
[30] According to Mr. Simaamba, the son of the late chief Simaamba, "the *nakalindi* is the central place where the chief meets his *sikatongos* whenever he wants to find out how they are doing in their respective places. It is a place where each *sikatongo* makes a report and advice is given to, and by the chief." Simaamba, Interview, Nov. 25, 2006.

After drinking the water, the chief takes a roll call of his people. Whenever each neighborhood is called, the people from that area shout with joy. Simaamba then addresses his senior *sikatongos* starting with Nambwele:

*Ndakwaanzya Hacihibi!*     (I greet you, Hacihibi).
Nambwele responds:     *kukaita ku kajiba* (you greet me because you know me).[31]

He then greets *Sikatongo* Hakuyu:

*Ndakwaanzya Hakuyu!*     (I greet you, Hakuyu).
Hakuyu responds:     *Tulinamuntengwe tutandila busi* (We are like the Southern black flycatcher, we follow the smoke).[32]

After these greetings, the chief asks his *sikatongos* about the ecological wellbeing of their neighborhoods. During the 2006 ceremony, for example, the *sikatongos* complained that their neighborhoods were suffering from hunger. They appealed to the chief to supplicate the *basangu* for good rains so that people can have enough to eat.

The *sikatongos'* requests are followed by dancing women who similarly solicit the chief for rain in an artistic fashion. Unlike the *sikatongos* who simply make verbal supplications, women do it through dancing, clapping, and kneeling before the chief. After receiving all their requests, the chief, on behalf of all living elders, leads the procession toward the royal graves, leaving behind *Sikatongo* Nambwele—who is traditionally prohibited from visiting Simaamba's sacred graves.

Simaamba graves resemble a Tonga village with small huts. The procession checks individual huts to determine whether their gifts

---

[31] According to *Sikatongo* Nambwele, it was a taboo for him and Simaamba to meet face to face except during the *lwiindi*. "In the past, if I saw him (Simaamba) coming, I would change direction. Today, however, we meet." Interview, Feb. 2009. By responding, "You greet me because you know me," Nambwele seems to be pointing to this belief.
[32] The greeting illustrates Hakuyu's role in Simaamba's neighborhood; always prepared to aid whenever needed.

(beer left the previous night) were accepted. As Alexr G. MacAlphine noted more than a century ago about the Tonga of Nyasaland (Malawi),

> If the frothy scum on the beer has been disturbed, or if any of the offering seemed to be less in quantity than when they had been placed in position, the omen was good. If no change was noticeable, they judged that they and their gifts had been unfavorably received, and they set themselves to gain favor by larger and better sacrifices.[33]

This observation applies to some extent, but because the Tonga of Simaamba supplicate their ancestors individually, they check each hut and if the beer is consumed or the scum is disturbed, that specific ancestor is said to be pleased with them. However, should they find the scum undisturbed on another grave, they conclude that the specific ancestor is unhappy with them. At the 2006 *Iwiindi*, for example, the gift that was untouched belonged to the immediate late chief, who happened to be the reigning Simaamba's uncle. According to informants, the rejection of gifts indicated the unfavorable relationship between the current Simaamba and his late uncle.

To bring about reconciliation, the chief did not make another sacrifice, but employed verbal confessions to implore his late uncle to accept the gifts. He reminded his uncle that when he was alive, he too made mistakes and annoyed the ancestors. However, when he asked for forgiveness, they forgave him. He then continued, "If we, your people, have done wrong, we ask for your forgiveness and implore you to accept our gifts." Thereafter, he danced around the shrine for several minutes.

After visiting all shrines, the chief reminds the ancestors of their moral responsibilities to their descendants. Then a general request to all *basangu* for abundant rain, harvest, and help to control rats

---

[33] Alexr G. MacAlphine, "Tonga Religious Belief and Customs: 4. Worship," *Journal of the Royal African Society* 6, no.24 (Jul., 1907), 380.

(*mbeba*), insects, birds and anything that can thwart good harvest is made.

After this general request, the chief leads his party back to *nakalindi*, where *Sikatongo* Nambwele rejoins the procession back to the *ganda*. Since children are not generally allowed to visit the *malende*, they eagerly await the chief's return outside the vicinity of the *malende*. When the party emerges from the *malende*, the children, young people, and nursing mothers rejoin the procession back to the *ganda*. Upon reaching the *ganda*, the chief performs his final dance around it for several minutes. Thereafter, he retires into the *ganda*, where the *mulela* reclaims the spears and all the royal artifacts. The chief is now free to go back to the palace and the *lwiindi* celebrations continue with feasting.[34]

## Relating the *Lwiindi* to Anthropological Literature

Lee M. Brown observes that central to African traditional thought is the conviction that the intentions of ancestors can be known.[35] While ancestors do not will evil for their descendants, they can punish them if they go against established norms. The rejection of the ritual beer by chief Simaamba's late uncle pointed to some form of moral lapse among the living. In fact, the chief's prayer pointed to the moral authority of ancestors. As Mutukuzi shows, ancestors upheld ethical standards during their lifetime and know the consequences of ignoring traditional norms; thus, their moral guidance is sought in times of community crisis. So what is the relationship between ancestors and God? Does the absence of God in the *lwiindi* suggest *Leza* is totally non-existent in Tonga worldview?

---

[34] For the descriptions of other *lwiindi* ceremonies, see Colson, *Tonga Religious Life in the Twentieth Century*, 2006; "Rain Shrines of the Plateau Tonga of Northern Rhodesia," *Africa: Journal of the International African Institute* 18, no.4 (Oct.,1948), 272-283; O'Brien and O'Brien, "The Monze Rain Festival," 1997.

[35] Lee M. Brown, "Understanding and Ontology in Traditional African Thought," *African Philosophy: New & Traditional Perspectives*, Oxford University Press, (2004), 158-193.

Only special examination of Simaamba Tonga worldview can answer these questions. To start, Simaamba Tonga believe that nobody can become a chief without the protection of the *basangu* and *mizimu*. Just as elders supplicate to the ancestors, in this worldview, ancestors and the *basangu* are the ones with power to approach *Leza* on behalf of their descendants. However, should these forces be deemed not able, then the living would bring their supplications directly to *Leza*. On the household level, however, family ancestors exist to protect their descendants from individual calamity. As *Sikatongo* Nambwele explained, "When I move in the forest and see a snake, I say the ancestor has protected me. I can't say, o my Lord, but *mizimu yandi* (my ancestors)....I believe that if somebody dies in my family, he is the one watching after my movements. He is protecting me."[36] So the question raised at the beginning of this Chapter is worth repeating: "To whom is Mutukudzi appealing?"

The holding of the *Iwiindi* after the first rains is indicative of how people understand the role of ancestors and God in their daily life. The fact that the first rains have fallen does not translate into abundant harvest. Since God is the only giver of rains, remaining connected to the *basangu* and other vital spiritual forces through the *Iwiindi* is critical to the realization of abundant life on Earth. In this regard, the *Iwiindi* is not only meant to implore the *basangu* for more rains, but also to ask them to prevent nonhuman creatures from destroying the harvest.

Just as Mutukudzi called on the elders to intervene in the ecological crisis, the Tonga believe that the ancestors and God have power to intrude in any life-threatening situation. They also believe it is only "through their intervention with *Leza*, a god who controls all things" that rain is given.[37] Equally important is the

---

[36] The Muzambi independently made a similar statement on February 27, 2009. See also Colson, *Tonga Religious Life*, 51.
[37] Colson, *Tonga Religious Life*, 277; Elisabeth Colson and Max Gluckman, (eds), *Seven Tribes of Colonial Central Africa* (Manchester, England: Manchester University Press, 1959), 156.

belief that despite the negative effects of rats, birds, and insects on human life, they are nevertheless part of the sacred universe of life. Rather than destroying them through pesticides, the Tonga entreat their *basangu* to control nonhuman activities. So what is the role of ancestors in this worldview?

As early as 1936, J. H. Driberg argued that the ancestor cult is purely a secular act. In his article, "The Secular Aspect of Ancestor-Worship in Africa," Driberg argues that Africans do not generally apply the words, "worship, sacrifice, offerings, and prayer" to the ancestral system. Accepting the fact that it is difficult or even impossible to find English words that will convey the real meaning of the words employed by Africans to the cult, Driberg contends that "no African 'prays' to his dead grandfather any more than he 'prays' to his living father."[38] He insists, "the words for "prayer" and "worship"...are strictly reserved for...religious dealings with the Absolute Power and the divinities. The Latin word *pietas* probably best describes the attitude of Africans to their dead ancestors, as to their living elders."[39]

Almost thirty years later, anthropologist and Africanist Meyer Fortes, built on Driberg's argument in his analysis of the Tellensi of the Sudan. He contended that the cult is an act of mutual *pietas* or obligation between parents and their children.[40] It is expected that children respect their parents not just when they are alive, but even when they die. Nonetheless, he departed from Driberg's argument when he observed that the Tallensi differentiate between living elders and ancestors. Maintaining that ancestors occupy a higher position than living elders in Tallensi cosmology, Fortes argues that ancestors constitute "the ultimate tribunal and

---

[38] J.H. Driberg, "The Secular Aspect of Ancestor-Worship in Africa," *Journal of the Royal African Society* 35, no.138 (Jan., 1936), 6.
[39] Ibid. See also Bolaji E. Idowu, *African Traditional Religion: A Definition* (London: SCM Press, 1973), 181-182.
[40] Meyer Fortes, "Pietas in Ancestor Worship: The Henry Myers Lecture, 1960," *The Journal of the Royal Anthropological Institute of Great Britain and Ireland* 91, no.2 (July – Dec., 1961), 166.

the final authority in the matters of life and death."[41] Hence, they deserve ultimate reverence and worship.

Accordingly, he insisted that the authority of ancestors depends on the world of the living to be realized. Since only the living kin can make one an ancestor, he argues, filial reciprocity between the dead and the living is an ontological requirement. For this very reason, filial piety is crucial to the cult since "a person becomes an ancestor not because he is dead but because he leaves a son, or more accurately, a legitimate filial successor, and he remains an ancestor only so long as his legitimate lineal successors survive."[42]

Unlike Fortes who concluded that Africans worship ancestors, Igor Kopytoff reverted to Driberg's original argument that the ancestor cult should be understood as a cult of "elders living and dead."[43] He noted that most Bantu languages do not distinguish between living elders and dead ancestors. Hence, the authority of elders is the same whether they are dead or alive. Consequently, any argument that seeks to view ancestors as objects of worship (as Fortes did) fails to comprehend the phenomenon of ancestors in Africa. Differently stated, African ancestors are part of the living community of elders who deserve respect from their kin. "If I am young, I go to my elders who happen to be alive. The old people go to their elders; but since these are dead, they are to be found at the grave or at the cross-roads at night."[44] He further argues that:

> Ancestors are vested with mystical powers and authority. They retain a functional role in the world of the living, specifically in the life of their living kinsmen; indeed, African kin-groups are often described as communities of both the living and the dead. The relation of the ancestors to their living kinsmen has been

---

[41] Ibid., 176. To Fortes, the ancestors are the Supreme authority in Africa. But Bolaji Idowu argues that Africans make a distinction between Deity, the divinities, and the ancestors. Idowu, *African Traditional Religion*, 184.

[42] "The Tallensi believe that a man who dies sonless has wasted his life, and the Chinese compare such a one to a tree without roots." Fortes, *Pietas in Ancestor Worship*, 181.

[43] Igor Kopytoff, "Ancestors as Elders in Africa," *Africa: Journal of the International African Institute* 41, no.2 (Apr., 1971), 133.

[44] Ibid., 131.

described as ambivalent, as both punitive and benevolent and sometimes even as capricious.-- In some sense the elders are the representatives of the ancestors and the mediators between them and the kin-group.[45]

Jomo Kenyatta independently reached a similar conclusion. He argued that just as the community respects the living elders for their seniority and wisdom, they too must respect "the seniority of the ancestral spirits."[46]

Kenyatta and Kopytoff's arguments are evident in the *Iwiindi* when the two *sikatongos* and women present requests to the chief, who later presents them to the *basangu*. Since African ontology demands that elders protect or discipline their juniors, ancestors dispense both favors and misfortune. Hence, the people interpret the ancestors' actions as possible responses to their actions. Like chief Simaamba's address to the ancestors, the living appeal to their ancestors for forgiveness and support in this world.

Responding to Kopytoff's critique of his original argument, Meyer Fortes countered that the linking of the authority of ancestors to that of the living elders does not address the issue fully.[47] This is because Africans differentiate between the authority of the living and dead elders. They employ the word "elder" in the secular sense and "ancestor" in a ritual sense. Thus, the elders' influence is limited to the secular sphere, while the ancestors' authority is in the spiritual realm. Thus, ancestral rituals reveal the continuous presence of the ancestors in a state of existence that "represents a transformation of secular parenthood."[48] While this argument is plausible, it is already established that in African worldviews, the secular and the spiritual are intrinsically interconnected.

---

[45] Kopytoff, "Ancestors as Elders in Africa," 140.
[46] Jomo Kenyatta, *Facing Mount Kenya: The Tribal life of the Gikuyu* (London: Secker and Arburg, 1938), 255.
[47] Meyer Fortes, "The Authority of Ancestors," *Man, New Series* 16, no.2 (Jun., 1981), 301.
[48] Ibid., 301-302.

## Theological Discussion of the Cult of Ancestors

According to Bolaji Idowu, ancestors are the primary objects of African supplications. In fact, they are considered:

> [A]s heads and parts of the families or communities to which they belonged while they were living human beings; for what happened in consequence of the phenomenon called death was only that the family life of this Earth has been extended into the after-life or super sensible world. The ancestors remain, therefore, spiritual superintendents of family affairs and continue to bear their titles of relationship like father or mother.[49]

While accepting that the difference between the authority of the living elders and ancestors is complex, Idowu argues that the anthropological theory that "ancestor worship is the root of all religions" controlled scholars' positions on the ancestor cult. Those who argue that Africans worship ancestors seek to prove this theory, while those who favor veneration over worship want to reject it. From a theological standpoint, however, Idowu argues that the differentiation of veneration from worship seems to ignore the complex nature of the human mind. Worship and veneration, he argues, are psychologically close and the human mind swings between the two depending "on the spiritual climate of the moment."[50]

Contrary to Idowu, who does not favor one position over the other, Gabriel Setiloane agrees with J.H. Driberg and Igor Kopytoff that ancestors are not worshipped. "Even after death, 'the vital participation' of the deceased is experienced in the community in general and in the home clan circle in particular. What has been described as, 'the ancestral cult of the Africans,' refers to this experience in the life of the people."[51] Nonetheless, it is misleading, Setiloane argues, to associate ancestors with the

---

[49] Idowu, *African Traditional Religion*, 184.
[50] Ibid., 182.
[51] Gabriel M. Setiloane, *African Theology: An Introduction* (Johannesburg: Skotaville Publishers, 1986), 17.

Divinity. Africans give service (*tirelo*) to the ancestors, which he argues is the same service rendered to one's parents while they are alive. The Tswana speak of fulfilling their duties to *Badimo* (ancestors) and "pray" to *Modimo*.[52]

Consequently, ancestors are a vital link between various forces in Bantu cosmology. According to Setiloane, their rank "spans the various levels of being in this life, across the homes and clans in the total community of village and tribe as well as the unseen world of *BoModimo* (Divinity) which is strongly inclined to be identified with the underworld."[53] Placide Tempels also asserts that ancestors "are spiritualized beings; beings belonging to a higher hierarchy, participating to a certain degree in the divine Force."[54] Thus, they are uniquely moral and just; and by default guardians of morality.

Here, it is vital to note that the authority of ancestors is derived from the religious worldview that informs African cosmologies. Although ancestors rank above the "living elders" in the hierarchy of beings, they are directly connected to the living elders. In an interdependent universe, ancestors and living elders constitute the court of the *vakuru*, whose guidance and wisdom is sought, especially in the time of national crisis. In this regard, the basis for the primacy of the ancestor cult is the ancestors' ontological position in Bantu ontology. As guardians of the land and morality, the *vakuru* are expected to monitor people's actions on Earth.

However, the *Iwiindi* ceremony does not put one role over the other, but accepts multiple or pervasive roles. Like the royal ancestors of Simaamba,

> [ancestors] do not occupy a single 'position' in a structural sense but are embodied in a number of different ways in a wide range of activities and material culture. These multiple manifestations

---

[52] Ibid., 18.
[53] Ibid., 19.
[54] Tempels, *Bantu Philosophy*, 42.

suggest a variety of possible identities for ancestors rather than a unified model.[55]

Again, despite their higher ontological positions, ancestors on their own cannot send rain or ensure the salvation of their descendants.

## We Share One Earth with our Ancestors

The cult of ancestors makes one point clear: Ancestors share this Earth with us. This belief is crucial to the development of African ecological ethics. As American theologian Daniel Maguire warns, a theology that denies Earth as our home,

> might do more harm than opiate the social conscience with hope for the sweet by and by. It can make our Earth-life the prologue, not the text and context of our being. It can de-territorialize our identity. It can make us strangers in this paradise, and estrangement is the gateway to enmity. If we have a claim on afterlife, and the plants and the animals do not, we are not kith and kin, nor do we share their perils. Earth as prolegomenon and Earth as destiny are the ultimate in divergent worldviews and ethics.[56]

The *Iwiindi* illustrates this very fact. Ancestors are resident with us on Earth and equally depend on the produce of Earth for their continual existence. To destroy Earth is to destroy their life force, that of future generations and ultimately our own. For an African therefore, there is no afterlife without Earth. The underworld is not evil, but the most feared place for its moral sanctions; it is from this world that life and blessings flow. As the *sikatongo* pointed out above, protection for the living flows from the world of ancestors and God. Since what happens to this world affects the underworld, those in the underworld have the duty to defend Earth from human abuse.

---

[55] John C. McCall, "Rethinking Ancestors in Africa," *Journal of the International African Institute* 65, no.2 (1995), 258.
[56] Daniel Maguire, "More People: Less Earth," in *Ethics for a Small Planet,* (ed.), D. Maguire and L. Rasmussen (New York: State University of New York Press, 1998), 44.

Any African Christology that utilizes the paradigm of ancestor ought to take the ecological role of ancestors into consideration. Mutukuzi's appeal to the ancestors/elders to intervene in the ecological crisis is an excellent example of the role of ancestors in primal imaginations. In times of crisis, Africans seek the directions of ancestors/elders, since their insights, "reflect the ancestors' experiences; they give wisdom and life. Whoever lives in accordance with ancestral ethics chooses life. To reject them means death, that is, the destruction of one's own life and that of the clan, both in their visible and invisible dimensions."[57]

Questions of land, fertility, water, and other ecological issues are matters of ancestral concerns. To treat the cult of ancestors as merely addressing social, religious, and political issues is to ignore the ecological significance of the cult in African religions. In fact, one can go further and say that the ancestor cult is the cult of Earth since it seeks to uphold the ecological balance of the ecosphere. Thus, to associate Jesus with ancestors is to invite him into people's earthly experiences.

## Ecological Dimensions of the *Lwiindi*

Across Africa, ancestor cults are usually linked to the fertility of the land. For groups like the Shona, Tonga and Chewa, rain-calling is not just central to their religion, but also an expression of their social and economic norms. Among the Tonga of Simaamba, for example, the *lwiindi* ceremony is an avenue through which the community communes with each other, the living dead as well as the Earth community. While the *lwiindi* of Simaamba has limited geographical appeal, *Sikatongo* Monze—a well-known rain caller and healer—transcended geographical confines of the Gwembe. The prominence of Monze, for example, forced the O'Brien to conclude that Tonga life was politically organized around him.[58]

---

[57] Bujo, *African Theology*, 27.
[58] To the O'Briens, the trial of Monze (the rainmaker in 1902), the evidence that David Livingstone speaks about chief Monze, and the fact that Monze invited the Ndebele to

But, such an argument fails to see that the Tonga were ecological as opposed to political communities. And, as already noted, the power to perform the *lwiindi* was a prerogative of *sikatongos*. It is therefore highly duplicitous to force the modern concept of "chief" over traditional Tonga eco-social organization. The power of a *sikatongo*, that is the ability to uphold the ecological balance of his vicinity, was not political; though it often possessed political overtones. As Colson states,

> The sikatongo is not per se a leader or ruler of men. He is of importance only in relation to his katongo which is specific to a neighborhood. Through him [people] relate themselves to the land on which they live, which provides their sustenance. In any other neighborhood, he is powerless. He cannot take his ritual position with him.[59]

Colson's observation needs emphasizing. Monze's power to call rain and to heal would have placed him at the center of Tonga cosmology within the confines of his neighborhood and not beyond.[60] As a successful rain caller, however, *sikatongo* Monze confronted ecological disasters and unexplained illnesses in his community; the very issues that mattered most to his people.[61] Thus, he could have had a larger following in the valley. In this sense, Monze could have been viewed as a chief by the Europeans. At the advent of colonialism, Monze was conferred with "political" authority.

The Tonga people are aware of this colonial interpretation since they refer to such chiefs as "chiefs of the book" (pointing to the role of collecting hut taxes, which such *sikatongos* played in colonial times). To gain traditional legitimacy in the new political order, these *sikatongos* turned their *lwiindis* into regional cults; thereby including other neighborhoods in the process. Charles

---

join his fight against the Lozi King Lewanika, suggest the political role and the leadership of Monze in the valley. O'Brien and O'Brien, "The Monze Rain Festival," 519-522.
[59] Colson, *Social Organization of the Gwembe Tonga*, 65.
[60] According to Chief Chipepo, it is impossible for his people to celebrate the *lwiindi* in a foreign land; hence they have no *lwiindi*. Interview, Lusaka, 2006.
[61] Ibid.

Halubanje's (Nambwele) insistence that he is the rightful person to perform the *lwiindi* points to this historical tension.

Just as critical were the effects of the forced resettlement on the *lwiindi*. The loss of ancestral land, coupled with the completion of the dam and resettlement, apparently indicated the failure of the *basangu* to protect their land, as noted earlier. Worse still, Colson and Scudder have argued that between 1960 and 1963, the relocatees had much better harvests than they used to get in the valley. That Earth could still produce without the help of Earth priests created a cognitive dissonance among the Tonga who now interpreted the *basangu* as powerless in the new land. But, once the ecological conditions changed and droughts became common in their new land, the belief in the *basangu* was revitalized.[62]

## Ecological Aspects of Tonga Holy Shrines

Despite being displaced from the valley, the people of Simaamba reestablished a new *malende* (shrine) within the vicinity of their new neighborhood. Aside from multi-dimensional psychological, physiological, and socio-cultural insults that characterized the resettlement, the current shrines were developed as a security mechanism in the foreign land.

The Tonga consider the *malende* as sacred spaces of community memory (*lieux de memoire*) where an individual encounters the spiritual powers of life. Accordingly, new chiefs are expected to spend a week in the *malende* before they are enthroned. Being the burial places of the royal *basangu* and homes to the owners and guardians of the land, only those who win the approval of the *malende* can inherit the Simaamba throne.[63]

As a sign of respect, it is a taboo to harvest natural goods from such groves. Doing so is considered an attack on ancestors and other spirits and tantamount to being a witch. From this

---

[62] Colson, *The Social Consequences of Resettlement*, 233.
[63] Should one die or be attacked by animals in the *malende*, it is believed that the *basangu* have rejected him. Such a person cannot become a chief.

perspective, the sacredness associated with the groves can enhance the conservation of nature mostly out of reverence for spiritual forces resident therein as opposed to instrumental motives. Like most sacred groves across the continent, Tonga sacred groves are protected from human exploitation as compared to other areas in the land which are virtually turning into a desert.

In addition, religious beliefs tend to inform the social construction of power and shape ecological relationships in any community. Customs surrounding sacred groves maintain orderly ecological, social and moral relationships in a specific community. Such relationships, however, do not present sufficient motivation for ecological responsibility. In situations where poverty is high, sources of income and land are limited, the poor are forced into exploiting the groves as a survival issue.

Nevertheless, the *malende* still hold promise for ecological diversity. Michael J. Sheridan and Celia Nyamweru are correct to contend that African sacred groves are not relics of pristine forests as previously held. Rather, they are constructed over a period of time as people impute sacredness to them. In short:

> [The] sacredness of groves is not the result of cultural values abstracted from their contexts in human lives. It is not in trees, plants, vines, springs, pools, rivers, and rocks. Sacredness is embedded in the social institutions that sacred groves manifest in African landscapes, which means that the ecological status of these patches follows from the shifting social organization of African societies and the flux of historical change on the continent.[64]

But, there is another reason why Africans respect sacred groves. Disrespect of the sacred groves endangers not just the offender, but the entire community. As Colson rightly notes, gathering roots or wood in the *malende*, and burning the grass without the

---

[64] Michael J. Sheridan and Celia Nyamweru, *African Sacred Groves: Ecological Dynamics and Social Change* (Oxford: James Curry, 2008), 20.

consent of the Earth priest is viewed as an insult to the entire community.[65]

It is important to note that even newcomers are not exempt from such injunctions. As already noted, the Tonga attribute the Lusitu condition to the abuse of the Goba *malende*. Because Africans fear spirits more than government law enforcement officials, most of Simaamba's area shows signs of degradation due to overpopulation and deforestation, but the sacred grove is relatively undisturbed. Thus, placing sacredness on Earth can inform ecological action and sensibility. Amid the ever increasing populations, land shortages, and poverty in Simaamba's area, however, it remains to be seen how long this sacred grove will remain undisturbed.

But, the sacredness associated with groves also changes over time; hence overpopulation, unplanned resettlements, and poverty are real threats to sacred groves. One example of how poverty and landlessness can destroy sacred groves is reported by Marthinus Daneel. Speaking about the sacred grove of Mount Mugabe (not related to President Robert Mugabe), Daneel observes that commercial interests and unplanned resettlements desecrated sacred groves around Lake Kyle in Masvingo, Zimbabwe. Whereas traditional sanctions protected sacred groves (*murambatemwa*) and prohibited the cutting of ancestral trees, commercial interests and land shortages led to the destruction of sacred groves, which he contends, are the "epitome of human hubris in the face of ultimate forces of life."[66]

These ultimate forces manifest in natural phenomena—snakes, animals and other sacred creatures. In Samfya, Zambia, the Chundu sacred grove has been maintained due to the number of

---

[65] According to Colson, misuse of *malende* invites "general disaster for the community, unless the offenders were punished and a ritual of cleansing performed. If it is discovered that someone has cut the wood in the immediate vicinity of a shrine he is ordered to pay a black chicken." Colson, "Rain Shrines of the Plateau Tonga," 275.
[66] Marthinus Daneel, *African Earthkeepers: Wholistic Interfaith Mission* (Maryknoll, New York, Orbis Books, 2001), 9.

snakes that reside in it. Although the grove is just next to a high school, the sacredness associated with it has protected it from human abuse. In Raffingora, Zimbabwe, Dr. Gift Makwasha narrates a story about the sacred grove which was protected due to the sacredness associated with it. The grove was home not just to snakes but to a number of abandoned animals—goats, and chickens (*huku* or *mbudzi, yekurasira* or *yechikwambo*), which were used in traditional cleansing ceremonies and later released into the wild. The person who did not share this community history killed a sacred snake (he later became mentally handicapped thereby increasing the belief about the sacredness of the grove) and a White farmer took all the animals away.[67] Such stories show that the role of sacred groves in conservation is not only dependent on the level of sacredness people associate with them, but also on the economic wellbeing of the community and the shared values in that specific society.

Finally, the eco-political implications of the ancestor cult deserve further investigations. Jesus, our ancestor is, by default, the guardian of the land *par-excellence*. Africans will adequately relate to a depiction of Jesus who assures them of abundant life within their life worlds. That most Africans depend on the land for their daily needs invites an ecological face of Jesus in Africa today. Among the Tonga of Simaamba for example, Jesus should become the *sikatongo*, the charismatic rain caller, who intercedes with *Leza* on behalf of God's people. These Christian themes and perceptions will be explored in depth in the Chapters that follow.

---

[67] Gift Makwasha, Interview, Boston, MA, 2010.

## Chapter Three
## Morality in the Face of Progress:
## Civilization, Christianity, and Commerce

The mission theory of Civilization, Christianity, and Commerce ("the three Cs") led to the evangelization and colonization of Africa. European missionaries sought to save Africans from hell, but unwittingly promoted imperial powers' interests on the continent. David Livingstone's missionary activities exemplify how some missionaries unwittingly and enthusiastically worked as colonial agents. This unclear demarcation of missionary work from colonial responsibilities compromised missionary activities.

Missiologist Brian Stanley links Christian mission to the Enlightenment. He argues that Protestant mission theories in the eighteenth and early nineteenth centuries shared five distinct assumptions. They assumed: first, that all non-Western people were heathens; second, that all other religions were false; third, that Western civilization was superior to any other form of civilization; fourth, that rational knowledge was necessary for proclaiming the gospel; and finally, that the Christian message was one of individual responsibility.[1]

The Enlightenment-inspired belief that rationality was necessary to evangelization was behind the emphasis placed on education. Educating Africans to read the Bible was essential to civilization.[2] But, while missionaries evangelized Africans for the heavenly kingdom, colonial governments sought mission-educated Africans to aid their colonization agenda. Since to be "civilized" meant

---

[1] Brian Stanley posits that English Evangelicals believed Christianity was God's appointed engine of civilization. Brian Stanley, "'Commerce and Christianity': Providence Theory, the Missionary Movement, and the Imperialism of Free Trade, 1842-1860," *The Historical Journal* 26, no.1 (Mar., 1983), 76; *Christian Missions and the Enlightenment* (Surrey, Curzon Press: 2001), 8.

[2] William Carey's views on the gospel as a means of civilization represented just one position of the established Evangelical mission theories. See Alexander Duff, *Missions as the Chief End of the Christian Church* (Edinburgh: John Johnstone, 1840).

rejecting traditional African values, colonial governments (with the help of missionaries) prohibited certain rituals and customs, some of which were essential to African morality. African drums, taboos, names, customs, rituals, and even folk-stories often were termed "barbaric" or simply sinful. One telling example was requiring that all converts take on Western names as Christian names. To be a Christian meant to become a John or a Dickson, but never a Kapya.

To some extent, the rejection of religious and cultural values aided the process of decolonization across sub-Saharan Africa. As George Reid notes, "European missionaries in Africa were a symbol of economic uplift, private enterprise, technology, Christian values, Western schools, hospitals and Churches. Nevertheless, the missionary, one of the largest supporters of European rule, unwittingly began the process of decolonization."[3] Missionaries paved "the way for European governmental occupation," he argues,

> and the introduction and perpetuation of unequal European Christianity. Consequently, the Church became a provocateur of African Nationalism, but unwittingly so. Because the Christian church permitted a paradox between what it preached and what it practiced, Africans began to regard missionaries as tricksters whose Christianity was a means to an end.[4]

Jean Comaroff repeats this very point. She argues that early missionaries represented what life could look like under the new order. They taught equality of all human races, but benefited from racial segregation.[5] The disparity that existed between the colonial minority (missionaries included) and African Christians made the teaching of equality before God self-defeating.

From a Christian social ethical perspective, however, it is the paradoxical relationship between "Christ" and "culture" that began

---

[3] Reid W. George, "Missionaries and West African Nationalism," *Phylon* 39, no.3 (3rd Qtr. 1978), 225.
[4] Ibid., 232.
[5] Jean Comaroff, *Body of Power, Spirit of Resistance: The Culture and History of a South African People* (Chicago: University of Chicago Press, 1985), 23-25.

the process of decolonization. Some missionaries were quick to realize that colonization and Christianity were not bedfellows. So they joined Africans to challenge colonialism. In addition, the theory of civilization worked against colonialism, since it alerted Africans to some European democratic values which were in line with African cultures. In short, missionaries promoted the "civilization" of Africans, but unknowingly opened themselves and their colonial counterparts to religious, social, economic, and moral critique. So, in which ways is African morality different from Western values, if at all?

## Understanding African Morality

In Chapter Two, we observed that African ontology of God, spirits, humanity, animals, plants, and the nonliving has something in common with the Christian doctrine of creation. In both religions, each ontological category has intrinsic value to be protected and defended. This is even more apparent when we realize that to destroy one is to break the harmony of the universe and therefore to invite the wrath of the Creator God. For this reason, although colonialism negatively affected African morality, many people remained faithful to the moral codes of their ancestors while practicing the codes of the new order—a trend that has continued to this day.

African moral order is ontologically interconnected; hence, it is hard to differentiate between social and religious norms. Ogbu Kalu is correct; the goal of African morality "was the preservation of a religious moral order. Likewise, religious rituals were instruments of preserving social order."[6] Because spiritual beings police human actions, tradition "supplies the moral code and indicates what people must do to live ethically."[7]

---

[6] Ogbu U. Kalu, "Religion and Social Control in Igboland," in *Religious Plurality in Africa: Essays in Honor of John Mbiti* (ed.), Olupona K. Jacob and Sulayman S. Nyang (Berlin: Mouton de Gruyter, 1993), 115.

[7] Ibid.

Laurenti Magesa concurs:

> African Religion's conception of morality is steeped in tradition; it comes from and flows from God into the ancestors of the people. God is seen as the Great Ancestor, the first Founder and Progenitor, the Giver of life, the Power beyond everything that is. God is the first Initiator of a people's way of life, its tradition. However, the ancestors...are the custodians of this tradition.[8]

In African cosmologies, he adds, "spirits are active beings who are either disincarnate human persons or powers residing in natural phenomena such as trees, rocks, rivers, or lakes."[9] By default, therefore, God, ancestors and spirits are active moral agents and guardians of morality.

Subsequently, Bantu morality promotes the recognition of the harmony and interaction of vital forces in the universe, and respect for them. Along these lines, the utilization of natural goods has ethical implications. As Tempels observed,

> [the Bantu] have a notion of what we may call immanent justice, which they would translate to mean that to violate nature incurs her vengeance and that misfortune springs from her. They know that he who does not respect the laws of nature becomes...a person whose inmost being is pregnant with misfortune....This ethical conscience of theirs is at once philosophical, moral and juridical.[10]

Consequently, an individual exists in a web of eco-social moral obligations. Against the assumption that such obligations were limited to one's community, Tempels contends otherwise. He insists that however hostile intertribal relations may be, it is forbidden to kill an outsider since "the diminution and destruction of an outsider's life involves the disturbance of the ontological

---

[8] Laurenti Magesa, *African Religion: The Moral Traditions of Abundant Life* (New York: Orbis Books, 1997), 35.
[9] Ibid., 35-36.
[10] Placide Tempels, *Bantu Philosophy*, [translated from *La Philosophie Bantouein* 1945 by A. Rubbens] (Paris: Presence Africaine, 1952), 88.

order and [divine wrath] will be visited upon him who disturbs it."[11]

Finally, in Bantu communities, moral obligations increase with the vital rank, experience and knowledge. It is one thing for a young person to fell a sacred tree and it is another for an adult to do so. While the living elders and chiefs are the visible moral custodians, their authority is never above that of the ancestors or the Supreme Being. One is always reminded that nobody can deceive the "living dead."

## The Ethics of Interconnectedness

All norms are culturally conditioned and are informed by human identifications with particular community values.[12] Generally, African morals are expressed in proverbs, rituals, myths, oral literature, folktales, songs, customs, and other cultural symbols. Among the Bemba, it is said, *umukulu apusa akabwe tapusa cebo* (elders can miss a blow; never a word). Again, *akanwa kamwenfu, takabepa* (a mouth with a beard does not lie). Such proverbs were meant to induce respect of the elders in African societies. As Ogbu Kalu observes, "age is crucial to African social relations because with age, wisdom, proximity to land of the spirits, and closer contact with the ancestors go together."[13] Thus "ancestorship primarily implies moral activity."[14]

Across Africa, living elders are the visible figures of morality. Although chiefs and elders are expected to guide the living to make correct moral choices, the ancestors (whose sphere of knowledge

---

[11] Tempels, *Bantu Philosophy*, 88. Among the Shona, the *ingozi* (avenging spirit) of a foreigner is highly feared. See Marthinus Daneel, *Zionism and Faith Healing in Rhodesia* (The Hague: Morton, 1970). Also James Pfeiffer, "African Independent Churches in Mozambique: Healing the Afflictions of Inequality," *Medical Anthropology Quarterly* 16, no.2 (2002), 176-199.
[12] Amina Mama, "Is it Ethical to Study Africa? Preliminary Thoughts on Scholarship and Freedom," *African Studies Review* 50, no.1 (April 2007), 6.
[13] Kalu "Religion and Social Control in Igboland," 115.
[14] Ibid., 48.

is far superior to that of chiefs and living elders) are the just judges of human conduct. As the *lwiindi* illustrated, Africans construe natural disasters to the disturbance of "the whole order of beings."[15] So how do Africans understand moral duty?

In African worldviews, duty includes reciprocal obligations. Just as the elders have the duty to protect their young, so must the young respect the elders. Good life "depends not only on the ancestors, but also on the degree of esteem which a person shows for parents and the clan elders."[16] The elders have an obligation to hand over community wisdom to their young; in return, the young must respect their elders. Thus, the welfare of the living depends on their obedience to the elders both living and dead.

The moral term *"ubuntu"* aptly summarizes the meaning of duty among the Bantu. But, part of *ubuntu* includes how one relates to the land. A person with *ubuntu* cannot mistreat nonhumans or destroy Earth. Yet, despite the eco-theocentric bias of African ethics, some Western theologians and African philosophers alike have too often concluded that African ethics is anthropocentric. But as Bujo contends,

> It is hardly conceivable that the African, whose thinking is always set in a religious context, could have a morality without God. Though the human person stands in the center of African morals, the position of God is distinctly emphasized, since as creator he has to intervene in the moral order if the human person does not follow the laws set up by him.[17]

Elsewhere, he adds,

> God is not far from the African world; all relationships, between person and person, living and dead and between persons and nature, are rooted in God and point toward God and toward the end of all things in God....Every person's future lies with God... for

---

[15] Tempels, *Bantu Philosophy*, 98.
[16] Bénézet Bujo, *African Theology in its Social Context* (Maryknoll, New York: Orbis, 1992), 34.
[17] Bénézet Bujo, *The Ethical Dimension of Community: The African Model and the Dialogue between North and South,* Translated from German by Cecilia Namulondo (Nairobi: Paulines Publications Africa, 1998), 23.

the African, God cannot be imagined without God's creation, nor without God's saving will for humankind.[18]

William R. O'Neill seems to agree with Bujo when he notes that "the ideal of abundant life serves as a rich, polyvalent symbol in traditional moral wisdom, integrating what in the West have emerged as discrete cognitive, moral, and expressive modes of knowing....African moral wisdom is irreducibly religious."[19]

The above observations are vital to understand the foundation of African morality. As observed in previous Chapters, African ontology views God as the source of morality, but ancestors, spirits and elders are the guardians of ethics. This philosophy directs the morality of abundant life. To confirm this ontological reality, Africans trace creation to the Supreme Being, who is the origin of ancestors and all life. Thus, an eco-theocentric rather than an anthropocentric focus ought to be taken as the true representation of African ethics.

The Bantu used animals and other natural goods, but cruelty to animals or misuse of nonhumans were regarded as an affront to the ancestors. Even wild animals were morally and spiritually protected. Only a certain number of edible animals were killed, and hunting for pleasure was unheard of. This is because animals were creatures of God or simply *children of God* with rights to life. Among the Tonga of the Gwembe for example, domestic animals are named after their dead relatives. Apart from the spiritual significance of such naming, the act shows how Africans relate to the natural world.

In addition, Africans experience life in community relationships. Due to this community emphasis, however, African ethics can be declared "deeply anthropocentric," an assertion many theologians and philosophers have supported. Charles Nyamiti argues that African religion is "centered mainly on man's life in this world, with the consequences that religion is chiefly functional, or a means to

---

[18] Bujo, *African Theology*, 32.
[19] William R. O'Neill, S.J., "African Moral Theology," *Theological Studies* 62 (2001), 127.

serve people to acquire earthly goods (life, health, fecundity, wealth, power and the like) and to maintain social cohesion and order."[20] Magesa adds: all creation is "intended to serve and enhance the life force of the human person and society."[21]

Indeed, humanity (including the living and the yet to be born) is the beneficiary of God's love in creation. Yet Africans understand that although Earth was given to the founding ancestors as a gift, it was conditional on how they related to other vital forces in creation. This is because Earth belongs to God, who is the Supreme ontological guardian of creation. Mbiti puts this in context:

> God is the Originator and Sustainer of man; the spirits explain the destiny of man; man is the center of this ontology; the animals, plants and natural phenomena and other objects constitute the environment in which humanity lives, provides a means of existence and if need be, humanity established a mystical relationship with them.[22]

Although Mbiti argues that humanity is at the center of this ontology, in African cosmologies, humanity is connected to other vital forces. In fact, the center depends on other forces to hold itself together. Mbiti seems to suggest this very point—humanity is at the center, but

> [African] anthropocentric ontology is a complete unity or solidarity which nothing can break up or destroy. To destroy one of these categories is to destroy the whole existence including the destruction of the Creator, which is impossible. One mode of existence presupposes all the others, and a balance must be maintained so that these modes neither drift too far apart from one another nor get too close to one another.[23]

From the above analysis, it seems the conclusion that African ethics is deeply anthropocentric was reached too quickly and without paying attention to the concept of interconnectedness on

---

[20] Cited in Magesa, *African Religion*, 51.
[21] Ibid.
[22] Mbiti, *African Religions and Philosophy*, 16.
[23] Ibid.

which African ontology rests. One of the many factors that led to this conclusion could be the Western anthropocentric ideologies that informed African theology in its early days.

In the West, human beings were, and to some extent still are, at the center of the universe as well as the focal point of ethical analysis. In a Latin American context, however, Brazilian theologian Leonardo Boff advocates the rejection of this paradigm since:

> [E]cology requires that we humans advance beyond our anthropocentric viewpoint, which is deeply embedded in Western culture and continually reaffirmed by a certain type of interpretation of the Hebrew and Christian Scriptures. We believe ourselves to be the focal point of everything. We see all other beings as existing for our purposes, and all creatures as finding their meaning and praising God through human beings, at the mercy of human beings, to be dominated and where convenient to be used.[24]

What Boff advocates is in line with African cosmologies, where not all creatures can be said to be at the mercy of humanity. As previous Chapters illustrated, some creatures represent God, the ancestors, and the spirits in the universe and are thus deeply integrated with the human community.

But, morality has community implications in African society. Whereas in Western ethics emphasis is placed on individual actions, rights and obligations, African ethics emphasizes the consequences and rewards of individual actions on a wider community. That which benefits the community is favored over that which favors an individual. Crime is not committed against an individual, but the entire community. Thus, when one kills another person, for example, the entire clan is guilty of murder. What then is the role of the individual in community?

As upcoming chapters will show, an individual has a duty to transmit community life from one generation to another. Unless given to spiritual forces as ritual wife or husband, generally, every individual is expected to get married and have children. O'Neill

---

[24] Leonardo Boff, *Ecology and Liberation: A New Paradigm* (Maryknoll, NY: Orbis Book, 1995), 85.

observes that procreation is an "intergenerational transmission of...the vital forces uniting those living with the ancestors (remembered dead) and those yet to be born reflect[ing] the inseparability of the Spiritual and the natural domains."[25] Bemba proverbs, like *mayo mpapa naine nkakupapa* (my mother carry me today, and I will also carry you) and *kolwe akula asabilwa nabana* (when the monkey grows old, young ones take care of him/her), point to the instrumental value of children on one hand and the transmission of life on the other. Hence, infertility, impotency, and same-sex marriages are likely to be viewed as evil.

Since African life is "collective," being ethical or possessing *ubuntu* means upholding community values and norms. Among the Bemba, for instance, human actions qualify one to be human or not. As the following Chapter will insist, possessing *ubuntu* implies acting in the interest of the community. *Umuntu* with *ubuntu* is expected to build community life, while the one who lacks *ubuntu* destroys it. As Nkafu Martin Nkemnkia concludes, "the African community is that entity which gives account of everything and everyone. The African being is not being-in-oneself but a being-with-everyone. This is African vitalogy."[26]

Tempels expressed this "African vitalogy" when he observed that in the Western world, children or descendants may exist apart from their parents or ancestors and still have the right to their support. Among the Bantu, by contrast,

> To say that ancestors or parents have a duty of vital strengthening can be understood only as an intrinsic duty, an ontological duty to preserve the clan, a duty toward that force which is superior to them....In his vital action on behalf of his dependants, the ancestor or the elder is strengthening himself in a line of numerous descendants.[27]

Hence, questions of population growth, economics and poverty should be addressed from this collectivist moral perspective.

---

[25] O'Neill, "African Moral Theology," 127.
[26] Ibid., 121.
[27] Tempels, *Bantu Philosophy*, 99-100.

## Ecological Themes in African Worldviews

Ecological issues are not widely addressed in African theology, yet African cosmologies possess ecological themes that can inform Christian ecological awareness and responsibility.

## Land as a Commons

Throughout Africa, land is a commons or community trust that belongs to the past, present, and future generations. While the people work the land, the living dead safeguard it for their own ontological wellbeing as well as for the sake of future generations. As ontological guardians of the land, the "living-dead" ensure that the rights of future generations to the land are protected. Although this subject will be explored in detail in Chapter Six, the theme of land as an ancestral trust is crucial to ecological ethics.

## Sacred Spaces

As discussed in Chapter Two, the sacred spaces (*malende*) can inform ecological and action. G. Parrinder observes that Shona sacred groves (*murambatemwa*) are refuge spaces for every creature. The Zimbabwe ruins, he argues, are "uncanny and sacred places. It is said that if one tries to break a twig from a tree, it cries out 'do not break me.' No living creature may be killed there, and if an animal is pursued into the ruins it calls out, 'do not kill me.'"[28] In the *malende*, all creatures have natural rights to be protected.

## Vital Force: The Spirit that Holds the Universe Together

Despite the criticisms that Tempels' theory has received from scholars like Mbiti, Africanists have not discussed African theology, philosophy, or ethics without referring to the concept of vital force. Among the Bantu, God or the Supreme Being is the vital force-self, but has shared this force with all creatures. It is this force that connects creation to a web of dynamic and intricate relationships.

---

[28] Geoffrey Parrinder, *Religion in Africa* (London: Penguin Books, 1969), 59.

Put differently, God created the founders of the clan who, behaving according to God's laws, founded community cultures. Belonging to a community culture implies participating in the vital force of the clan founders. Those who live a long life possess, in greater intensity, the reality of the vital force.

Nkemnkia illustrates this notion when he follows Tempels to argue that the vital force is expressed in relationships with God, the ancestors, humanity and the natural world. Africans do not accept the theory that things happen without a cause. One should look for answers in this world before resigning one's fate to God. Only afterwards can Africans accept that "God has given and God has taken away."[29] Therefore, humanity alone does not constitute the entire vitalogy since God, spirits, ancestors, and nonhuman beings are equally vital forces.

Africans believe that humanity and nonhumans share the same elements that constitute the material world. It is from this perspective that Earth is called the mother of all living beings. While some scholars argue that humanity is the highest form of all living beings and that all other creatures find their meaningful existence in the human world, Nkemnkia insists that "humanity finds meaningful existence in a spiritual dimension through his relationship with others, the world and with God."[30] To this effect, Africa has many creation myths that illustrate the origin and interdependence of creation.

## Creation Myths

The creation of Earth is a given among Africans. Humans, animals, and the entire Earth community are creatures of God—that is what they were meant to be and always will be. According to a Sudanese Bassa myth of creation, for example, God created the world and all creatures including humanity. At that time there

---

[29] Nkafu Martin Nkemnkia, *African Vitalogy: A step Forward in African Thinking* (Nairobi: Paulines Publications Africa, 1999), 117.
[30] Ibid., 121.

were no animosities between humanity and nature; people and nonhumans lived in peace. Unlike other myths that blame animals for death, the Bassa attribute death to human disobedience. The ever working and watching Supreme Being *Lolomb* had warned humanity to resist sleeping. That humanity chose to fall asleep is the reason death came into this world. This led to hostility between humans and nature.

The Bassa are not the only community culture that views animals as closely related to humanity. The Chewa people of Malawi have a myth of *Kaphiri-Ntiwa*. According to this myth, human beings, animals, and God lived together in harmony until one person "invented fire and set the grass ablaze. The animals fled in terror and God too escaped into the sky, leaving humans alone with their disastrous power and knowledge."[31]

The Lozi of Zambia attribute death to human arrogance toward other creatures. In a fashion similar to that of St. Francis of Assisi in distant Europe, the Lozi argue that humanity and other creatures were meant to exist as God's family. The failure to abide with the family principle forced God out of Earth and brought about death. According to the myth, *Nyambe* created Earth and all creatures. Sadly, one creature called *Kamonu* (human being) imitated God, forged iron spears and killed an antelope. *Nyambe* was very annoyed with *Kamonu* for killing his own brother. *Nyambe* forgave him, but *Kamonu* did not repent.

Armed with his spears, he killed a buffalo and other animals. *Nyambe* was very upset and sent misfortune on Earth and then retired to the sky. To date, the Lozi believe that it is evil to kill certain animals and birds.[32] And, closely related to such myths is

---

[31] Christopher Wrigley, "The River-God and the Historians: Myth in the Shire Valley and Elsewhere," *The Journal of African History* 29, no.3 (1988), 378-379.

[32] Parrinder, *Religion in Africa*, 32. Also in John Kaoma, "God, Humanity and Nature: Reflecting on the Relational Approach," *Listening Journal of Religion and Culture* vol. 35, no.3 (Fall 2000), 233. "Kuomboka," Zambia National Broadcasting Corporation documentary. February 2000. The documentary called the Lozi people traditional environmentalists.

the belief in totems, through which many African cultures affirm their connectedness to the natural world.[33]

## *Mukowa*: the Principle of Interconnectedness

The concept of totem or clan (*mukowa*) can enhance ecological awareness in Africa. Among the Bantu, for example, totems are generally associated with nature—plants, other creatures, or natural phenomena. It is the *mukowa* that links individuals to each other and to the entire universe.

The Bantu identify themselves through *mukowa*. Totems symbolize belongingness; they define and interconnect families, clans and kingdoms. The value of symbols is that they act as a bridge between the past and the present. As Theo Sundermeier rightly discerns, "Symbols are mirrors of real life, mirrors of people in society and the cosmos.--Symbols make Africans aware of themselves, and of the world in which they have a part." What genealogies are to westerners, totems are to the Bantu.

That even children know their *mukowa* explains the significance of totems among the Bantu. As we discovered in Chapter Two, the Chieftainship of Simaamba identifies itself as "*bagande* royal establishment clan."[34] Since *bagande* means frog, one wonders why the establishment can pride itself in a frog. Yet to the Tonga, life cannot be envisaged without *totems*. As a schoolboy assured Colson, "The clan is the most important thing we Africans have."[35]

Consequently, Tumani Mutasa Nyejeka asserts that totems (*mutupo*) are vital to how the Shona and Ndebele community

---

[33] Kalu argues that among the Igbo, tabooed acts were an offense to Earth and Divinity alike. Since life depends on Mother Earth, the Earth Goddess (boa) is given great prominence. Thus "offenders would propitiate the Earth Goddess, and the cost of the propitiatory rituals could serve as deterrence. While totems relate more to myths of origin and ancestral symbolism, taboos are used by the Igbo to restrict individuals; taboos and cleansing rituals are religious, because they under-prop a religious worldview." Kalu, "Religion and Social Control in Igboland," 119.

[34] From the letterhead of His Royal Highness Chief E. M. Simaamba the XI, Bagande Palace, Box 67, Siavonga, Zambia.

[35] Colson, "The Plateau Tonga of Northern Rhodesia," 132.

cultures conceive social relations. Aside from affirming the interconnectedness of creation, the uniqueness and individuality of species is well pronounced in this principle. That is to say, m*utupo* affirmed and rationalized diversity of life and interconnectedness in the universe.[36]

Although Africans did not know the theory of evolution as propagated by Charles Darwin, it goes without saying that they were aware of their relationship to the natural world. They understood that humanity existed *in* nature rather than *above* nature; thus, the often celebrated concept of "I am because I belong" should become "I am because I have *mukowa* and because I have *mukowa*, I am interconnected to the Earth community." When two people meet, for example, their first obligation is to seek how they could be related through *mukowa*. Among the Bemba, people who share the same *mukowa* cannot get married no matter how distant they might be.[37]

Since Bantu relationships are built around the natural world, observing *mukowa* principles means honoring the ecosphere. Clans are obliged to protect their totem and may not eat the meat of that totem. The Shona, the Ndau, the Baganda, and the Luvale cultures, among many others, do not allow consumption of totemic animals. However, some cultures eat their totems. The Bemba *bowa* (mushroom) people consume mushrooms. That they eat mushrooms does not mean that they disrespect their totem. On the contrary, they do so with reverence and gratitude to their totemic ancestors for sacrificing themselves up as food to their own people.

*Mukowa* principles also foster social relationships among people who are not directly related otherwise. Among the Bemba

---

[36] Tumani Mutasa Nyajeka, "Shona Women and the Mutupo Principle," in *Women Healing Earth* (ed), Rosemary R. Ruether (Maryknoll, NY: Orbis *Books*, 1996), 135.

[37] Karla O. Poewe, "Matriliny in the Throes of Change: Kinship, Descent and Marriage in Luapula, Zambia, Part One," *Africa: Journal of the International African Institute* 48, no.3 (1978), 210. In other African cultures, however, marriage between people who share the same totem is encouraged.

and Chishinga of Zambia, for example, the concept of *ubwali* or *ubunungwe* (traditional cousins) is used to connect various clans. The *nsoka* (the snakes), *mbeba* (rats) [which, by the way, is my late father's mukowa], *mumba* (soil), *bowa* (mushrooms) and *imfula* (water) can be said to be socially related based on the workings of the ecosystem. The *mbeba* (rats) make their homes in the soil (*mumba*); hence they are cultural cousins with the *mumba*. We do not expect the mushroom to grow without water; hence their relationship with *mfula* (water/rain) is evident. Snakes (*nsoka*) are a threat to rats (*mbeba*); therefore, they are cultural cousins. All this goes to show that the totem is the most pronounced symbol of community interconnectedness in Bantu worldviews.

The value of *mukowa* is that it creates intimate relationships in Bantu communities. For this very reason, it does not die since it "is handed on from father to son [among the matrilineal societies, from mother to daughter] throughout the ages."[38] But, the *mukowa* does not just bind humanity to each other in an anthropocentric sense; rather it reminds humanity of its interconnectedness to the natural world. Humanity, despite its celebrated intelligence, can hardly exist outside the natural world; the *mukowa* emphasizes this. The Bantu people knew of nodal affiliations of the web of life long before this came to be understood in Western consciousness.

The above ecological themes reinforce the understanding that God cares for all creatures. They further suggest that African myths relate to biblical perspectives on creation (see the creation story in Genesis 1, God's covenant with all creation in Genesis 9, and so forth) and can inform Christian ecological ethics. It follows that ancestors, spirits and the Supreme Being must enforce the natural rights of nonhumans in time and space.

---

[38] Dora E. Earthy, "The VaNdau of Sofala." *Journal of the International African Institute* 4, no.2 (Apr., 1931), 226.

## The African Concept of Time: John Mbiti

John Mbiti is held as the voice behind the thesis that Africans conceive time differently, but other scholars struggled with the African notion of time long before he did. Arguably, Edward E. Evans-Pritchard was one of the first European scholars to realize that Africans reckoned time differently. In his work on the Nuer, published in 1940, Evans-Pritchard argued that the Nuer notion of time could be divided into two: "ecological time," which had more to do with the rhythm of nature; and "structured time," which dealt with age-related developments.[39] Ecological time constitutes days, months, and years; birth, marriage, death, and other rites of passage constitute structured time. He finally concluded that Africans understood time differently; this is the very point John Mbiti explored later.

Mbiti contended that African time is event-oriented. That which has not happened, or "what has no likelihood of an immediate occurrence falls in the category of no-time. What is certain to occur, or what falls within the rhythm of natural phenomena is the category of *inevitable* or *potential time*."[40] Unlike Evans-Pritchard, however, Mbiti asserts that African time is two-dimensional:

> [Time consists of] a long past (*zamani*), a present (*sasa*) and virtually no future. The linear concept of time in Western thought with an indefinite past, present and infinite future is practically foreign to African thinking. The future is virtually absent because events which lie in it have not taken place, they have not been realized and cannot, therefore constitute time. If, however, future events are certain to occur or if they fall within the inevitable rhythm of nature, they, at best constitute only *potential time*, not *actual time*.[41]

---

[39] Booth argues that prior to Mbiti's discussion of the concept of Time, Edward E. Evans-Pritchard and Paul Bohannan had already pointed out some of what Mbiti observed. Newell S. Booth Jr., "Time and African Beliefs," *Journal of Religion in Africa* VII, Fasc. 2 (1975), 85-87.
[40] Mbiti, *African Religions and Philosophy*, 17.
[41] Ibid.

Mbiti nonetheless agreed with Evans-Pritchard on the aspect of natural phenomena. "People expect the years to come and go," he insisted, "in an endless rhythm like that of day and night, and like the waning and waxing of the moon. Each year comes and goes, adding to the time dimension of the past. Endless time or eternity for them is something that lies only in the region of the past."[42] It is for this reason that time is not spent—but made. It matters less what time the event begins as long as it has taken place. Africans, Mbiti contended, have "little or no active interest in events that lie in the future beyond, at most, two years from now; and the languages concerned lack words by which such events can be conceived or expressed."[43]

Since the future does not constitute actual time, Mbiti argues, Africans consider only a relatively short future, which is part of the present (*sasa*). The *sasa* is the "now period," and the center of existence. It "is the time in which people are conscious of their existence, and within which they project themselves both into the short future and mainly into the past (*zamani*)."[44]

The *sasa* is the most meaningful period since it carries personal recollection of life events. Before an event enters the *zamani*, it must be actualized in the *sasa* period. As for the *zamani*, it "is the period beyond which nothing can go. Zamani is the graveyard of time, the period of termination, and the dimension in which everything finds its halting point. It is the final storehouse of all phenomena and events, the ocean of time in which everything becomes absorbed into a reality that is neither after nor before."[45]

---

[42] Ibid., 21.
[43] Ibid., 17-19. Booth compliments Mbiti's findings about the Kikamba language. The Luba of southern Democratic Republic of Congo are similar to the Akamba. Quoting H.W. Beckett's *Handbook of Kiluba* of 1951, he notes that the Kiluba tenses belong to three times groups: the present, near from present and further from present. The Kiluba "pay careful attention to the past and present, but are much more vaguely interested in the future….The further tense practically exists only in the past, and…is rarely found in connection with future time." Booth, "Time and Change," 81.
[44] Mbiti, *African Religions and Philosophy*, 22.
[45] Ibid., 23.

In short, the *zamani* provides the sense of security to the *sasa* through myths, customs, and rituals. In ecological terms, one can add, the *zamani* binds creation together.

Mbiti further argues that the African concept of history moves backwards and there is no expectation of a "golden age" in the future.

> People look more to the past for the orientation of their being than to anything that might yet come into human history. For them, history does not move toward any goal yet in the future: rather it points to the roots of their existence, such as the origin of the world, the creation of man, the formation of their customs and traditions, and the coming into being of their whole structure of society.[46]

From this perspective, he concludes that:

> African peoples have no 'belief in progress,' the idea that the development of human activities and achievements move from a low to a higher degree. The people neither plan for the distant future nor 'build castles in the air.' The center of human thought and activities is the Zamani, since for them there is no 'World to come,' such as found in Judaism and Christianity.[47]

## Revisiting the African Concept of Time

With the advent of ecological consciousness and spirituality, Mbiti's observations on time deserve critical re-examination. If Africans lack a sense of the future, it is very difficult to elaborate on or defend an ethical rationale for human responsibility toward future generations of life and the natural world.

Mbiti did not address why most Africans consider the living dead as those who have gone ahead. Although Africans appear to emphasize the past (*zamani*), all customs and norms associated

---

[46] John S. Mbiti, *New Testament Eschatology in an African Background: A Study of the Encounter between New Testament Theology and African Traditional Concepts* (London: Oxford University Press, 1971), 24. Unlike in African Philosophy, Mbiti limits himself to the study of his own people, the Akamba.

[47] Mbiti, *African Religions and Philosophy*, 23.

with rites of passage are future-oriented. Missing one stage undercuts one's future life. Death, in particular, is a future event through which one enters into the *zamani*.[48] The *zamani* is not the graveyard of time, but time past the grave from where the living dead accompany their descendants into the future.

So, because we live in time and continue to exist in space, death does not end time; rather, it moves time beyond the grave. In African cosmologies, for somebody to be born, grow, marry, have children, die in old age, and become an ancestor, future-oriented rites should have been performed. In fact, it is the duty of those who have gone ahead (dead) to ensure the future security of their descendants. Among the Bemba, for example, the dead are said to have gone *kuntanshi* (ahead) as opposed to *kunuma* (backwards). This notion is also found among many African cultures.

In addition, not all Africans languages have words for past, present, and future. Among the Bemba for example, *mailo* and *masoshi* can refer to yesterday and tomorrow and the day before or after tomorrow respectively. It is therefore misleading to argue that the absence of these words means that they don't exist— rather it points to the difference in our conceptions of time.

Africans may put emphasis on the past (tradition), but that does not demote them to a futureless peoples. Undeniably, Africans do not have an eschatology that moves humanity from this Earth, due to their Earth-affirming religions. But, to suggest that they do not plan for the future is an overstatement. Similarly, some African cultures may lack "expressions [that] convey the idea of a distant future," but they do plan for the yet to come.[49]

It is also misleading to argue that Africans do not believe in progress as Mbiti did. The pyramids in Egypt, the *n'gombe Ilede* ruins, the great Zimbabwe ruins, and many other historical ruins

---

[48] Ibid.
[49] Mbiti, *African Religions and Philosophy*, 17. In eschatological terms, Mbiti's argument is to the point. Africans do not expect a golden age in the future, nor do they await one. The golden age is in the past, when people observed traditions of the elders without the corruption of Western civilization.

throughout Africa suggest that Africans believed in progress and planned for the distant future.

One of the major reasons why Africans opposed the selling of land is based on the belief that it belonged to future generations and the ancestors. That the rights of unborn generations to land were considered, suggests that Africans had a strong sense of the future. Dominique Zahan concurs with this point when he argues that Africans conceive time in relation to future generations. Giving an example of human succession to illustrate the African concept of past, present, and future, he maintains,

> The human being goes backward in time: he is oriented toward the world of ancestors, toward those who no longer belong to the world of the living, while he turns his back on what is to come, the future. Future and past are thus determined in relation to the two major sides of the human body, the back and the front. Between them, the flanks, containing the ribs, are analogous to the present, connecting the two extremes.[50]

Mbiti's futureless notion of time is contradicted by Zahan's observations. This is because the African concept of time is circular and not linear. Due to the interconnectedness of "periods" of time, or moments in time, Africans experience the future in the dance of life. Events take place in the circle of time as illustrated below.

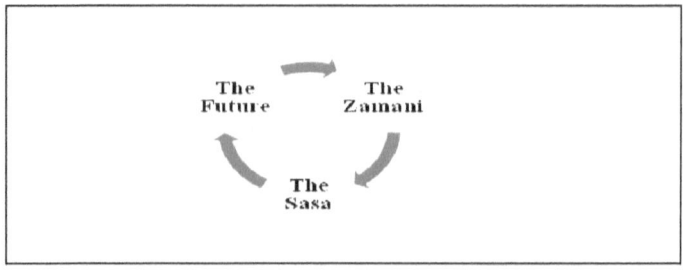

*The circle of Time*

---

[50] Dominique Zahan, *The Religion, Spirituality, and Thought of Traditional Africa* (Chicago: University of Chicago Press, 1970), 45.

The Church father's Greek concept of *perichoresis* (from the word *peri*, which means around and *choreo*, meaning to dance, thus dance around), which describes the relationship of the Father, Son and Spirit in the Holy Trinity can equally be employed to explain the concept of time in Africa. To a great extent, African cosmologies follow this circular pattern. There is no future without the past, and no past without the future in this notion of time.

## The Ecological Implication of Time

African theologians are correct to contest that African traditional thought pays more attention to the past, but it is a past that plants and is planted in the future. The *zamani* cannot exist without the future and vice versa. For this reason, just as the *zamani* overlaps with the *sasa*, it also transcends it into the future. By implication, "it is not time that moves into the past, but events….time as such, does not run anywhere."[51] In this way, the *zamani* is the *telos* of events. In fact, while Africans fear death, they also accept it as an entry into future life. In other words, death does not necessarily break the dance of life. The dead are not dead; they continue to exist in, and influence the circle of time and space. By dying, one enters a spiritual world and therefore, has the power to influence the future activities of the *sasa*.

As alluded to in previous Chapters, the cults of ancestors and high Gods spring from the belief that spiritual beings can alter the future. The dead are buried according to the traditions so that they can direct future events and life. It is to this reality that even Mbiti points when he speaks of the ancestors and unborn (future generations) as part of the present (*sasa*) human community. The living depend on Earth, but equally so do the dead and the unborn. Thus, how Earth is cared for is of great concern to the ancestors and Supreme Being.

Furthermore, Mbiti's analysis of time was based on the Western concept of time, which seems to break time into periods. But, as

---

[51] Booth, "Time and Change," 84.

Newell S. Booth Jr. observes, the separation of periods into past, present, and future is foreign to Africans:

> Actually, the whole distinction of "stages" due to an abstract notion of "time" as an entity is alien to African thought. There are not "times" but "events." These are completed and "perfect," or still developing and thus incomplete or "imperfect." If one wished, one might say that these incomplete events are in all three "times": past, present and future. The "past" of an incomplete event is quite different from the "past" of a completed event; it may have less in common with completed past than it has with the "present" and the "future." The distant past or the [*zamani*] period is not simply past in a linear sense; it transcends our distinction of past, present and future and provides the basis for a timeless communal life.[52]

Indeed, Africans did not emphasize the future, because it depends on how the living behaved toward these forces. Disrespecting the guidance of the *zamani* can destroy one's future.

Further, the prominence of diviners in African cultures also suggests the future orientation of African time. Diviners have the powers to transcend time and space, a point both Mbiti and Zahan overlooked. Among the Tonga and in other African cultures, diviners, like ancestors, have some power to know the mind of the *zamani* and the future alike; as the Bembas say, *ebaishiba ifya kuntanshi* (they are the ones who know the future). It is here that the interconnectedness of African spirits and ancestors becomes important. If diviners can communicate with the ancestors, it follows that they can migrate into the *zamani*. Likewise, if they have the power to read the mind of ancestors, they can migrate into the future. In this case, human life is a dance in time and space; any attempt to break this dance jeopardizes the future.

Being human implies having limited knowledge of timeless communal life, as illustrated by the Bemba saying, *beshiba uko wafuma tabeshiba uko uleya* (we know where we are coming from but we do not know where we are going). This does not mean that

---

[52] Ibid., 92.

the future is absent; rather, it is the future that the *sasa* can alter, based on its relationship with the *zamani*. Again, this conceptual understanding has critical implications for ecological action.

## The Interconnectedness of Morality and Religion

Since the time of Plato, philosophers have grappled with his Euthyphro dilemma: "Is what is ethical commanded by gods because it is moral, or is it moral because it is commanded by gods?"[53] Although Plato had wrestled with this dilemma, it is the promotion of Christian norms that led Enlightenment era thinkers to explore the relationship between religion and ethics.[54]

While gods played a vital moral role in Plato's world, the Enlightenment belief in human capacity to make right choices reduced the power of religion in morality. Aside from aiding the separation of the sacred from the secular, the Enlightenment led people to envision a moral society without religion.[55]

Some scholars have contested the assumption that African morality and religion are one and the same. Because Africans are extremely religious, religion is not just an ontological phenomenon, but "pertains to the question of existence or being."[56] Thus, a person is immersed into religious participation even before birth; hence everything in life is understood religiously. As Laurenti Magesa asserts, "religion is far more than 'a believing way of life' or life itself, where a distinction or separation is not made between religion and other areas of human existence. If one is to speak of 'revelation' or 'inspiration,' it is not to be found in a book, not even

---

[53] See Plato, *The Last Days of Socrates*, reprinted and translated, and with an introduction by Hugh Tredennick (London: Penguin Books, 2003), 20ff.

[54] As early as 1896, Otto Pfleiderer concluded that "religion and the ethical ideal, so far from being in conflict, stands in as close a relationship to each other as underlying reality and appearance, as root and tree." Otto Pfleiderer, "Is Morality without Religion Possible and Desirable?" *The Philosophical Review* 5, no.5 (Sept., 1896), 451.

[55] Stanley J. Grenz, *A Primer on Postmodernism* (Nashville: Wm. B. Eerdmans Publishing Co., 1996). See also Gabriel C. Rochelle, "Aphophatic Preaching and the Postmodern Mind," *St. Vladimir's Theological Quarterly* 50, no.4 (2006), 397-419.

[56] Mbiti, *Africans Religions and Philosophy*, 15.

in the people's oral tradition, but in their lives."⁵⁷ Therefore, to speak about African Christian ethics is to accept the community in which life is experienced as normative for ethical behavior. So, when studying African ethics one needs to study a particular culture.

## The Non-Religious Basis of Ethics

In 1910, American sociologist Charles A. Ellwood published an article in which he argued that human conduct is based upon social interactions. According to his analysis, moral ideals reflect the values of specific community cultures. The moral, he suggested, is simply the normative aspect of the social. Therefore, moral virtues are concrete community values. In his words, "moral ideals must lie within the limits of social survival, social efficiency, and social harmony of humanity, and not outside of them....Ethical ideals are derived genetically from the social life and they must fall within certain limits which...human society imposes."⁵⁸

By 1929, another American intellectual Walter Lippmann, who viewed morality as a trial of social living, had concluded that morality is based on societal interaction. He contended that "in the world where no man desired what he could not have, there would be no need for morality."⁵⁹

Robert A. Hinde, Professor of Biological Science at St. John's College, Cambridge, however, expanded this argument when he maintained that,

> Morality is a product of basic human psychological characteristics shaped over pre-historical and historical time by diachronic dialectical transactions between what individuals do or what they are supposed to do in the culture in which they live. That is, throughout human history, the behavior, values and attitudes of

---

⁵⁷ Magesa, *African Religion*, 25.
⁵⁸ Charles A. Ellwood, "The Sociological Basis of Ethics," *International Journal of Ethics* 20, no.3 (Apr., 1910), 326.
⁵⁹ Walter Lippmann, *A Preface to Morality* (New York: Macmillan, 1929), 145.

individuals have continuously influenced and been influenced by the culture in which they live.[60]

Because morality points to group *distinctiveness*, it is learnt through the interaction of biological, cultural and psychosocial forces upon an individual. Thus, it originates from society.[61]

Likewise, William Warren Bartley, III, questions the extent to which morality and religion are interdependent.[62] While accepting that religion influences morality, Bartley argues that in certain moral issues, "no directive of a religious character is available. So that, even if we are to accept that one ought to do what God wills, one would still have to ascertain by moral reasoning independent of religious teaching what to do with those situations concerning which God had not spoken."[63] In such cases, reason and other social faculties are consulted when making moral decisions.

Bartley's questions led some non-theological scholars to accuse ethicists of forcing religion on morality. Kwame Gyekye and J. N. Kudadjie are representative of the many voices that advocate society as the source of morality. Gyekye argues that in Akan thought, for example, the "right is not that which is commanded by God or any supreme being; what is right is not that which is pleasing to a spiritual being or in accordance with the will of such a being."[64] Rather, the good is "decreed...by human beings within the framework of their experiences in living in society."[65] His

---

[60] Robert A. Hinde, "Law and the Sources of Morality," *Philosophical Transactions: Biological Sciences* 359, no.1451, Law and the Brain (Nov. 29, 2004), 1685-1690. Hinde sees the interplay between biological and cultural influences in moral development. He addresses other major positions, among them the argument that morality is God-given (which we discussed under the *Euthyphro* dilemma) and that it is handed down by culture (the position advanced by Bujo and other African scholars).

[61] Ibid., 1691.

[62] W.W. Bartley, III, "The Reduction of Morality to Religion," *The Journal of Philosophy* 67, no.20, Sixty-Seventh Annual Meeting of the American Philosophical Association, Eastern Division (Oct. 22, 1970), 756.

[63] Ibid., 764.

[64] Kwame Gyekye, *An Essay on African Philosophical Thought: The Akan Conceptual Scheme*, Revised Ed. (Philadelphia: Temple University Press, 1995), 131.

[65] Ibid., 132.

argument is that "what is morally good is generally that which promotes social welfare, solidarity, and harmony in human relationships.--The good is identical with the welfare of society, which is expected to include the welfare of the individual."[66] This is because the Akan understand evil as anything that hinders social harmony. Although he cites traditional proverbs that point to the divine origin of Akan ethics, Gyekye maintains that spiritual forces do not determine morality but society does. For instance, some acts are prohibited not because they trespass the authority of supernatural beings, but due to their undesirable consequences on society. Thus, the Akan hold morality to be logically independent of supernatural powers.[67]

Ironically, Gyekye observes that in communal societies, parents, "heads of lineage" and "clan founders" powerfully influence the moral behavior of the individual. Probably, Gyekye employed the phrase "heads of lineages" as opposed to ancestors to avoid addressing the supernatural origin of African ethics.

Similarly, Kudadjie argues that morality among the Akan can be traced to the community rather than to gods. He contends that while religion plays a vital role in African morality, ethical values do not stem from religion since not all norms are said to be religious. To him, the ethics of solidarity and sharing have to do with customs and traditions. Therefore, the "claim that morality in African societies is wholly dependent on religion is, therefore, unacceptable."[68] Kudadjie carefully employed the phrase "wholly dependent on religion" in his argument. Like Gyekye, he asserts that religion is among the many factors that influence morality—customs, tradition, socialization, social structures, conscience, and climate. These factors consciously or unconsciously inform ethics and are equally sources of morality. Religion, he maintains, is not the only "cause or determinant" of morality and not all ethical

---

[66] Ibid.
[67] Ibid., 136-143.
[68] J.N. Kudadjie, "Does Religion Determine Morality in African Societies? A View Point," in *Religion in a Pluralistic Society*, (ed.) John S. Pobee (Leiden: E.J. Brill, 1976), 67.

sanctions are that of "the religious traditions manifest in that society."[69]

The above positions can be misleading, nevertheless. Aside from the fact that African worldviews are interconnected, the human community is under the control of spiritual forces. Human beings are part of the universe of life forces, and to the greater extent dependent on such forces in life. Hence, to be moral is to abide by the authority of such forces and not vice versa. In terms of actions, however, humanity plays a central role. Humans are expected to act responsibly to maintain the harmony of the cosmos. The consequences of human actions determines right and wrong—only life enhancing actions are good and the opposite is evil. Therefore, to be moral is to increase life while to be immoral is to decrease it.

## The Religious Basis of Ethics

Some scholars accept the religious basis of ethics. According to American theologian Shailer Mathews, for example, the ultimate basis of morality is religion.[70] Mathews' conclusion applies to African ethics as well. In his work on the Nyakyusa of Tanzania, Godfrey Wilson argues that morality and religion are one and the same. Having defined morality as "a right custom that is sanctioned by religion," Wilson maintains that the cult of ancestors, the belief in witchcraft, and the use of medicines are the three areas that unite religion and morality.[71]

Although Wilson advocates the interdependence of religion and morality among the Nyakyusa, he nevertheless distinguishes between morality and social ideals. Unlike morality, he argues, social values such as generosity, courtesy and the care for the old

---

[69] Ibid., 69.
[70] Shailer Mathews, "The Religious Basis of Ethics," *Journal of Religion* 10, no.2 (April. 1930), 229.
[71] See also Robin W. Lovin and Frank E. Reynolds (eds), "Ethical Naturalism and Indigenous Cultures," *Journal of Religious Ethics* 20 (Fall 1992), 267-413.

and the crippled carry moral sanctions. Any person who falls short of these ideals is guilty of sin.[72]

Wilson further asserts that the Nyakyusa understand sin as a breach of morality. "Whenever a man or his wife, child, or beast falls sick or dies; when his crops fail, or his cows go dry, he usually goes at once to diviners (*ondagosi*) to confess all his remembered sins and to find out whether any of them is responsible for the misfortune or not."[73] This is because the Nyakyusa believe that ancestors can punish people for trespassing social customs. Thus, any attempt to separate morality from religion among the Nyakyusa, he contends, is for academic purposes only, since these divisions "are undistinguishable in life. There is at times, however, a conflict between them; and in any case to understand how they unite in life we must first see them each distinctly."[74]

Most pioneers of African theology promoted the idea that African ethics is dependent on religion. According to Bolaji Idowu, African ethics "is basically the fruit of religion and...it is dependent upon it. [The human] concept of the Deity has everything to do with what is taken to be the norm of morality. God made man; and it is He who implants in him the sense of right and wrong."[75] Since ethics and religion are interconnected in Yoruba belief, Idowu maintains that separating ethics and religion will have negative consequences on society.

Unlike Gyekye above, J.B. Danquah argues that God or *Nana* (the Great Ancestor) is the source of morality among the Akan since their morals are usually inclined toward the demands of the Great Ancestor.[76] Because of the pivotal role ancestors play in Akan community, Danquah states that people are expected to live

---

[72] According to Wilson, "Custom is not only sanctioned by religion but also by public esteem and disapproval." Godfrey Wilson, "An African Morality," *Africa: Journal of the International Institute* 9, no.1 (Jan., 1936), 75-76.
[73] Ibid., 80.
[74] Ibid., 76.
[75] Bolaji Idowu, *Olodumare, God in Yoruba Belief* (London: Longmans, 1963), 145-146.
[76] J. B. Danquah, *Akan Doctrine of God* (London: Frank Cass, 1968).

by certain rules set down by the Great Ancestor. Failure to do so implies destroying life.

Like Idowu and Danquah, Mbiti argues that for Africans, religion influences every aspect of life. "[T]o be is to be religious in a religious universe. That is the philosophical understanding behind African myths, customs, traditions, beliefs, actions and social relationships. Up to a point in history this traditional religious attitude maintained an almost absolute monopoly over African concepts and experiences of life."[77]

According to Mbiti, Africans experience modern developments as a religious phenomenon. They consider social order and peace as vital to and sacred to community life. Anything that threatens social harmony is highly discouraged. Although an argument can be made that the good is not always decreed by supernatural forces, in Africa, the secular world is surrounded and permeated by the spiritual forces. Hence, if the goal of African ethics is social welfare, harmony, and solidarity in the secular world, then the social rather than the religious origin of African morality can be defended. But, African religion permeates all aspects of African sociology in which God, ancestors, the cosmos and humanity are active moral agents.

Similarly, Vivigi L. Grottanelli, who conducted his field-study among the Akan (Nzema), concluded that religious beliefs are the basis for morality. He argues that the Nzema uphold gods as the owners and masters of nature, more specifically rocks, rivers, and forests. The gods have power over life and death hence they are staunch supporters of the fundamental social values.

> Their actions enforce clan solidarity and respect for hierarchy, protect private property, and safeguard sexual morality; they provide penalties for infringement to these in cases where human justice might prove incapable of intervening efficiently....They protect people who have suffered wrong by unknown enemies

---

[77] Mbiti, *African Religions and Philosophy*, 262.

and bear witness to God's supremacy, being his children and obeying his laws.[78]

Grottanelli's observations demonstrate the symbiotic relationship between religion and social life. Moral values are important to social order, but they also have strong religious overtones. In short, although the divine origin is not literally pronounced, human actions can invite the wrath or blessing of ancestors or gods. For example, Grottanelli, in contrast to Gyekye, attributes the sanctions against adultery to the gods. He contends that among the Akan, certain diseases are associated with adultery.[79]

While Gyekye and Kudadjie limit their application of moral taboos and customs to human society, Grottanelli extends it to the natural world. He notes that the Akan have taboos that protect Earth from human abuse, because nature is viewed as the abode of gods and ancestors. Humanity must relate to nature with respect or else incur divine punishment. The common punishment for going against the rules of the gods is illness, and in some circumstances death.[80]

Importantly, however, among Africans, religion is crucial to morality. The fear of punishment and the expectations of rewards encourage or deter certain human actions. As Kalu rightly notes, "Medicine, magic, divination, oath taking, cursing, and blood pacts were rather direct modes. Indirectly, the fear of witchcraft, sorcery and poisoning kept the populace alert to moral misdemeanors."[81]

It is tempting to argue that the fear of spiritual forces is the primary goal of African morality. On the contrary, certain acts were done out of community obligations rather than religious sanctions. But, the interconnectedness of life suggests that morality exists within the religious sphere just as water exists in a waterfall. Thus,

---

[78] Vinigi L. Grottanelli, "Gods and Morality in Nzema Polytheism," *Ethnology* 8, no.4 (Oct.,1969), 402.
[79] Ibid., 383.
[80] Ibid.
[81] Kalu, "Religion and Social Control in Igboland," 119.

religion infuses all aspects of human life and any attempt to dismiss this link is rejecting the interconnectedness of African life.

Although Africans understand morality as linked to abundant life, they do not think that morality is absolute to the point that it will never change. African values can change over time. However, these values do not just change for the sake of progress or development. Rather, change is negotiated between the spiritual and human worlds. As repeatedly pointed out, the center of African religion and morality is the community—where the living dead are the moral guardians. Among the Bantu, how one behaved toward the new religion and colonial settlers was an ethical issue. In fact, those who easily cooperated with colonial masters and missionaries were said to had lost *ubuntu* (immoral) and worse than *indoshi* (witches); thus, a threat to the community's future. The next Chapter will discuss the ethics of *ubuntu* in detail.

# Chapter Four
## The Ethics of *Ubuntu*:
## Africa in Early European Eyes

In Chapter Three, we discussed how the mission theory of the "three Cs" (civilization, Christianity, and commerce) worked to colonize Africa. Because African cultures were perceived as barbaric and in need of Western enlightenment, missionaries and colonial settlers insisted that African life needed transforming. Thus, civilization was directly linked to moral, economic, and religious progress; but missionaries also insisted that civilization needed the gospel to be complete.

Just as African traditional beliefs influenced African worldviews, so did the Western beliefs control the values of missionaries. For example, some Western superstitions played a vital role to define the relationship between non-Westerners and Westerners. As Okot p'Bitek observes, the notion of the *wild man* controlled Europeans' perception of Africans. In fact, the idea of the primitive or the *noble savage* was the official lens through which African cultures were analyzed. p'Bitek explains: The reason for "this primitive critique was to make Western man live up to his supposed 'civilized nature.'"[1] But, missionaries soon realized that Africans had their own cultural norms.

## Civilization, Commerce and African Morality

The emphasis civilization and Christianity placed on individual accountability displaced African morality from its community focus. As already observed, in Africa a person of virtue is expected to

---

[1] Okot, p'Bitek, *African Religions in Western Scholarship* (Kampala: East African Literature Bureau, 1970), 38-39; Robin W. Lovin and Frank E. Reynolds argue that the use of the word "primitive" to refer to indigenous people "suggests, falsely, that their beliefs and practices are either simple or lacking in historical development. Robin W. Lovin and Frank E. Reynolds, "Ethical Naturalism and Indigenous Cultures," *Journal of Religious Ethics* 20 (Fall, 1992), 268.

enhance community life. Wisdom was not something one got from school, but obtained through community associations. The new world, however, promoted the acquisition of academic knowledge and degraded community based education. Only those trained in Western thought were said to "know," while the elders were said to be ignorant. This role reversal, whereby the young (who are traditionally ignorant in matters of life) became knowledgeable in modern issues, and elders (who are the holders of community wisdom and knowledge) were, and are still, demoted and labeled "ignorant," created social and moral crises in African communities. Apparently, some Africans revolted against Western education and blamed it for corrupting African morals; a trend that has continued to this day.

In addition, Western civilization brought a new understanding of time and life in general. Events and seasons constituted time and it mattered less whether the rainy season began in September or December. What was important is that the season comes and goes. If drought, floods, and other natural calamities occurred, Africans interpreted them as a result of their moral failure. As the *lwiindi* illustrated, special rituals were performed to ensure that such shortfalls are addressed. However, the new cosmology explained natural calamities from secular perspectives. Droughts, illnesses, and other social ills were not caused by gods, but by natural events. This displaced the role of ancestors not only from policing morality, but also from ensuring the fertility of the land. This paradigm shift negatively impacted African morality.

Moreover, the Christianization of Africa was aimed at destroying African traditional religions. From the Congo, Mutombo Mpanya, for example, insists that the creation of mission stations and Christian villages undermined traditional beliefs, since to be a convert to Christianity implied giving up one's traditional identity and cultural obligations.[2] Traditionally, such converts could have

---

[2] Mutombo Mpanya, "The Environmental Impacts of a Church Project," in *Missionary Earthkeeping*, (ed.), Calvin DeWitt and Ghillean T. Prance (Macon: Mercer University Press, 1992), 102-106.

suffered community isolation, but colonialism and Christianity shielded them and turned social misfits in traditional societies into powerful individuals in the new social and economic order.

Surprisingly, while colonial authorities outlawed most ancestral practices, Africans persisted to live between the world of ancestors and colonialism. Gift Makwasha shows how the old world provided and continues to be the foundation for understanding the new world for many Africans.[3] Bujo also captures this existential reality when he argues that despite Western advancements,

> [the] African religious tradition continues to survive. In existentially critical situations, even the intellectual elite and the royal church-goers return to their [ancestors'] practices. Apparently, to them the challenges to existential problems cannot be solved within the technologically oriented society or within the churches of foreign origin. Considering this, it seems right to admit that the ancestral tradition still influences the African down to his very roots.[4]

Admittedly, ancestral beliefs still play a role in Africa today, albeit a changed one.

Equally disruptive was the introduction of "commerce." Of course, trade around the Congo River, the Sahara and the interior of Southern Africa preceded the European invasion. The excavation of *Ingombe Ilede* (sleeping Cow) site in the Gwembe Valley revealed that Africans traded with other continents long before the fourteenth and fifteenth centuries.[5] Trade was nothing new to Africans, but the Enlightenment theory that viewed trade as

---

[3] Gift Makwasha, *The Repression, Resistance, and Revival of the Ancestor Cult in the Shona Churches of Zimbabwe: A Study in the Persistence of a Traditional Religious Belief* (New York: The Edwin Mellen Press, 2010).

[4] Bujo, *African Theology*, 15.

[5] *Ingombe Ilede* (sleeping Cow) is in the Lusitu area, where the Tonga were resettled. The excavations of burial sites revealed glass beads, copper, a single cowry shell, gold, wire, cotton cloth, wire-drawing equipment, and vast quantities of glass beads. These foreign products point to foreign trade long before the coming of the Portuguese. W. Phillipson and Brian M. Fagan "The Date of the Ingombe Ilede Burials," *Journal of African History* 10, no.2 (1969), 204.

individual and competitive, rather than a community enterprise, was alien.[6] Natural goods that had been used to build community life were exploited for individual economic benefits. Since competition rather than cooperation became the norm, Africans were forced to abandon their community values for Western ones.

Whereas the barter system was the norm in traditional Africa, commerce brought with it the money economy, and African cultures were forced to adopt this new system. Those who made more money were considered powerful regardless of age, while those who made less money—mostly the women and the elderly—were termed powerless.

Another consequence of the money economy was that it distanced people from Earth. It was one thing for an individual to make money without being connected to his or her community, but it was another for that person to do so without being connected to the land. Land, which was once considered a "commons" and a trust, was now understood as a commodity to be sold and bought. This shift transformed how many Africans understood life. Abundant life was no longer linked to how one related to the ancestors, but to how an individual worked his or her way up into this new economic ladder. Again, this new understanding of abundant life reduced the value Africans put on Earth and the ethics of *ubuntu*.

## Understanding *Ubuntu*

Early works of missionaries and anthropologists are usually accused of generalizations in their presentation of Africa. This is true, bearing in mind that like other continents, Africa is too big and too complex to be studied as one homogenic unit. Each community culture has its own heritage and customs, and one needs to be careful not to be caught in a colonial consolidation of cultures. Despite this awareness, Elias K. Bongmba argues that

---

[6] C.S. Lancaster and A. Pohorilenko, "Ingombe Ilede and the Zimbabwe Culture," *The International Journal of African Historical Studies* 10, no.1 (1977), 1-30.

there is a need to consider broad themes or principles that Africans confront while articulating particular ideas. He notes that those who are enthusiastic about broader themes usually err on the side of generalization, while particularists risk ignoring the common themes that Africans share.

> A balanced approach that emphasizes local ideas, as well as universal principles, is necessary because an essentialist perspective of Africa will not work. Such a perspective might reject the common themes and issues shared by African communities, which scholars turn to when making broad generalizations about the nature of African societies.[7]

One of these broad themes involves linguistic similarities. As John Gunther posits,

> [M]ost Bantu languages have similar qualities, and the roots of many words are the same, or approximately the same, all the way from Kenya to the Cape. The word for [person] is umu-ntu in Zulu, um-tu in Xhosa, oma-ntu in Luganda, and m-tu in Swahili. The plural form, aba-ntu is the same in a number of languages, and from this comes the word "Bantu" itself, meaning "Human Being." [African] languages on the other flank of Africa are totally dissimilar. They differ from Bantu almost as much as English does from Japanese.[8]

Although Gunther bases his linguistic analysis on *umuntu*, the Bantu have similar words for nonhumans: *icintu* in Bemba, *chinhu* in Shona, and *kinto* in Tswana. Rather than following the daily usage of these words in the Bantu context, translators imposed a Western juxtaposition of "thing" versus "man," and rendered *kinto* or *icintu* as "thing" while *umuntu* became "man." Unfortunately, this Western imposition has become the lenses through which Bantu philosophy has been discussed and analyzed. However, a

---

[7] Elias K. Bongmba, "Reflections on Thabo Mbeki's African Renaissance," *Journal of Southern African Studies* 30, no.2 (June 2004), 294.

[8] John Gunther, *Inside Africa* (New York: Harper, 1953), 287. A later theory says that the forest and southern Savannah languages of West Africa form a large group called Niger-Congo along with the Bantu languages, but that the Nilo-Saharan languages are different.

closer look at the word *umuntu* reveals that *mu* refers to human, while *ntu* points to "being," hence human being. Likewise, *icintu*, while translated as "thing," can be broken into two parts: *ici* points to nonhuman while *ntu* refers to "being;" thus, nonhuman being. Linguistically, *umuntu* and *icintu* confirm the interconnectedness of humanity and the natural world. What *umuntu* and *icintu* have in common is *ntu*. Thus, humans and nonhumans are not only intrinsically bound but also ontologically interdependent. This linguistic phrasing indicates that humans and nonhumans are not just connected by *ntu*, but have intrinsic value to be protected.

The phrasing also points to the ecological fact that both nonhumans and human beings are products of the common origin which Tempels identified as *ntu*. *Ntu*, one can argue, is the vital force that holds the universe together.

This observation was further elaborated on by Janheinz Jahn. Jahn divided Bantu philosophy into four categories based purely on the linguistic stem *ntu*. He argued that *ntu* is the universal force manifested in *muntu* (human being), *kintu* (thing), *hantu* (place and time), and *kuntu* (modality). Jahn insists that *ntu* expresses the being of forces, and hence "*NTU* is what *Muntu, Kintu, Hantu* and *Kuntu* all equally are. Force and matter are not being united in this conception; on the contrary, they have never been apart."[9] Thus,

> Muntu includes God, spirits, the departed, human beings and certain trees. These constitute a force endowed with intelligence. Kintu includes all the forces, which do not act on their own but only under the command of Muntu, such as plants, animals, minerals and the like. Hantu is the category of time and space. Kantu is ... 'modality,' and covers items like beauty, laughter, etc.--NTU is that point from which creation flows, where I suspect there is a formula for man, beast, plant, earth, fire, water, air and all circling forces at once.' NTU expresses, not the effect of these forces,

---

[9] Jahn, *Muntu*, 101.

but their being. But forces act continually, and are constantly effective. Only if one could call a halt to the whole universe, if suddenly life stood still, would NTU be revealed.[10]

Jahn's observation shows the substantial difference between Bantu and Western philosophy. Whereas Western philosophy puts humanity at the top of creation, in Bantu philosophy, humanity, animals, snakes, and certain trees can equally be on the top. Nevertheless, Jahn's argument that *kintu* includes all beings that act under human command is influenced by Western thought rather than Bantu philosophy. The Bantu did not differentiate between humans and nonhumans based solely on intelligence. If this were the case, Jahn's analysis that certain trees can be called *muntu* does not hold.

Consequently, Jahn's argument, though informative to Bantu philosophical thought neglected relating *ntu* to every creature, but demotes nonhumans to things, which is in opposition to African thought. This conceptual understanding reduces the inherent value of nonhuman beings to "things" to be exploited.

Despite the fact that linguistically *ntu* is shared by both human and nonhuman beings, some African theologians rush to associate *ubuntu* with the image of God.[11] Michael Mnyandu posits that "[u]muntu is regarded as the center of the world and the main concern of the Creator (Tixo) in all creation. Umuntu is not only the representative of God in creation, but also shares in the divine being (*NTU*). This special kinship between Umuntu and Tixo

---

[10] Ibid., 101. In *African Religion and Philosophy* (11), John Mbiti leaves out the following statement: "NTU is that point from which creation flows, where I suspect there is a formula for man, beast, plant, earth, fire, water, air and all circling forces at once."

[11] Gabriel Setiloane argues that Motho (*muntu*) "is that Energy or Force, that is Modimo—Divinity. The word used to describe the human person in this saying is the same as employed to describe the mysterious, all pervasive Energy-Force which is in fact the source of life." Gabriel M. Setiloane, *African Theology: An Introduction* (Johannesburg: Skotaville Publishers, 1986), 13.

(God/Creator) is demonstrated in the fact that Umuntu participates in Tixo's divine intelligence and skill of creativity."[12]

Following Thomas Aquinas (the fact he does not acknowledge), Mnyandu argues that humanity is God's special creature based on reason. Indeed, *ubuntu* should advocate the respect for humanity, but like Jahn, Mnyandu did not connect *ntu* to nonhumans. Etymologically, every creature shares this divine being, *ntu;* and as Bembas say, is *cana ca kwaLesa* (God's child).

## *Ubuntu* and the Power in Nature

Africans deem that the power resident in nature can be tapped to influence or determine one's destiny in life. Such power can increase or decrease one's physical vitality when used properly. Among the Bembas, for example, specific potions used to empower or disempower somebody are called *ifishimba* (power enhancers). Potions from leopards, dangerous snakes, lions, certain parts of specific animals, and many rare creatures are considered important to trap the power of the universe. Kings, diviners, and hunters receive the help of the natural world by using *ifishimba* for most of their endeavors.

In fact, certain animals are known to enhance luck, wisdom, and, more popularly, marriage stability. In some cases, it is believed that carrying certain roots will make dangerous animals run away from the carrier. Others believe that eating certain parts of a python can make one live longer. Such beliefs are so pervasive that they have found themselves noted in popular culture and music. A music group named "Glorious Band" became famous in Zambia for its hit entitled *BanaMayo Mufyupo* (Married Women). The song accuses women of giving love potions to their husbands, which as the group argues, has led to the extinction of *fikolyo-*

---

[12] [Michael] Mnyandu, "Umuntu as the Basis of Authentic Humanity," in *Perspectives on Ubuntu: A Tribute to Fedsem: Papers submitted at the Theological Colloquium at the Federal Theological Seminary in Pietermaritzburg, on the Occasion of its 30th Anniversary, August 1993* (ed.), M.G. Khabela and Z.C. Mzoneli (Alice: Lovedale Press, 1998), 68.

*kolyo* (blueheads, another species of lizards), chameleons (*fulunyemba*), and different species of trees in the country. The song ends with a theological statement that Jesus is the only true love potion for marriage (*umuti wacupo ni Yesu*).[13]

The insertion of Jesus at the end of what appears to be a purely traditional song is not accidental. As already established, Africans turn to their traditional religions for solutions first, before turning to Christ. This is as true with marriage as it is with other life challenges, from soccer to employment. The invocation of the traditional worldview does not mean the rejection of Christianity; rather, it points to the fact that for Africans, nature possesses powers that can alter human situations for better or for worse. Therefore, the attribution to human overuse the extinctions of blueheads, chameleons, and the drying of trees (deforestation), simply suggests how African traditional worldviews affect and influence people's interpretation of contemporary life.

Ecologically, the African dependence on the world of plant, insect, and animal species for remedies to social and psychological problems seems to confirm the unity and involvement of all living species in human life. Humanity may claim to be the crown of creation, yet without the power resident in nature, *umuntu* is highly vulnerable. From this perspective, *ifishimba* or the power potions resident in the natural world become another reason for protecting biodiversity in the world where human relationships are ecologically sustained.

## *Ntu* as the Concept of Ecological Interconnectedness

The understanding of *ntu* as "being" is similar to Paul Santmire's *Fns* cosmic conceptuality whereby nonhumans are viewed as "beings" as opposed to "things."[14] This reduction of nonhumans to

---

[13] Glorious Band, "Bana Mayo Mufyupo," *Isambo Lya Mfwa*, Lusaka, 2000.
[14] Paul Santmire, *Nature Reborn: The Ecological and Cosmic Promise of Christian Theology* (Minneapolis: Fortress Press, 2000), 64.

things has negatively contributed to irresponsible attitudes toward the natural world. But, as Santmire argues,

> Both nature and humanity...have their ontological ground in Being itself, in their own ways undoubtedly, but neither one has what might readily be thought of otherwise as a privileged relationship to God. That is to say; no longer are God and humanity in the same ontic class, while nature is in another, lesser class. According to hyper-personalistic way of thinking, both nature and humanity are in the same ontic class, while God is in another. God is the "Ground Being"...of every finite creature.[15]

Santmire advocates a new paradigm in human–nature relations. He posits that the "I—It" cosmic conceptuality assumes human - nature relations to be distant, manipulative, instrumental and to some extent exploitative. Building on Martin Buber's "I—Thou" cosmic conceptuality which promotes cooperation and mutuality with nature, Santmire proposes a third alternative: The "I—*Ens* cosmic relation from the Latin participle for being."[16] The *Ens* places moral accountability on human beings since the *Ens* is no longer an it (thing), but a being. Most importantly, the *Ens* has ethical claims on I. Like *icana ca kwaLesa* among the Bemba, the *Ens* can never be human property but "the Creator's and the Creator's alone."[17]

Santmire's cosmic conceptuality is closer to the *I—ntu* conceptuality of the Bantu. The interplay between *ici—ntu* and *umu—ntu* reminds us that a *ntu* (being) cannot be reduced to a "thing" since every being is a reflection of the Supreme *Ntu*. In addition, a *ntu* does not belong to humanity, but to the larger universe of the Ground of Being. That is to say, creation as a whole is a true witness of the Creator Spirit in the universe.

Generally, the Bemba would speak of *icintu candi*, "my thing," when referring to a computer or a car, but not to domestic animals

---

[15] Ibid.
[16] Ibid., 68-69.
[17] Ibid., 71.

or plants. The reason behind this distinction is that, unlike manmade objects like cars, animals share the Creator's being.

Africans cannot accept the reduction of animals to automata, as Descartes did. Nonhumans are not moved by mechanical power like clocks, but share the same divine character with humanity. Neither can they accept the assumption that ecosystems are "lifeless, mechanical, and distinct from people, but as fully alive and encompassing humans."[18] In African worldviews, nonhumans are "beings" that bring about ecological completeness and remind us that we are all Earth and to Earth we shall all return (Gen. 3:19).

African worldviews uphold the belief that all biota is part of the sacred web of life, with sacred links to the ancestors and the Supreme Being. For Africans, how the land and nonhumans are treated says much about the nation or community's values. As Bembas say, *icalo bapata abantu, ba mwena kunkoko* (The way chickens are treated tells much about that community's values).

According to Jacob Olupona, indigenous people relate with nature on a spiritual level. No Africanist, he asserts, can dispute the fact that in African tradition, nature is sacred and "wild animals are the most pure expression of God's power."[19] Thus, Christian ethics ought to promote relationships of *ubuntu* in an interconnected universe. *Ubuntu* should respect other creatures as independent beings with moral demands on human community. The killing of animals for meat is only justifiable if such slaughtering meets the demands of *ubuntu*. A person with *ubuntu* cannot pollute rivers, shoot animals for pleasure or even abuse God's Earth.

## Creation as the Sacred Offspring of the Supreme *Ntu*

The belief that nonhumans are sacred creatures of God is common in Africa. To the Bemba, for example, every nonhuman is regarded

---

[18] Frikret Berkes, Mina Kislalioglu, Carl Folke, and Madhav Gadgil, "Exploring the Basic Ecological Unit: Ecosystem-Like Concepts in Traditional Societies," *Ecosystems* 1, no.5 (Sept.–Oct. 1998), 412.
[19] Jacob Olupona, "Comments on the Encyclopedia of Religion and Nature," *Journal of the American Academy of Religion* 77, no.1 (March, 2009), 63.

as *icana cakwa Lesa* (a child of God) or *icana cabene* (someone's child). *Ifilengwa naLesa* (creatures of God) is another phrase employed to express the sacredness of all creation. Such phrases are used to caution people against destroying nonhuman creatures as well as to remind us of our common origin.

In traditional Africa, certain customs protected nonhumans from human abuse. For instance, only the number of animals needed for community consumption were killed. The motive was not just "sustainable" use. Rather, it was due to the belief that Earth belonged to the Original Being, *NTU*, who is also the origin of life and, by extension, the origin of our ancestors. Therefore, the excessive killing of animals, deforestation and pollution are attacks on our common being and ultimately on the supreme *NTU*.

Furthermore, *ubuntu* emphasizes right relationships in the universe; it recognizes that we are all inextricably bound up in each other's being, and we are one family in creation. For this reason, the ethics of *ubuntu* has the potential to address corruption, environmental degradation, genocide and other social evils. After all, *ubuntu* echoes much of the values of African cultures as well as principles of good governance and respect for human rights for all people. In South Africa, *ubuntu* contributed to the establishment and later the success of the Truth and Reconciliation Commission (TRC) in the post-apartheid era. Since the TRC was also based on Christian beliefs, it is suggestive that *ubuntu* is in line with Christian ethics. After all, both ethical traditions promote forgiveness and reconciliation; and restorative over retributive justice.

The value of *ubuntu* to transform social and political conditions is not limited to South Africa. *Ubuntu* can potentially transform global relations as well. Accepting the ethics of *ubuntu* implies acknowledging our common vulnerability, allowing others to exist so that together we can be said to be powerful. Yet *ubuntu* recognizes the humanity of each individual while insisting that the distinctiveness of each person depends on one's connection to other forces. All humans are born with the potential of *ubuntu,* but this potential can only be realized fully through relationships. So, to possess *ubuntu* is to proactively seek the transformation of human communities into welcoming, hospitable and caring societies. Here, the success of one is celebrated by the greater whole, and the diminishment of one's humanity affects the whole.

Apparently, the Bantu are aware that *ubuntu* can be present or absent in an individual or community. As Desmond Tutu rightly asserts, "we can tell when *ubuntu* is there and when it is absent. It has to do with what it means to be truly human, to know that you are bound up with others in the bundle of life."[20] If the awareness to our interconnectedness constitutes *ubuntu*, then recurring eco-social crises on the continent is indicative of its absence.

On the theological front, however, Michael Battle adds that in *ubuntu* theology, true human identity is discovered through "our common imago Dei."[21] Thus, fully realized *ubuntu* theology can "overthrow all forms of exploitation and, in the context of South Africa, the residue effects of apartheid."[22] Although Battle ignores the ecological potential of *ubuntu* theology to transform human attitudes toward nature, Tutu observes that the maintenance of harmonious relationships with nonhuman members of the cosmos is crucial to *ubuntu*:

> When Africans said, "Oh, don't treat that tree like that, it feels pain" others used to say, "Ah, they are pre-scientific; they're primitive." It is wonderful now how we are beginning to discover that it is true—that that tree does hurt, and if you hurt the tree, in an extraordinary way, you hurt yourself.--Every shrub and by extension every creature has the ability to be a burning bush and to offer us an encounter with the transcendent.[23]

---

[20] Desmond Tutu, *God Has a Dream: A Vision of Hope for Our Time* (New York: Doubleday, 2004), 27; *No Future Without Forgiveness* (New York: Doubleday, 1999), , 26.

[21] Michael Battle, *Reconciliation: The Ubuntu Theology of Desmond Tutu* (Cleveland, Ohio: The Pilgrim Press, 1997), 40.

[22] Ibid.

[23] Tutu, *God Has a Dream*, 29.

What comes out of Tutu's *ubuntu* theology is that the exploitation of nature hurts Earth and dims divine glory. Because *ubuntu* values creation as part of the sacred web of life, any *ubuntu* theology or ethics that ignores this interdependence misrepresents Bantu philosophy.[24]

Ecologically, the Bantu understand social life as interlinked through daily greetings. When we Africans ask, "How are you?," we are not inquiring about an individual, but the entire community. Usually, we respond in the plural since one can be well but his/her relative or animal is sick. To Africans, humanity exists in a delicate network of interdependence with the Earth Community. According to Tutu, this interdependence is called *ubuntu*, which "is difficult to translate into English. It is the essence of being human. It speaks of the fact that my humanity is caught up and inextricably bound up in yours. I am because I belong. It speaks about wholeness: it speaks about compassion."[25]

The values of *ubuntu* have vital implications for both interpersonal and global relations. All socio-economic and political systems that encourage competitiveness rather than cooperation work in conflict not only with God's will, but also with the ethics of *ubuntu*. After all, the global economy cannot exist in isolation. For as Tutu insists:

> [T]o share prosperity of affluent countries with indigent ones is not really altruism. It is ultimately the best kind of self-interest, for if the poor countries become prosperous in their turn, then they provide vigorous markets for the consumer goods produced elsewhere. The debt burden is a bomb that could shatter the economy of the globe to smithereens. And so a new and just economic order would benefit both the rich and poor nations.[26]

From this perspective, Tutu proposes the model of *the family of God*, as another way of conceiving the world. Understanding the

---

[24] Battle, *Reconciliation,*, 41.
[25] Ibid., 26.
[26] Ibid., 36.

world as the family of God means that we are all insiders. If we embrace this model, we will acknowledge the eco-social injustices,

> that cause a small percentage of our world to consume the vast majority of its resources—not unlike what happened in apartheid South Africa—while the vast majority lives in poverty, with over a billion people living on less than a dollar a day.--And every 3.6 seconds someone dies of hunger and three quarters of these are children under five. If we realized that we are a family, we could not let this happen to our brothers and sisters.[27]

The model of the family of God has rich implications for global relations. Asserting that our destinies are interlinked means that caring and compassion are *ubuntu* ideals to which global communities ought to aspire:

> If we could but recognize our common humanity, that we do belong together, that our destinies are bound up in one another's, that we can be free only together, that we can survive only together, that we can only be human together, then a glorious world would come into being where all of us lived harmoniously together as members of one family, the human family, God's family.[28]

As God's family, we will proudly join the Bantu in declaring that I am because I am interconnected to vital forces of life. Thus:

> Harmony, friendliness, and community are great goods. Social harmony is for us [Bantu] the summum bonum—the greatest good. Anything that subverts, that undermines this sought after good is to be avoided like the plague. Anger, resentment...even success through aggressive competitiveness are corrosive of this good.[29]

While Tutu does not extend the family model to Earth community, the extension is natural. An African family is an interdependent structure of the living, the ancestors, the living to come, the Supreme Being, and the natural world.

---

[27] Tutu, *God Has a Dream*, 23.
[28] Ibid., 23-24.
[29] Ibid., 31-32.

Since the scientific, traditional, and biblical worldviews are agreed on the interconnectedness of the universe, the family of God metaphor places ecological obligations on every individual. God's Earth is God's family of interconnected sacred beings with a common sacred origin in the Creator Spirit.

Viewing creation as the family of God also puts extra moral responsibilities on humanity and especially on faith communities. Since the living members of an African family do not constitute the entire family, it matters how we relate to other members of the Earth family. We are related to nonhumans through the history of creation and evolution; so the exploitation of one part of the family has direct effects on all relationships.

The conception of the Earth community as the family of God is in conformity with Santmire's extended family model. Santmire argues that we should uphold relationships of "mutuality and cooperation between persons and other creatures of nature."[30] Following St. Francis, he argues, we ought to view nature as *Ens* (being) and members of our "extended family."[31]

The "family of God" model can equally be derived from Sallie McFague's model of *The Body of God*. She asserts that conceiving the cosmos as the body of God confirms both the immanence and the transcendence of God. It is another way of viewing God as "the inspirited body of the entire universe, the animating, living spirit that produces, guides, and saves all that is."[32]

The richness of this model is that God's body unites, and makes everybody and every creature an image of divine transcendence. Since humans are part of the body of God, they have a moral responsibility to the fragile Earth, including the suffering and oppressed. For McFague, our unwillingness to stay in our place, to

---

[30] Santmire, *Nature Reborn*, 73; Cf. S. Samkange and T.M. Samkange, *Hunhuism or Ubuntuism: A Zimbabwe Indigenous Political Philosophy* (Salisbury: Graham Publishing 1980), 73ff.
[31] Ibid.
[32] Sallie McFague, *The Body of God: An Ecological Theology* (Minneapolis: Fortress Press, 1993), 20.

accept our proper limits so that other individuals of our species, as well as other species, can also have needed space, is sinful. She defines sin as denying our interconnectedness and the rights of others to exist. In many respects, McFague's model seeks to challenge dominant theological metaphors that disconnect humanity from Earth.

Despite the fact that the above models present a challenge to our anthropocentric conception of creation, these three models are quite different. To begin, Santmire and McFague's metaphors are planted in Western Christian mysticism and Western theology respectively, while Tutu's is built on the Bantu understanding of the family. Aside from these contextual differences, the emphasis of Santmire and McFague's models differs from that of Tutu whose emphasis is on family obligations. While Santmire promotes the extended family structure which is somehow lost in the West, and McFague proposes a positive view of the individual body in Western philosophy, Tutu bases his model on the positive socio-economic obligations to the family among the Bantu.

## Revisiting *Umuntu Ngubuntu Ngabantu*

The Xhosa, like many Africans, understand life as interconnected. This is expressed in a maxim: *umuntu ngubuntu ngabantu* (a person is a person through other people). Although the Xhosa proverb is the one which is widely known, other cultures have similar sayings. Among the Shona, it is said, *munhu munhu nekuda kwevanhu* (a human being is only human through other people). The Sotho say *motho ke motho ka batho* (a person is a person through other persons).

The anthropocentric focus of these proverbs is clear. The Bemba say, *icalo bantu* (Earth is people) which equally suggests that the value of Earth is dependent on people inhabiting our planet. *Icalo* can be rendered as the world, country, land, ecosystems or simply Earth. So to think that humans are what make the ecosphere is a fallacy.[33] Sadly, such anthropocentric interpretations of these sayings influence Southern Africa's (to some extent sub-Saharan Africa) socio-political analysis and application of *ubuntu*.

Africa should accept that some of the wisdom it received had some flaws and the ecological age demands that we right them. If *ubuntu* encouraged caring and compassion for others, then the adage *umuntu ngubuntu ngabantu* points at the interdependence of human life. In this regard, Bantu cosmology can be said to be environmentally bankrupt. Yet the African ontology of "I am because I am interconnected" points to the interrelatedness of all forces in community. Since an African community includes the natural world, limiting *ubuntu* to human relations is definitely misleading. Unfortunately, some African theologians and scholars interpreted *umuntu ngumuntu ngabantu* without questioning its application to the African traditional life style. By itself, the proverb does not meet the requirements of *ubuntu*.

Furthermore, the current understanding of the adage fails to address the ecological nature of African communities. It follows that a person is a person when in loving and just relationships with other *ntus* (*ens*). Thus, *ubuntu* should address the existential reality of life. African traditional wisdom is not environmentally bankrupt, rather its interpreters are. For the Bantu, humanity and nature are ecologically interconnected; to destroy one is to destroy them all.

Following the traditional African consciousness, it is vital that humanity acts ecologically rather than "humanely" in the sense of the proverb *umuntu ngumuntu ngabantu*. To live ethically implies upholding the ideals expressed in this proverb; yet, in a world where the exploitation of Earth and the poor shows no sign of slowing down, the ethics of *ubuntu* invites us to live ecologically on Earth.

---

[33] Berkes and others observe that indigenous words usually translated as land often encompass the living environment, including humans. Mostly, this idea is based on the concept that "everything in the environment has life and spirit." Berkes and Others, "Exploring the Basic Ecological Unit," 410.

The Bantu perceive themselves to be spiritually connected to the world of nature. Because ritual representation of resource management can enhance the proper stewardship of natural goods, environmental policies should capitalize on the African spirituality of nature. In other words, religious beliefs are crucial to the formation of ecological moral codes and values. For example, many Africans are still to find the spiritual rationale for respecting government-protected game reserves. While the reasons for such reserves are ecologically and economically sound, Africa lacks a spiritual basis for game parks. Unless game reserves are accorded spiritual value, poaching will continue across Africa.

Here, the ethical model of *ubuntu* can definitely redirect Africans to loving nature. To possess *ubuntu* is to accept that *abantu* (people) are on Earth as well as Earth; it entails accepting our moral responsibility to Earth on behalf of future generations of life, and it enforces the idea that humans are "earth that thinks, hopes, loves and has entered into the no longer instinctive but conscious phase of decision making."[34] "We are because we are connected" to the sacred web of life.

The *etymological link between nonhuman beings (ifi-ntu) and humans (aba-ntu) should not deceive us into believing that our species is safe simply because we think*. Neither should we underestimate the consequences of destroying Earth. Poverty, hunger, disease, social unrest, and violence are among the many effects of this crisis. Unfortunately, these effects are not felt equally across the globe since the poor are the most affected. For example, water pollution is likely to affect poor children more than rich ones. Subsequently, demanding eco-justice is critical to the ethics of *ubuntu*.

Yet, if one hoped that the end of colonialism would signal a return to the ethics of *ubuntu*, experience shows that post-independence Africa lacks *ubuntu* at many levels. Gauging by the

---

[34] Leonardo Boff, and Elizondo Virgil eds. *Ecology and Poverty* (Maryknoll, New York: Orbis Books, Concillium, 1995), 69; Also with slight variation in Leonardo Boff, *Cry of the Earth, Cry of the Poor* (Maryknoll, New York: Orbis Books, 1995), 106.

level of ecological destruction that has taken place after independence, an argument can be made that some missionaries such as Robert Moffat, David Livingstone and Albert Schweitzer exercised *ubuntu* toward the natural world more than post-independence African religous and political leaders. Our leaders should accept that *ubuntu* demands eco-social accountability, too.

## Disintegration of Eco-Social *Ubuntu*

The above understanding of *ubuntu* can paint a naïve picture of contemporary Africa. The truth is, contemporary Africa shows that the ethical system of *ubuntu* is disintegrating while Christianity is growing. As Mwenda Ntarangwi has shown, Christianity in Africa ought to address issues of corruption, bad governance, genocide, and other social ills.[35] Our young men and women may fill our churches, but in most cases, they remain unemployed or are underemployed. Can *ubuntu* address the eco-social and political crisis in Africa today?

Many scholars advocate *ubuntu* as fundamental to good governance and by extension to the wellbeing of the whole world. It was not surprising that the 2009 U.S. Episcopal Convention in Anaheim, California, had *ubuntu* as its theme.[36]

Malegapuru William Makgoba, however, argues that Western democracy does not address the central values of African communities. Aside from its foreignness, the European context in which Western democracies developed was nationalistic and closed to outside cultures. Ideologically, he argues, Western democracy found it hard to negotiate racial and cultural differences in non-Western contexts. In addition to the oppression of masses, in its early days, Western democracy promoted individualism, competition, corruption, and exploitation of the Earth and the Earth's poor. From this analysis, he concludes that

---

[35] Mwenda Ntarangwi (ed.), *Jesus and Ubuntu: Exploring the Social Impact of Christianity in Africa* (Trenton, NJ: Africa World Press, 2011).
[36] Ubuntu. http://www.episcopalchurch.org/gc2009.html. Accessed August 17, 2009.

Southern Africa's political ideology should be built on the philosophy of *ubuntu*, which he argues:

> Emphasizes respect and harmony of the non-material order that exists in us and among us; it fosters man's respect for himself, for others, and for the environment; it has spirituality; it has remained non-racial; it accommodates other cultures and it is the invisible force uniting Africans worldwide. Therefore, unlike Confucian or European philosophies, it transcends both race and culture.--It must deliver freedom with opportunities while addressing values and cultural systems."[37]

Sociologically, *ubuntu* should be understood within the context of communalism, in which Africans exist. But, as Penny Enslin and Kai Horsthemke rightly assert, the values of *ubuntu* are not unique to African cultures. Rather, "*ubuntu* as a philosophical approach to social relationships must stand alongside other approaches and be judged on the value it can add to better human relations in our complex societ[ies]."[38] In short, the values of *ubuntu* are universal and have global application.

This is not to turn a blind eye to genocides, sexism, corruption, xenophobia, and homophobia that have overtaken sub-Saharan Africa today. Nhlanhla P. Maake suggests that these vices are not only due to the disintegration of the values of *ubuntu*, but also to the introduction of half-baked Marxism. These developments have led to "a downtrodden people oppressing each other with hardly any moral compunction."[39] While Maake's point is valuable, it is important to realize that *ubuntu* is an ethical ideal and not an existential reality. In addition, it is tempting to view "*ubuntu* as the *deus ex machina*,"[40] with automatic powers to magically erase historical and contemporary problems in Africa. But, to deny

---

[37] In Penny Enslin and Kai Horsthemke, "Can Ubuntu provide a Model for Citizenship Education in African Democracies?," *Comparative Education* 40, no.4, Special Issue (29): Philosophy, Education and Comparative Education (Nov., 2004), 547.
[38] Ibid., 548.
[39] Nhlanhla P. Maake, "Multi-Cultural Relations in a Post-Apartheid South Africa," *African Affairs* 91, no.365 (October 1992), 295.
[40] Bongmba, "Reflections on Thabo Mbeki's," 300.

*ubuntu's* usefulness based solely on such vices is akin to rejecting the usefulness of democracy due to its failure in Hitler's Germany.

Africa's contemporary problems demand a new analysis and application of *ubuntu*. Economic status, sexual identity, gender, and bad governance demand analyzing. As Van Binsbergen argues, in the context of South Africa,

> the discourse of ubuntu revolves around textual violence, but scholars must realize that 'the concept of ubuntu is historically determined to constitute a bone of contention, to remind us of past violence and to lead us into new violence, until we realise that above all, ubuntu is the invitation to confront this determination and, together, rise above such violence.[41]

South African scholars are not the first to advocate *ubuntu* as a political ideology. At the time of Zimbabwe's independence in 1980, Stanlake Samkange and Tommie Marie Samkange asserted that *hunhu* is the basis of African morality and indigenous political philosophy of the Shonas of Zimbabwe. The moral virtues of sharing, solidarity and interdependence, and respect for elders, they argue, are characteristics of *hunhu*. In contrast with the philosophy of "democratic" capitalism that values wealth over people, *hunhu* emphasizes the sacredness of the land and the interdependence of humanity.[42] It is *hunhu* that links one's being to the family, clan, village, district, province, and wider universe.[43] Therefore, a person with *hunhu* cannot allow another human to be homeless, starve, be dehumanized, or violated.

Consequently, possessing *hunhu* involves accepting one's cultural and social roles; sidetracking from these traditional roles is unethical. While this aspect could have led to the oppression of

---

[41] Ibid.
[42] According to Stanlake Samkange and Tommie M. Samkange, the Shona consider land as sacred (*zvinoyera*) and "the real owner of the land [to be] the tutelary spirit, *Mwari* and, to a lesser extent, the various tribal spirits." Samkange and Samkange, *Hunhuism or Ubuntuism*, 51-55.
[43] Ibid., 72-79.

women and young people in community, the Samkanges maintain that *ubuntu* should be analyzed within communal roles.[44]

South African President Thabo Mbeki explored the role of *ubuntu* in rebuilding Africa. Mbeki has written much on the African Renaissance, but it is his 1998 speech entitled "The African Renaissance, South Africa and the World," presented to the United Nations University, that closely examined the *ubuntu* concept. Mbeki did not even mention *ubuntu* in that speech, but it was in the background. For example, he asserted that globalization illustrates the interconnectedness of humanity. The world

> is an interdependent whole in which none can be truly free unless all are free, in which none can be truly prosperous unless none elsewhere in the world goes hungry, and in which none of us can be guaranteed a good quality of life unless we act together to protect the environment.[45]

Telling by the wave of human rights abuses, civil wars, and corruption that characterize post-colonial Africa, however, one can safely conclude that the ethical system of *ubuntu* is yet to permeate contemporary African life.

That said, *ubuntu* remains a conceptual tool to redress the current economic and socio-political injustices, thereby leading to a better Africa. As a conceptual tool, *ubuntu* can hold African leaders accountable to their people and to the entire global Earth community. Finally, the emphasis *ubuntu* places on rights and responsibilities of every person to advance community wellbeing makes it attractive to Christian theologians and ethicists alike.

## *Ubuntu* in the Face of Corruption

The catastrophic levels of corruption in Africa contradict the rapid growth of Christianity and Islam on the continent. Across Africa,

---

[44] Ibid., 61-63. The Samkanges argue that *hunhu* jurisprudence upholds community responsibility. They insist that a leader with *hunhu* is humble, and seeks the interests of his/her subjects. Ibid., 103.

[45] Thabo Mbeki, "The African Renaissance, South Africa and the World," 9 April, 1998, http://www.unu.edu/unupress/mbeki.html. Accessed 11/27/08.

corruption has become a new societal norm in post-colonial, socio-political, and economic life. Because this vicious virus threatens the future of the continent, there is need to revisit the values of *ubuntu* in Africa.

You Jong Sung, Sanjeev Khagram, and Morris Szeftel define corruption as the abuse or misuse of public office, public resources, or some public obligation or duty for purposes of private (personal or group) gain.[46] This definition assumes that only public officials are guilty of corruption. In most African countries, however, private individuals are equally involved in this vice.

The negative effects of corruption on the socio-economic and political life of Africa is frightening. "An insidious plague that has a wide range of corrosive effects on societies," is what the then UN Secretary General Kofi A. Annan called corruption in his foreword to the United Nations Convention Against Corruption (UNCAC). While this insidious plague is found across the globe, in Africa, it undermines good governance and economic development.

In addition, corruption erodes trust among the electorate, thereby compromising the rule of law. Today, corruption has almost become the only viable path to public office. Aside from a number of Parliamentary elections nullified in Zambia and Uganda, among many African countries, due to vote buying in cash and kind, the UNCAC advocates enhancement of "transparency in the funding of candidatures for elected public office and, where applicable, the funding of political parties."[47] Yet the funding of political parties remains secretive across the continent.

But, there is another bad side to corruption; it diverts funds intended for development and undermines the Government's "ability to provide basic services, feeding inequality and injustice

---

[46] Morris Szeftel, "Between Governance and Underdevelopment: Accumulation and Africa's 'Catastrophic Corruption," *Review of African Political Economy* 27, no.84 (Jun., 2002), 298; You Jong Sung and Sanjeev Khagram, "A Comparative Study of Inequality and Corruption," *American Sociological Review* 70, no.1 (Feb., 2005), 153.

[47] U.N., *Convention Against Corruption*. http://www.unodc.org/documents/treaties/UNCAC/Publications/Convention/08-50026_E.pdf. Accessed 12/15/2012.

and discouraging foreign aid and investment."[48] In 2002, for example, the African Union (AU) report revealed that the continent was losing over $150 billion annually due to corruption.[49]

Noting the urgency of the matter, the AU advocated the establishment of Anti-Corruption Commissions on the continent—leading to the establishment of the "African Union Convention on Preventing and Combating Corruption," adopted in Maputo, on July 11, 2003. Article 19 of the Convention, for instance, criminalizes "secret commissions and other forms of corrupt practices during international trade transactions," but these practices are still prevalent in many African countries.[50] In short, African countries have in place anti-corruption agencies. But, as S. O. Osoba contends, in Nigeria as elsewhere, these structures are "controlled and operated by, and in the interest of, members of the ruling class who have a vested and entrenched interest in sustaining and even extending corrupt practices."[51]

Indeed, amidst extreme economic inequalities, even poor people are victims as well as beneficiaries. As Sung and Khagram assert, the poor are forced to depend "on petty corruption and bureaucratic extortion in their efforts to secure basic services."[52]

## The Roots of African Corruption

African corruption has many roots. Colonialism, bad governance, underdevelopment, African traditional heritage, and religious affiliation have been suggested as factors that promote

---

[48] Ibid., iv.
[49] Elizabeth Brant, "Corruption 'costs Africa billions'," BBCNEWS, Sept., 18, 2002. http://news.bbc.co.uk/2/hi/africa/2265387.stm. Accessed 04/16/2009.
[50] African Union, *Convention on Preventing and Combating Corruption*, http://www.africaunion.org/root/au/Documents/Treaties/Text/Convention%20on%20Combating%20Corruption.pdf. Accessed 04/16/2009.
[51] S. O. Osoba, "Corruption in Nigeria: Historical Perspectives," *Review of African Political Economy* 23, no.69 (Sep., 1996), 385.
[52] Sung and Khagram, "Between Governance," 39-140.

corruption.[53] To some extent, Blaine Harden's description of an African leader in the early 1990s still rings true:

> His photograph hangs in every office in his realm. His ministers wear...tiny photographs of Him on the lapels of their tailored pin-striped suits.--His every pronouncement is reported on the front page.--He scapegoats minorities to shore up support. He rigs elections. He emasculates the courts. He cows the Press. He stifles academia. He goes to church.....He awards competitive, overprized contracts to foreign companies which grant...his family and his associates large kickbacks....He affects a commitment to free-market economic reforms to secure multi-million dollar loans and grants from the World Bank and International Monetary Fund...His rule has one overriding goal: to perpetuate his reign as Big man.[54]

Needless to say, no African leader accepts being "corrupt." Thus all African leaders—many of whom fit this embarassing description—are signatories and parties to the Convention against Corruption.[55] Harden's point about African leaders' commitment to economic reforms to secure multi-million dollar loans deserves highlighting. While corruption is linked to bad governance, almost all African countries have held "democratic" elections. Aside from allowing the ruling elite to accumulate more wealth at the expense of the poor, these elections increase corruption as noted above.[56]

## Impact of Corruption on the Environment

The catastrophic levels of corruption are threatening Africa's eco-social wellbeing. International trade in diamonds, oil, gas, coltan,

---

[53] Osoba, "Corruption in Nigeria," 371-386.
[54] Blaine Harden, *Africa: Dispatches from a Fragile Continent* (New York: W.W. Norton & Co., 1990), 217-218.
[55] U.N., *United Nations Convention against Corruption.* http://www.unodc.org /unodc/en/en/ treaties/CAC/signatories.html. Accessed 10/10/09.
[56] Szeftel rightly argues that in Africa, the Western Corruption Perception Index (CPI) misrepresents how corruption is perceived. "The values by which corruption and honesty are judged are those of the people who manage the globalisation process, who lend money, reschedule debts, and conduct business and diplomatic activities." Szeftel "Between Governance and Underdevelopment," 293.

gold, and timber are among the many natural goods that have fostered civil wars, environmental degradation, and violence across Africa. In Zimbabwe, for example, the land redistribution program sought to address colonial inequalities, but failed dismally. After an attempt to redistribute the land through a referendum failed in 2000, President Robert Mugabe called on his followers to invade white owned farms. Similar to situations in Liberia, the Democratic Republic of the Congo, and the Sudan, the ecological impact of Mugabe's rule is now visible. His followers viciously destroyed wildlife, polluted rivers, and felled trees without remorse.

In addition, African leadership's business dealings with international companies are compromising the future of the continent. These companies are interested in profit; human and environmental wellbeing matters less. As the UN Expert Panel's October 2002 report on the exploitation of natural goods alleged, natural goods were behind the atrocities committed in the Democratic Republic of Congo. Five African governments and 85 businesses operating in Europe, Asia, and the U.S. were involved.[57]

African countries may have environmental monitoring bodies that ostensibly seek to protect the ecological wellbeing of the continent, but these bodies are usually compromised. In most cases, they approve projects that undermine ecological integrity to satisfy political interests of the day: African wetlands in Uganda, Kenya, and Nigeria, parks and other ecologically sensitive areas in these and other African countries have been converted to human settlements. Land conversion is likely to increase as Africa's population explodes—the subject we will explore in the following Chapter.

---

[57] Michael Renner notes that while "political oppression or the denial of minority rights," may initiate civil wars, "the pillaging of oil, minerals, metals, gemstones, or timber allows wars to continue that were triggered by other factors." For instance, diamonds were behind the civil war in Angola (with the total value of $4–4.2 billion) and Sierra Leone ($25–125 million/year). Timber ($100–187 million/year) and oil ($400 million/year) propped the wars in Liberia and Sudan respectfully. Coltan (250 million total) was behind the war in the Congo. Michael Renner, *The Anatomy of Resource Wars* (New York: WorldWatch Paper 162, October 2002), 7.

# Chapter Five
## Christianity and Population Growth: Conservation of Africa's Natural Goods

In Chapter Four, we explored the impact of civilization, Christianity, and commerce on African morality. We also noted that while the moral fiber of *ubuntu* is slowly being compromised, this ethical concept has potential to transform peoples' attitudes to the environment and to one another. In this Chapter, attention is paid to the question of population growth and its impact on the ethics of *ubuntu* and the environment.

As early as July 1968, African Independent States called for the protection and conservation of the continent's natural goods during the fifth summit of the Organization of African Unity (now known as African Union) in Algiers, Algeria. The countries jointly adopted "The African Convention on the Conservation of Nature and Natural Resources" (ACCNNR) out of the conviction that natural goods were "capital of vital importance to mankind."[1] Despite viewing natural goods from a purely instrumental perspective, African leaders acknowledged that most natural goods are "irreplaceable" and limited. They argued that "the utilization of the natural resources must aim at satisfying the needs of man according to the carrying capacity of the environment."[2]

The ACCNNR was later revised and modified in Maputo, Mozambique, in 2003 to take into consideration the concept of sustainable development. Although the Convention did not shift from its anthropocentric and instrumental focus with regard to human attitude toward Earth, it nevertheless provided a very strong moral reason for conserving nature. The revised ACCNNR

---

[1] The Convention entered into force on October 9, 1969. African Union, *African Convention on the Conservation of Nature and Natural Resources* (Revised Version). http://www.au.int/en/content/african-convention-conservation-nature-and-natural-reso urces -revised-version. Accessed 02/16/2013.
[2] Ibid.

admonished States to employ "the precautionary principle, and with due regard to ethical and traditional values as well as scientific knowledge in the interest of present and future generations" in their exploitation of natural goods.[3] The expanded Convention specifically admonished African states to protect both plant and animals species which were threatened with extinction.

The Convention's concerns are reflected in the *Earth Charter*, which was launched in the Hague in 2000. But, unlike the ACCNNR, the Charter places humanity in nature. According to the Charter, humanity is part of a vast evolving universe, and "Earth, our home is alive with a unique community of life."[4] Warning of the dire consequences which awaits us if we do not change our attitudes, the Charter insists:

> We stand at a critical moment in Earth's history, a time when humanity must choose its future. As the world becomes increasingly interdependent and fragile, the future at once holds great peril and great promise. To move forward we must recognize that in the midst of a magnificent diversity of cultures and life forms we are one human family and one Earth community with a common destiny. We must join together to bring forth a sustainable global society founded on respect for nature, universal human rights, economic justice, and a culture of peace. Toward this end, it is imperative that we, the peoples of Earth, declare our responsibility to one another, to the greater community of life, and to future generations.[5]

The Charter's invitation to uphold human responsibility toward Earth is crucial to our future. Life is "dependent on preserving a healthy biosphere with all its ecological systems, a rich variety of plants and animals, fertile soils, pure waters and clean air."[6]

The *Earth Charter* has been endorsed by tens of thousands of individuals, and publicly supported by numerous heads of States.

---

[3] Ibid., Article IV.
[4] *The Earth Charter*. http://www.earthcharterinaction.org/content/pages/Read-the-Charter.html. Accessed 02/03/2009.
[5] Ibid.
[6] Ibid.

While the December 10, 1948 *United Nations Human Rights Charter* and the June, 1981 *African Charter on Human and Peoples' Rights* have been incorporated into African moral discourse, the ACCNNR and the *Earth Charter* are yet to find space in theological literature and discourse as a whole. Ironically, African ecological values, predate and anticipate most of these documents' ideals.

## Population Growth in the Gwembe Valley

As observed in Chapters One and Two, the building of the Kariba Dam was born from a theory that economic progress was key to civilization. The relocation of the Tonga from the valley to selective areas on both sides of the Zambezi River was viewed as saving the uncivilized Africans from perpetual underdevelopment. Aside from disrupting the harmonious relationship that existed between nature and humanity, the dam created a demographical crisis in the Gwembe valley.

Prior to the construction of the dam, the Gwembe population on the Zambian side was about 52,000. At that time, the population density was about eight residents per square mile. After resettlement, the Tonga were forced into population densities three times the density of their original communities, and their population increased by 140 percent within 29 years; this situation increased pressure on the land.

The Kariba situation is common across Africa. According to Ezekiel Kalipeni, uncontrolled demographic growth is "one of the major factors that have greatly contributed to the declining economies and food production in most African countries."[7] While Kalipeni pays attention to the impact of population growth on Africa's economies, he barely addresses the ecological effects of resettlement which are critical to Africa as a whole. Resettled people adjust negatively to their new environments since they are not ecologically and spiritually connected to it.

---

[7] Ezekiel Kalipeni, *Population Growth and Environmental Degradation in Southern Africa* (Boulder: Lynne Rienner Pub.,1994), 19.

Back in the valley, however, the Gwembe Tonga practiced a mixed economy, with animal husbandry and farming. Those resettled brought their economic practices with them, and increases in demographics were matched by that of their animals. Unlike in the valley where food and habitat for their animals was in abundance, it was limited in this new environment. This led to over-grazing and over-cultivation of their small fields, creating severe land degradation. Today, the Lusitu area (where some Gwembe Tonga were originally resettled) is severely degraded.

Lisa Cliggett argues that while some portions of the Gwembe remain forested and uninhabited, areas close to the lakeshore and tributaries are densely populated.[8] Aside from associating environmental degradation to overpopulation, Cliggett asserts that the poverty of the valley should be traced to land scarcity, poor soils, and HIV/AIDS. In her historical analysis, she notes:

> The Gwembe Valley is known throughout Zambia as a drought-prone, isolated, and impoverished region of scarcity. The difficult living conditions in the Gwembe are linked closely to the local changing environment, agricultural practices, and changing social institutions. Although the Gwembe climate and ecology have always challenged local people's food procurement strategies, the resettlement in 1958 caused additional pressures for both the Tonga and their hosts in new areas. People were forced to compete for the same limited resources, and in most cases, resettlers had access only to poorer-quality soils than their hosts had in the new areas, and more than they had had before resettlement.[9]

What Cliggett addresses above is common across Africa. According to Lester R. Brown, rapid population growth is behind the reductions in per capita cereal production across the globe.[10] Tim Dyson makes a similar argument. Dyson links global human hunger to hasty population growth. "Slower population growth," he

---

[8] Lisa Cliggett, *Grains from Grass: Aging, Gender, and Famine in Rural Africa* (New York: Cornell University Press, 2005), 61.
[9] Cliggett, *Grains from Grass*, 59.
[10] Lester R. Brown, "Feeding six billion," *World Watch* (Sept./Oct. 1989), 32-40.

argues, "would probably eventually result in higher per capita food supplies. The world's most poorly nourished populations are generally growing the fastest. And in many locations—not just Africa...demographic pressures are damaging the resource base upon which people's livelihoods depend."[11]

It is threatening that Africa's food production is not keeping up with rampant population growth. It has become common for African countries to request food aid based on various reasons—from wars to harvest failures. While international agencies have provided such aid, suppliers are now finding it difficult to meet the demand. Unless the world addresses rapid population growth as a matter of priority, starvation of masses will soon become common.

## Neo-Malthusian and Neo-Böserupian Arguments

Is rapid population a threat to human life and the Earth? Two positions exist on how scholars have answered the above question. Thomas Robert Malthus presented the thesis that exponential growth will outstrip the means of sustenance on planet Earth.[12]

Ecologists who share the Malthusian narrative emphasize the negative impact of overpopulation on Earth and biokind. The Population Action International, Population Reference Bureau, the Worldwide Fund for Nature, and Conservation International, are among the many organizations that share the Malthusian hypothesis in their developmental activities. These organizations assume that overpopulation will lead to the death and starvation of other forms of life. For this reason, we must address population growth for the sake of the Earth and future generations.

If Malthus was alarmed by population growth, Ester Böserup argued that "necessity is the mother of invention." She viewed "agricultural intensification" as one way population growth will

---

[11] Tim Dyson, "Population Growth and Food Production: Recent Global and Regional Trends," *Population and Development Review* 20, no.2 (Jun., 1994), 407; See also Brown, "Feeding six billion," 32-40.
[12] Nash, *Loving Nature*, 46.

lead to new innovations and "agricultural growth."[13] To Böserup, investment in technology will avoid the Malthus catastrophe and resolve the challenges of overpopulation.

Neo-Böserupians like Valentina Mazzucato and David Niemeijer see the fulfillment of Böserup's theory. They argue that population growth has already forced African traditional institutions to adjust to better farming methods and enabled an environmentally sustainable land use within the context of a rising population and growing scarcity of natural goods.[14]

What Neo-Böserupians do not address, however, is the limited nature of natural goods. Technological changes do not happen out of the blue but on Earth, the very Earth being threatened by the forces of technology. As already observed, Böserup's hypothesis follows the economic assumption that Earth has unlimited goods to be exploited endlessly, which is ecologically false.

Needless to say, the exponential growth of human population in shorter and shorter periods threatens Earth's carrying capacity and our wellbeing. Rosemary Ruether rightly links population growth to other ecological issues—consumption, climate change, pollution, extinction, militarism, and wars. Unless we accept Earth as our home, and the destruction of Earth as self-annihilation, we are agents of self-destruction, she argues.[15]

John Holden and others equally attribute the destruction of the ecosystem to demographic growth (Malthus) and industrialization. They argue that until 200 years ago or so, humanity existed in harmonious relationships with nature. This relationship was disturbed by runaway population and ruthless exploitation of natural goods. Climate change may transform ecological systems,

---

[13] Ester Böserup, *The Conditions of Agricultural Growth: The Economics of Agrarian Change under Population Pressure* (Chicago: Aldine, 1965).

[14] Valentina Mazzucato and David Niemeijer, "Population Growth and the Environment in Africa: Local Institutions, the Missing Link," *Economic Geography* 78, no.2 (Apr., 2002), 171-193.

[15] Rosemary Ruether, *Gaia and God: An Ecofeminist Theology of Earth Healing* (New York: HarperCollins, 1992), 88. For detailed discussion, see "Part Two—Destruction," 61-114.

but as they argue, "The new factor in this dynamic relationship between plants and their environment is the greatly accelerated rate of change imposed by man, with which the response mechanisms of species are unable to cope, resulting in large-scale losses, not only of species but also of the whole ecosystem."[16] To them, human-related activities are responsible for the progressive disruption of the ecosystem on planet Earth.

## Is Africa's Population Growth Sustainable?

Although the ACCNNR challenged African states to conserve natural goods, the implication of rapid population growth on the ecosystems was not addressed. Ecologists are generally agreed that uncontrolled population growth has a negative impact on eco-social relationships. As Christians, we can celebrate the fact that over 633 million people in sub-Saharan Africa will be Christians by 2025, but what we should address is the fact that "under even the lowest of the U.N.'s projections, sub-Saharan Africa's population will nearly double in size to 1.2 billion by 2025."[17]

As we shall see below, there exists a body of scholarship that sees no link between rapid growth and environment degradation. James Oldham, the founder and director of Las Lianas Resource Center—an organization that supports indigenous communities in the Amazon region of South America in their efforts to protect their culture and natural environment—sees the Malthusian arguments as flawed.[18]

---

[16] John Holden, James Peacock, and Trevor Williams, *Genes, Crops and the Environment* (Cambridge: Cambridge University Press, 1993), 3.
[17] New York Times, *Magazine,* "The Population Explosion Is Over," December 14, 1997. http://www.nytimes.com/1997/12/14/magazine/l-the-population-explosion-is-over-52 6258.html. Accessed 2/16/2013. United Nations, *The World at Six Billion,* 6. http:// www .un.org/esa/population/publications/sixbillion/sixbilpart1.pdf. Accessed 5/25/2012.
[18] James Oldham, *Rethinking the Link: A Critical Review of Population—Environment Programs,* Population and Development Program at Hampshire College and the Political Economy Research Institute at the University of Massachusetts, Amherst, 2006. http://popdev.hampshire.edu/sites/popdev/files/uploads/publications/PEoldham_06.pdf. Accessed 5/25/2012.

But, given the rates at which Africa's population and poverty are growing, Africa is headed for disaster. For example, in 1910, Africa had about 133-150 million people. By 1950, the continent had reached 221 million. Africa hit 1 billion in 2009 and is expected to almost double within 40 years.[19] That the continent's natural systems will not be the same as in 1900, and the global economy will continue to favor the global North over the global South generally and Africa particularly, means that the continent should prepare for more civil and ethnic conflicts. Nations, ethnic and religious groups increasingly can be expected to seek control over limited resources.

African nations should acknowledge that Western-driven economic policies by their own are not the answers to the continent's economic and ecological woes. Mostly, these policies are tailored to maximize competitive exploitation of natural goods at the expense of the Earth community. Since colonial times, Africa has hoped for economic development, but has received soil erosion, land degradation, species extinction, forced migration, desertification and deforestation.

Although many of these problems are self-inflicted, Western exploitation is equally to blame.[20] As Chapter Four illustrates, then, Africa's future depends on how we revisit the ethics of *ubuntu* through which humanity lives sustainably in nature. Among other things, this will entail addressing the growing numbers collectively and responsibly. While some proposals have been made—ranging from mirroring China's one child policy to forced family planning— the current crisis demands that every individual on planet Earth live ecologically in an interconnected universe. This will entail addressing the global North consumption rates and global South population growth.

---

[19] UN., *World Population to 2300*, Department of Economic and Social Affairs, 27. http://www.un.org/esa/population/publications/longrange2/WorldPop2300final.pdf. Accessed 12/15/2012.
[20] Hugh McCullum, "Environment and Change in Post-Apartheid South Africa," in *Restoring the Land*, (ed.), Mamphela Ramphele, (London: Panos, 1991), 167.

Equally important, however, is addressing corruption and mismanagement of African economies. Rancorous corruption compromises not just the lives of millions of people, but also the ecological prospect of the continent. As long as Africa's natural goods remain in the hands of voracious dictators, the ecological catastrophe will worsen. Thus, African leaders should be compelled to uphold the ethics of *ubuntu* and share the wealth equitably.

Because the predicament has local and global repercussions, Africa and the rest of the world should work together to resolve the problem. It is of little importance to reduce population growth in Africa, while Western countries continue to lead ecologically destructive life-styles as evidenced especially in materialism and consumerism. Scholars might project that the world population will level off by 2050, but this estimate does not include a leveling off of consumption, which equally threatens Earth. Consumption can be expected to surge as long as global economic policies are predicated on growth, and are the current means by which GDP is figured.[21]

The doctrine of uncontrolled procreation could arguably have been sanctioned in the past by Sacred Scriptures, and African traditional religions, but Mother Earth has a limited capacity to sustain life. In line with the ethics of *ubuntu*, the ACCNNR, and *Earth Charter*, ecological harmony can only be attained through the exercise of common responsibility.

It needs to be understood that every person in the global North contributes to the destruction of rain forests in Brazil. Oil spills are problems created not just by owners of oil companies, but also by consumers throughout the world (especially in the global North) who use fuel for far too many activities. Therefore, the solutions to our ecological problem lie in all humanity fighting to make a difference: in nations through policies and laws, in communities by collaborative actions, and by each individual in his or her way.

---

[21] Severine Deneulin and Masooda Bano, *Religion in Development: Rewriting the Secular Script* (London: ZED Books, 2009).

Moreover, our ecological awareness ought to emerge from Africa's religious biasness. Rather than being downplayed, African religious worldviews ought to be integrated with Christianity and the sciences to develop concrete ecological programs and initiatives.

## Economic Development Amid Population Growth

According to the "2009 World Population Data Sheet," Africa has the world's highest birth rate as well as the highest projected growth rate—"growing by 24 million per year." Africa is projected to hit 2 billion by 2050.[22] Further,

> Africa has the youngest and fastest-growing population, increasing at an annual 2.15 per cent from one billion in 2009, with urbanization closely linked. While in 2010, 395 million people lived in urban areas, UN projections say this will reach 1.23 billion people—60 per cent of the total population—by 2050.[23]

Consequently, the *Global Environmental Outlook 5* noted that climate related displacements will accelerate urbanization—the very point made by the Intergovernmental Panel on Climate Change. The panel warned that between 70 million to 250 millions Africans and Asians will face water shortages by 2020.[24] In Africa, these demographic and climate related challenges will adversely impact the poor whose livelihoods depend on the land.

But, the negative impact of overpopulation are already being felt across the globe. According to the World Food Program, for example, "hunger kills more people in the world than AIDS, malaria

---

[22] Population Reference Bureau, *2009 World Population Data Sheet,* http://www.prb.org /Publications/Datasheets/2009/2009wpds.aspx. Accessed 06/05/2013. AllAfrica, "Africa: Continent's Population Reaches One Billion." 08/20/ 2009. http: //allafrica. com/ stories/200908200660.html. Accessed 06/05/2013.
[23] The United Nation Environmental Programme, *Global Environmental Outlook 5,* June 6, 2012. http://www.unep.org/geo/pdfs/geo5/RS_Africa_en.pdf. Accessed 06/06/2012.
[24] In Etienne Piguet, "Population," *Encyclopedia of Global Warming and Climate Change*, (ed) George Philander, 817-819 (Los Angeles: Sage,2008), 818.

and tuberculosis combined."[25] In 2010, the Food Agriculture Organization showed that almost 1 billion people—300 million children—suffer from hunger every year. Sadly, "98 percent of them live in developing countries."[26] Against the long held assumption that natural disasters and wars are the chief causes of starvation, the U.N. Millennium Project noted that "only eight percent are victims of famine or other emergency situations."[27] Hunger related illnesses kill over 11 million children a year while 146 million are underweight—again, most of them in developing countries.[28] As the Millennium Project vividly puts it,

> More than one billion people in the world live on less than one dollar a day. In total, 2.7 billion struggle to survive on less than two dollars per day. Poverty in the developing world, however, goes far beyond income poverty. It means having to walk more than one mile everyday simply to collect water and firewood; it means suffering diseases that were eradicated from rich countries decades ago. Every year eleven million children die—most under the age of five and more than six million from completely preventable causes like malaria, diarrhea and pneumonia.[29]

Perhaps the most disturbing fact is that over 114 million children have no access to basic education while almost 600 million women are still illiterate globally. Amid such alarming and depressing data, developed nations and the World Bank devote very little resources to addressing global poverty. In 2013, for example, the World Bank and International Monetary Fund set the year 2030 as "the global target" for eradicating global poverty.[30] But that goal has the

---

[25] "Every 3.6 seconds, one person dies of starvation and the majority are children under the age of 5." UN., "Fast Facts: The Faces of Poverty." http://www.unmillennium project.org/documents/UNMP-FastFacts-E.pdf. Accessed 06/06/2012.
[26] FAO, *News Release*, 14 September 2010.
[27] UN, "Fast Facts: The Faces of Poverty."
[28] UN, "Hunger Stats." http://www.wfp.org/hunger/stats. Accessed 5/25/2012.
[29] UN, "Fast Facts: The Faces of Poverty."
[30] Annie Lowrey, "Is It Crazy to Think We Can Eradicate Poverty?," April 30, 2013. http://www.nytimes.com/2013/05/05/magazine/is-it-crazy-to-think-we-can-eradicate poverty. html?pagewanted=all&_r=0. Accessed 05/15/2013.

"$1.25-a-day income threshold," which is an oxymoron. As Annie Lowrey explains, "In Zambia, an average person living in such dire poverty might be able to afford, on a given day, two or three plates of cornmeal porridge, a tomato, a mango, a spoonful each of oil and sugar, a bit of chicken or fish, maybe a handful of nuts. But he would have just pocket change to spend on transportation, housing, education and everything else."[31] This scenario illustrates the level of disconnectedness in our world.

This disconnection is what Leonardo Boff calls original sin, or the sin of the world that promotes domination of the poor and Earth.[32] To address this problem, he suggests returning to the concept of interconnectedness or "panentheism: God in all and all in God."[33] The belief that God is present in the cosmos and the universe exists in God suggests that we are all one family; God's family. Here, Christian and traditional religious foundations for procreation should be revisited. Admittedly, some groups within Christianity, Traditional religions, and Islam are opposed to family planning when contraception is the method. But, the current crises demand confronting the reality that endless multiplication is impossible on a limited Earth. It is one thing to advocate abundant life of many children in the world with 10 million people, but it is another to make a similar argument when faced with 14 billion. For this reason, Christian ethics ought to address population growth from an eco-ethical perspective.

Within African morality, anything that threatens life is evil. Spirits, for example, can be good or evil depending on how they act. Likewise, human beings can be good or evil depending on their

---

[31] Ibid.
[32] Leonardo Boff, *Cry of the Earth, Cry of the Poor* (Maryknoll, New York: Orbis Books, 1995), 81.
[33] Panentheism from the Greek *Pan* (all)—*en* (in)—*theos* (God). According to this eco-theological conviction, the Creator Spirit "is present in the cosmos and the cosmos is present in God." This theology, Boff argues, differs from pantheism—the belief that everything is divine. Ibid., 152.

actions. In this regard, our irresponsible attitudes manifested in unplanned population growth are immoral.

The question, however, remains as to how the ancestors will respond to the problem of land shortages amidst population explosion and poverty. As rural populations grow, so does the need for more land and effective distribution of community natural goods. This need creates another crisis for both humanity and other biokind and boosts environmental degradation. So will Africans remain on their ancestral lands amidst the growing populations and poverty?

As already illustrated, traditional African cosmovisions view prosperity quantitatively. Abundant life means having countless animals, unlimited fertile lands, plentiful fruit forests, vast water resources, and, above all, numberless children. The advent of the biblical command to "multiply and fill the Earth," and the Quran's injunction to "marry and procreate," amplified such sanctions.

## Population Growth: Ancestral Blessing or Curse?

Despite attempts to reduce population growth, world demography has continued to grow at a very alarming rate; from 1.6 billion in 1900 to 7 billion in 2013. Moreover, 85 percent of this growth was registered in developing nations, mostly in Africa.[34] Demographic studies further project that by the year 2050, the world population is likely to be between 10 to 14 billion. Africa alone will account for 40 percent of this growth.[35] Amidst such an alarming growth rate, desertification, global warming, shrinking cropland area, species extinction, and deforestation will continue to threaten Africa. This

---

[34] UN.*World Population to 2300*. http://www.un.org/esa/population/publications /long range2/worldPop2300final.pdf. Accessed 06/27/2013; U.N.*Sustainable Development Policy in Africa: Harmonizing Population and Economic Growth in the process of Implementing the ICPD Programme of Action*, ECA/FSSDD/POP/CSD/01/6. United Nations Economic and Social Council (27 August 2001), 2-9. See A. W. Clausen, *Population Growth and Economic and Social Development: Addresses by A.W. Clausen President, The World Bank and International Finance Corporation* (Washington, D C: The World Bank, 1984), 7.
[35] Ibid. See Clausen, *Population Growth and Economic and Social Development*, 5.

reality will hinder Africa's attempts to meet the economic needs of its growing population.

As early as 1974, the Bucharest Population Conference assumed that development would resolve the population problem. It noted that through development and education, for example, fertility rates would be reduced and the impacts of demographic explosion mitigated.[36] Yet Africa's population growth remains the world's biggest developmental challenge as the continent lags behind the rest of the globe in nearly every indicator of human wellbeing.

Africa's population growth has both social and economic implications, but to view it solely from an economic perspective is missing the point. Africa's population growth has a strong religious basis. Many Africans favor bigger families as opposed to smaller ones due to traditional beliefs that view children as blessings from the ancestors. Sadly, this religious aspect is lost or underestimated by Westerners when addressing Africa's exploding population.

Ruether, for example, argues that while achievements have been registered to increase human life expectancy in developing countries, little has been done to control population growth. "The burgeoning population in the third world," she contends, "reflects the fact that enough sanitation and expansion in food and industrial production has taken place to create the condition for more and more of those born to survive. But this 'death control' has not been matched by a corresponding birth control, especially among the poorest and most uneducated populations."[37]

Ruether's point that enough sanitation and expansion of food and industrial production has taken place to create the condition

---

[36] According to G. Letamo and O. Totolo, "the population-environment nexus has generated heated debates. Some link population growth to environmental degradation while others view demographic growth as "an advantage that generates wealth and therefore needs to be tapped." The first school of thought is often referred to as "Alarmists or Pessimists" and the latter as "Non-Alarmists or Optimists." G. Letamo and O. Totolo, "Population-Environmental Interface in Botswana," in *Human Impact on Environment and Sustainable Development in Africa*, (ed.), Michael Darkoh and Apollo Rwomire (Hampshire: Ashgate, 2003), 102.

[37] Ruether, *Gaia and God*, 91.

for more and more of those born to survive, though true, should be evaluated from a global perspective. In many African countries, the opposite is true. The advent of HIV/AIDS, political repression, corruption, and the worsening levels of poverty have all contributed to the reduction of Africa's life expectancy. This is despite the reduction of infant mortality rates.[38] Even for those who survive their teenage years, poverty robs them of a meaningful life. This analysis, however, does not dismiss the fact that Africa should control its population growth.

The question of birth control ought to be addressed within the framework of Africa's ontology. Isaac Addai's findings among women in Ghana revealed that religious beliefs influenced contraceptive use among married women. From this perspective, Addai advocates taking traditional religious beliefs seriously when developing population-related policies.[39] Those who view children as signs of divine and ancestral blessings are likely to oppose population control, so Addai contends.

However, a study conducted in Northern Ghana among the Kessena Nankana suggests that once the elders/ancestors are consulted, many Africans are likely to prefer smaller families. Phillip B. Adongo, James F. Phillips and Fred N. Binka discovered that some traditional leaders and ancestors favor smaller families as opposed to bigger ones due to land shortages in the area. They concluded that religious opposition against "family planning" will not be so systematic among the Kassena-Nankana due to their ancestors' openness to population control.[40] But this ancestral openness to smaller families does not imply that African religions' role in "family planning" is fast disappearing. On the contrary, the

---

[38] See 2008 Central Intelligence Agency, *The World Factbook*. https:// www.cia. gov/ library/publications/the-world-factbook/rankorder/2102rank.html.Accessed 01/17/2008.
[39] Isaac Addai, "Does Religion Matter in Contraceptive Use among Ghanaian Women?" *Review of Religious Research* 40, no.3 (Mar., 1999), 259-277.
[40] Philip B. Adongo, James F. Phillips and Fred N. Binka, "The Influence of Traditional Religion on Fertility Regulation among the Kassena-Nankana of Northern Ghana," *Studies in Family Planning* 29, no.1 (Mar., 1998), 23-40.

value of this study lies in the fact that the preference for smaller families is coming from the past (*zamani*) and not contemporary forces (*sasa*).

## Impact of Overpopulation on Human Communities

Rapid population growth is destroying the interconnectedness of human communities. In Africa, this is happening at multiple levels. Common sense demands that population growth should match growth in education, health care, food production, and other basic needs. Sadly, these basic needs are not readily met even for the current populations.

Besides, Africa's population growth is concentrated in regions of abject poverty; places without adequate social services and decent living conditions—shanty-towns and illegal compounds.[41] In these areas, most of the residents are poor and are likely to be female. Yet increasing professional opportunities for women is vital to controlling population growth.[42] Furthermore, Africa's population is outgrowing economic development, resulting in civil and ethnic wars, family breakdowns, xenophobic attacks, street children and genocides. Unless conditions of poverty are positively addressed, increasing the population beyond what it is now will only exacerbate the crisis to catastrophic levels.

In his 1984 address to the "National Leaders' Seminar on Population and Development" in Nairobi, Kenya, A. W. Clausen, (then president of the World Bank and International Finance Corporation) linked rapid population growth to lower education

---

[41] Clausen argues that population growth is creating urban economic and social problems. Between 1950 and 1980, the population of city dwellers in developing countries in cities of more than 5 million people increased from 2 percent to 14 percent. While some of this is due to rural-urban migration, Clausen argues that 60 percent of this growth was caused by natural increase. Clausen, *Population Growth and Economic and Social Development*, 11.

[42] Michael Lipton advocates the provision of quality education and employment to women as vital to voluntary infertility. Michael Lipton, "New Strategies and Successful Examples for Sustainable Development in the Third Word," *International Food Policy Research Institute* 170 (1989), 6-7.

standards, lack of contraceptives and poor living standards for hundreds of millions of people.[43] In addition to contributing to a breakdown in the social fabric, rapid population growth, Clausen observed, "threatens a precarious balance between natural resources and people. Where populations are still highly dependent on agriculture, continuing large increases in population can contribute to overuse of limited natural resources, such as land, mortgaging the welfare of future generations."[44]

Because population pressures force people to overwork their marginal lands, Clausen argues that "when undue stress is placed on traditional agricultural systems and the environment is damaged, the economic wellbeing of the poor is particularly threatened."[45] Arguing that strains on natural goods are already acute in some African countries among them, Burundi, Malawi, Eastern Nigeria, Rwanda, and some parts of the Sahel region, he contends that even countries that are rich in natural resources do not escape this problem.

In what appears to be a Neo-Böserupian argument, he argues that rapid population growth slows productivity due to the fact that governments are forced to divert resources from technological advancements (that would boost food production) to social services. Rather than placing the entire burden on the citizens, Clausen blames the continent's poor economic policies. To him, developing countries could cope better with the demographic problem "if the right economic and social adjustments could be made fast enough, if technical change could be guaranteed, and if rapid population growth itself inspired technical change."[46] To reduce fertility rates, he advocates educating women about population control methods, and the provision of some financial incentives to, and imposition of, disincentives on families.

Following the 1984 World Development Report, Clausen notes:

---

[43] Clausen, *Population Growth and Economic and Social Development*, 4.
[44] Ibid., 11.
[45] Ibid., 10-11.
[46] Ibid., 12.

> Economic and social progress helps slow population growth; but, at the same time, rapid population growth hampers economic development. It is therefore imperative that governments act simultaneously on both fronts. For the poorest countries, development may not be possible at all unless slower population growth can be achieved soon.[47]

Further, Clausen asserts that poverty and rapid population growth reinforce each other. While advocating government involvement in fertility control, Clausen argues that population policies should be "humane, non-coercive, and sensitive to the rights and dignity of individuals."[48]

Clausen's observations, though insightful, are a clear example of how some scholars want to view the issue of demographic growth. Such scholars are quick to point to the economic problems of over-population while ignoring the African traditional worldview, which is at the center of the population question. As the following section will reveal, Africa's population crisis lies in its socio-cultural and religious worldviews. In these worldviews, children are signs of power and wealth as well as divine approval. It is this cosmovision that needs confronting as we address rapid population growth.

## Arrest this Growth: Family Planning

By 1970, family planning programs were established across sub-Saharan Africa. Since then, there has been an increase in contraceptive use in the region. The advent of the HIV/AIDS pandemic and other sexual infectious diseases increased the use of condoms in various African countries. Ironically, despite many AIDS related deaths, Africa has not registered any proven fall in fertility or population growth.[49] So what does this say about methods employed to address population growth?

---

[47] Ibid., 25-26.
[48] Ibid., 26.
[49] John C. Caldwell and Pat Caldwell, "The Cultural Context of High Fertility in sub-Saharan Africa," *Population and Development Review* 13, no.3 (Sep, 1987), 415.

In her October 23, 2011 opinion piece to *The New York Times*, Helen Epstein observes that by the end of this century, the world population will be 10 billion, "a billion more than previously expected. Nearly all of these extra billion people will be born in Africa, where women in some countries bear seven children each on average, and only 1 in 10 uses contraception." Aside from noting that "some countries could increase eightfold in the next century," Epstein argues that this growth will have negative implications for Africa. "In many parts of Africa," she rightly observes, "people already scramble to obtain food, land and water, and discontent provides fertile ground for extremism. So it is important to think carefully about the response to Africa's exploding population."[50] Epstein praises Evangelical Churches for giving human voice to women on matters of family planning, which she suggests as a probable key to Africa's population control.

Epstein's conclusion is important to the future of the continent. While the phrase "family planning" is still associated with the Western world, Africans have long practiced it by employing different methods of reducing fertility. These traditional methods carry spiritual significance, so nobody dares trespass them. One traditional family planning method found across Africa is postpartum abstinence. In most societies, the Chishinga, the Bemba and the Ushi of Zambia for example, couples were expected to abstain from sex for a period of two to three years after childbirth. While postpartum abstinence provided time for the mother to nurse her baby, it was believed that the husband's semen would contaminate the child's milk and kill the baby.[51]

In addition, sexual abstinence was generally encouraged. In some cultures, once a woman became a grandmother, she was expected to abstain from sex. Because most women were married

---

[50] Helen Epstein, "Talking their Way Out of a Population Crisis," *The New York Times*, October 23, 2011.
[51] Caldwell and Caldwell, "The Role of Marital Sexual Abstinence in Determining Fertility: A Study of the Yoruba in Nigeria," *Population Studies* 31, no.2 (Jul., 1977), 193-217; "The Cultural Context of High Fertility," 424-427.

between the ages of 13 and 16, they usually became grandmothers in their 30s; again limiting the number of children one could have.[52] Sometimes, communities encouraged sexual abstinence before marriage. Among the Bemba, it was believed that sex before marriage would make a girl grow long fingers. Such taboos not only gave women power over their bodies, but controlled the number of children born in a given community. Since the community was part of an African family, postpartum and other sexual norms controlled fertility. In their study of African fertility, the Caldwells concluded that on average, African women ended up with six to seven children in their life time (which is still very high).

There is yet another reason for Africa's population growth. Generally, begetting more children means more human power for labor intensive agriculture methods. In addition, since one does not know how the child will turn out, having many children means increasing the chances of winning the economic "lottery." If one has 10 children, for example, chances are that one could become successful in modern life; some Africans believe. Because of the community nature of African life, such a person will be a source of income for the parents as well as his or her unfortunate kin.

So to address the threatening population crisis, it is important to put emphasis on educating Africa's young about the need for positive "reproductive health" and not just family planning. The wording here is important. Africans tend to view the concept of family planning as foreign simply because such policies emphasize individual choices and rights while sidelining the community. In a society where sexuality and fertility are understood within the

---

[52] Caldwell and Caldwell, "The Cultural Context," 411. The abstinence period is viewed as responsible for polygyny in African communities. However, Dominique Zahan argues that polygyny was both a solution to widowhood as well as an insurance against the infertility of women. It is "compared to the man who wants a drink and who digs several wells at different places to be sure of satisfying his thirst." Dominique Zahan, *The Religion, Spirituality and Thought of Traditional Africa* (Chicago: Chicago University Press, 1970), 10.

community context, emphasizing individual rights and choices violates community norms and values.

Nonetheless, family planning is not just a secular economic issue, it is religious. In a cultural context where the secular and the sacred are interdependent, contraception use should be addressed both socio-culturally and theologically if the population crisis is to be arrested. Put differently, the resistance to fertility decline in Africa is due to religious beliefs that emphasize high fertility.

Kevin McQuillan observes that religion can only influence fertility if it meets three basic conditions. First, religion should be central to the social identity of the community. Second, it must have power to articulate norms and values for the given community. Finally, it must have the power to communicate these norms and promote compliance in the specific context.[53] Although the first two are easily identifiable, the third condition is somehow veiled. African traditional religion derives its powers from the community. In fact, the community in which an individual is born, grows, dies, and is reborn, is the center of African religions.

That said, Alfred O. Ukaegbu observes that the Ngwa Igbo, like many other African cultures, agree with Christian traditions on at least one point—"increase and multiply!" One would add Islam as well. Numerous children are viewed as "the fulfillment of God's will as well as a sign of harmonious relationship with gods and the departed relatives who are happily reincarnating with their kinsfolk."[54] This religious worldview undergirds the assumption that high fertility is an "ideal" ethical standard sanctioned by tradition, ancestral spirits, and the Supreme Being. From this perspective, African societies will only tackle rapid population growth when traditional and spiritual motivations for higher fertility are adequately addressed. Failure to do so will mean that

---

[53] Kevin McQuillan, "When Does Religion Influence Fertility?" *Population and Development Review* 30, no.1 (Mar., 2004), 25-56.
[54] Alfred O. Ukaegbu, "The Role of Traditional Marriage Habits in Population Growth: The Case of Rural Eastern Nigeria," *Journal of African International Institute* 46, no.4. (1976), 394.

traditional family ideals will prevail over any population policy, foreign or domestic. As the Caldwells assert:

> The essence of the traditional belief system is the importance attributed to the succession of the generations, with the old tending to acquire even greater and more awe-aspiring powers after death than in this world and with the most frequent use of those powers being to ensure the survival of the family of descent.[55]

In Chapter three, we saw that fertility is also associated with African lineage eschatology. Since the African concept of family goes beyond this world, an individual belongs to a wider family, which as the Caldwells observe, stretches "infinitely far back and with an enormous spiritual investment in reaching indefinitely into the future. Only a small proportion is alive at one time. That extension into the future should be a central concern not only of those alive but also of their dead ancestors."[56] So unlike Mbiti who views Africans as futureless, the Caldwells assert that the lineage rolls "on into the future of a finite number of spirits, with ancestors being reborn as descendants." Generally, limiting the number of children is interpreted as denying one's "ancestors the right to rebirth and condemning them to eventual extinction."[57]

Ukaegbu makes a parallel point. Among the Ngwa Igbo of Nigeria, he argues, procreation is the only means by which "reincarnation and continuity of the family tree are effected in time and space."[58]

The importance placed on ensuring lineage extension account for the opposition Western family planning methods receive on the continent. Western methods address economic arguments, which have little to do with African traditional ontology. Africans will resist family planning programs aimed at addressing the needs of

---

[55] Ibid., 409.
[56] Ibid., 416.
[57] Ibid.
[58] Ukaegbu, "The Role of Traditional Marriage Habits in Population Growth" 393.

the *Homo Hierarchicus,* while ignoring *Homo Ancestralis.* The Caldwells and Pat Quiggin are right to emphasize that:

> In keeping with the aim of lineage perpetuation, emphasis is placed on fertility: by society, the ancestral spirits, and even the high gods who are otherwise of a little day-to-day importance. Virtue is related more to success in reproduction than limiting profligacy; and in many societies the initiation ceremonies allowing sexual activity to commence are ritually more important than allowing celebration of marriage.[59]

Since ancestors retain identity through their living descendants, lineage prolongation is a moral imperative an African can hardly escape. It is this virtue that assures someone of the protection of ancestors for daily survival as well as future life. Consequently, when births are slow to come or children die, ancestors are consulted for answers. One example in which this belief is expressed is when naming children. Africans usually give their children names that illustrate divine favor or the help of the living dead. For instance, my children's names (Dorothy, Natemwa, Namaka, and Takudzwa) carry divine overtones.

Sarah Pasque Margolis attributes the failure to reduce rapid population growth to policies that focus on individual rights in contexts "where religion and culture tend toward pronatalism."[60] An argument that population should be reduced to address the economic crisis or environmental degradation is likely to appeal to intellectuals, but not to traditionalists. "In a highly pronatalist society," she argues, "a population policy that casts family planning as a 'normative' means of protecting the health of children or of young people provides an invaluable counterweight to 'normative' religious or political opposition to family planning."[61]

---

[59] John C. Caldwell, Pat Caldwell and Pat Quiggin, "The Social Context of AIDS," *Population and Development Review* 15, no.2 (Jun., 1989), 188.
[60] Sarah Pasque Margolis, "Population Policy, Research and the Cairo Plan of Action: New Directions for the Sahel," *International Family Planning Perspective* 23, no.2 (June, 1997), 86.
[61] Ibid., 88. See also Caldwell, Caldwell and Quiggin, "The Social Context of AIDS," 189.

As noted above, the failure to control rapid population growth is not due to government ineffectiveness alone, but also to the promotion of programs that conflict with African religious beliefs. While the question of political opposition to family planning is beyond the scope of this book, it is important to note that most political and religious leaders prefer having many children despite being exposed to Western values and norms. This is because African anthropology and psychology favor bigger families as opposed to smaller ones. Sadly, this is the most overlooked factor when scholars, economic development staff, and Westerners in general address demographic growth in Africa. As the discussion on the concept of time illustrated, Africans experience life in the circle of time, in which procreation is a norm, while infertility is a social, cultural, and religious curse.

Traditionally, limiting of one's profligacy is unethical and evil at its worst. A person with *ubuntu* honors family obligations; chiefly, procreation. Dominique Zahan concurs:

> African thought assigns man different modes of time depending on his marital status. The bachelor is placed in a false human perspective; he registers his life in linear time and follows a straight path with no possibility of returning. In this, he resembles the infant whose eventual disappearance leaves his parents and society with only the regret of his lack of human development. The married man, by contrast, follows a curved line because he inscribes his life in cyclical time, and thereby finds himself in the true human perspective. Indeed, through marriage, and especially through fatherhood, man enters into a cycle of generations. He abandons the straight route in order to follow the gyrating movement of creativity and great undertaking; he becomes fully a man.[62]

Africans generally dread dying without leaving offspring behind—another reason Africans can forgive a celibate priest fathering children. To Africans, unless sanctioned by religion, childlessness is

---

[62] Dominique Zahan, *The Religion, Spirituality, and Thought of Traditional Africa*, Translated by Kate Ezra Martin and Lawrence M. Martin (Chicago: The University of Chicago Press, 1970), 10.

abnormal, a curse and the end of one's vital force. A woman capable of reproduction or anticipating that she will reproduce again is regarded differently from a woman who can no longer have children. As the Caldwells observe, "Not only is premature terminal barrenness abhorrent—whether it's caused by pathological or voluntary sterilization—but attitude or behavioral barrenness in arranging to have no more children or even starting the intention to have no more is abhorred as well."[63] Africans cannot conceive of marriage without children.

The issue of human sexuality is beyond this study, but it is important to note that Africa's opposition to same-sex relations and marriages partially lies in this understanding. As long as somebody had children, how he had sex is of little importance in African sexuality. In some way, this understanding explains why many well-known gay men across Africa can openly boast of being happily married to women. Neither would traditional African communities accept divorce on the account that the husband is gay as long as he has fathered children. Again, this situation accounts for why many African religious and political leaders claim to have had no gays in their jurisdiction as understood in Africa today. To be human meant to procreate and homosexuals do not, an African insists. Based on this social religious worldview, an African is skeptical as to whether fertility can endanger his family or national economy. The need for prolongation of life, the socio-political support and economic power and stability that big families can sometimes bring, make this problem even the more complex.

## Looking Forward

The Neo-Böserupian myth that economic and technological growth is the answer to Africa's population growth assumes that Earth, like the economy, grows; and, that Earth's goods can be extensively exploited without consequences to life. This assumption denies the basic point of ecology; most of Earth's goods are, to use Larry

---

[63] Caldwell and Caldwell, "The Cultural Context of High Fertility," 412.

Rasmussen's words, a "one-time endowment." In addition, Neo-Böserupians ignore the fact that once Earth is degraded, its capacity to sustain life is compromised. Thus, it is crucial that we understand that, "An expanding world needs to know the total activity the biosphere can tolerate and yet renew itself indefinitely. It needs to know the biosphere's 'carrying capacity' for the long haul."[64]

It is my contention that post-colonial African governments employ policies that reflect Western assumptions. These policies assume that natural goods can be recycled endlessly through the use of capital. However, human wellbeing ought not be measured in terms of the exploitation of natural goods alone. Rather, human development ought to foster positive attitudes toward the ecosystems. It must accept that Earth is "embodied energy with its own complex life, its own complex actions and needs, and its own economy."[65]

Africa inherited and promoted the instrumental view of Earth, which is in direct contradiction with traditional understandings of land. Land is home to sacred forces of life. We are allowed to use it in as much as we respect these forces. The Chief can claim to be the owner of the land, but in reality, land is a commons and "a sacred trust," which is permanently in the holding of ancestors. It is for this reason that land could never be sold; its value was priceless. The following Chapter will address this issue in detail.

---

[64] Larry Rasmussen, *Earth Community, Earth Ethics* (Maryknoll, New York, Orbis Books, 1998), 115.
[65] Ibid., 118.

# Chapter Six
## Capitalism:
## A Threat to Africa's Future

### The Question of Sustainable Development

Chapter Five explored the negative impact of rapid population growth on the Earth community. Aside from demanding more Earth's natural goods, demographic growth requires new land for human settlements. The fact that population growth compromises the quality of life on Earth is not disputed by most global South scholars. What is mostly disputed, however, is the assumption that poor nations should put measures in place to arrest this growth. Scholars—among them Murray Bookchin and Curtis Skinner—argue that population growth by itself does not threaten the quality of life on Earth; rather, global economic inequalities promoted through laissez faire capitalism do. Thus, as long as the majority of the world population survives on less than 20 percent of the world's natural goods, while a minority consumes over 80 percent, the current environmental crisis will persist whether we remain at 7 billion or not. Using Neo-Böserupian argument, Skinner contends that population growth encourages technological innovations. He blames the environmental crisis on the economic exploitation of developing countries by the developed world (and now China).[1]

James Nash supports the theory that human beings, especially those in the global North, are living beyond Earth's limit. Like Skinner, Nash argues that Earth has enough resources to meet

---

[1] Curtis Skinner, "Population Myth and the Third World," *Social Policy* (Summer 1988), 57-62. According to Murray Bookchin, "Land distribution is now so lopsided in the Third World in favor of commercial farming and a handful of elite landowners that one can no longer talk of a "population problem" without relating it to a class and social problem." Murray Bookchin, "The Population Myth—I," *Green Perspective, Newsletter of the Green Program Project* (8, July 1988). http://dwardmac.pitzer.edu/anarchist_archives/bookchin/gp/perspectives8.html. Accessed 01/16/2009.

everyone's needs. Sadly, the global North does not live by needs alone, but by wants; hence overconsumption rather than overpopulation is one of the biggest problems threatening Earth.[2] Nash insists that overpopulation is a factor in environmental degradation, but he also argues that the per capita consumption of each individual matters. To Nash, "the average additional person in affluent nations, particularly the United States, consumes far more and places far greater stress on the world's natural resources—some say 20–30 times more, on the average—than their counterparts in some poor nations."[3]

Nash accepts that poor nations ought to check their population growth, however, he equally advocates a morality of reduced consumption and an equitable redistribution of Earth's natural goods. Nash's argument is expressed in the context of what is going on in North America, but poverty, species extinction, overpopulation and resource exhaustion are being experienced across Africa. These problems are especially visible in urban areas where abject poverty and environmental degradation are at their worst.

Although Africa's colonial legacy bears some blame, unequal distribution of natural goods contributes to the ongoing crisis. Idi Amin in Uganda, Fredrick Chiluba in Zambia, Olusegun Obasanjo in Nigeria, Charles Taylor in Liberia, and Mobutu Sese Seko in the Congo robbed their nations of billions of dollars and left their countries' environment degraded. As Chapter Four insisted, unless corruption is addressed, Africa's future is dire.

Such arguments do not dismiss the fact that the effects of land degradation are already being felt across Africa—soil erosion, landslides, crop failure, and the overdependence on fertilizers are now a norm. In some cases, communities and families are fighting over the limited ancestral lands; occasionally at the cost of people's lives. In situations where such violent conflicts are absent,

---

[2] James Nash, *Loving Nature: Ecological Integrity and Christian Responsibility* (Nashville: Abingdon Press, 1991), 47.
[3] Ibid.

severe land degradation usually results. Is it not time to ask our ancestors for more land? But the real question is, "Which lands"?

Geographically, Africa is the second largest land mass on planet Earth, with approximately 30,000,000 sq km. The mere size of the continent can easily deceive us into believing that we have endless land for our ever growing population. The truth is, Africa has two large deserts; the Sahara desert covers almost a third of the continent with 9,065,000 sq km, while the Namib consumes almost 259,000 sq km. While this leaves out almost two thirds of the continent, not every piece of land is agriculturally friendly; hence, land degradation and desertification demand immediate attention. The effects of land degradation range from starvation to forced migration as environmental refugees seek productive lands.

Scholars have identified various causes of desertification and land degradation. These include climate conditions and human-related activities; farming, deforestation, over-grazing, and mining.

It is argued that desertification is not new to human history, but dates back several centuries when human populations were relatively small. Others argue, however, that desertification is a post-1970 Sahelian drought phenomenon connected with the advancing deserts; the hypothesis advanced by ecologist Hugh Lamprey who conducted his study in Sudan between 1958 and 1975. He concluded that the desert was advancing at the rate of 5-6 km per year; the position subsequently adopted by the Sudanese government. The government insisted that desertification starts in small patches and grows bigger due to human and climatic variations that reduce vegetation and expose soils to erosion. If this process is not arrested in time, small areas can develop into full blown deserts.[4]

Yet Lamprey asserted that human related activities and climatic variations are directly linked. For example, drought can precipitate land degradation in areas that are overexploited just as land

---

[4] O.B. Smith and S. Koala, "Desertification: Myths and Realities," in *Human Impact on Environment and Sustainable Development in Africa*, (eds), Darkoh, M.B.K, and A. Rwomire (Hampshire, Aldershot: Ashgate, 2003), 188-189.

degradation can cause drought "by the feedback mechanisms involving surface albedo, soil moisture and possibly dust."[5]

Admittedly, many factors contribute to desertification and land degradation. Poor agricultural practices—long term irrigation, slash and burn, overgrazing, insufficient crop rotation and short fallow periods—are among the factors that cause desertification. These human activities encourage water and wind erosion, which in turn reduce land productivity and foment desertification. This situation is worsened by overpopulation and poverty.

Of course, some peasant farmers' agricultural methods contribute to desertification, but to fault them entirely is to ignore the role of multi-national companies in this process.[6] These companies push the poor into arid areas while clearing large areas for monoculture and mining projects.[7] In the end, no African country is immune to this dire environmental despoliation.

In most African countries, land degradation is worsened by mining. According to Munyaradzi Chenje, the UN environmental assessment specialist, mining activities have minimal impact on the environment, except where the more environmentally harmful techniques are employed.[8] Nevertheless, due to lack of strong environmental monitoring and regulations across Africa, the exploitation of mineral goods has had negative impact on the land, the water, and other biokind. Copper, iron, gold, and diamond

---

[5] Ibid., 190.
[6] Church Collins and Mary Wright argue that in order to avoid paying the costs of ecologically sustainable processes and technologies, multi-national or global companies prefer to operate in the Global South where laws are often weak. As such, "precious water around the world is being consumed or contaminated at a startling rate. Forests are being leveled and factories belch pollution into the air. Biodiversity is being rapidly destroyed in order to meet [our] short-term economic needs." Chuck Collins and Mary Wright, *The Moral Measure of the Economy* (Maryknoll, NY: Orbis books, 2007), 112.
[7] David Korten, *When Corporations Rule the World* (San Francisco: Berrett-Koeher Publishers, 2001); Collins and Wright, *The Moral Measure of the Economy*, 109-112.
[8] Munyarazi Chenje, *State of the Environment 2000: Zambezi Basin* (Maseru: Lesotho, 2000), 122.

mines have scarred the landscape, polluted waterways, reduced land productivity, and in most cases displaced local people.[9]

African nations are aware of the effects of mining on the poor. However, they are forced to displace their people for foreign earnings. One example is that of the coalfields in Johannesburg, South Africa. While these coalfields produce sulfurous air pollution equal to that of all of Europe and continue to degrade the land's productivity and peoples' lives, the South African government (like most African governments) does not pay attention to the same.[10]

## Land Degradation and Food Security

Africa's land and environmental degradations are directly linked to the continent's food security. The 1991 Lusaka Southern African Development Community (SADC) declaration on the environment stated that land degradation is undermining agriculture, which is the mainstay of rural livelihoods in the region.[11] The 2007 United Nations Food and Agriculture Organization (FAO) document which warned that mining activities in Africa were reducing land's productivity confirmed this observation. FAO contended that "The potential of land to produce is set by soil and climatic conditions and by the level of inputs and management applied to the land. Any over-exploitation or mining of land beyond these limits results in degradation and declining yields and this is now happening in

---

[9] G. Letamo and O. Totolo's observation about Botswana is also true with regard to Zambia. Sulphur dioxide (one of the waste products in copper processing) once released into the atmosphere combines with water vapor to form sulphuric acid. "During the rainy season, this acid falls on trees, water resources and buildings. The environmental impacts which are discernible are, yellowing of tree leaves and corrosion of buildings." Letamo and Totolo, "Population-Environmental," 127. As Zambia continues to open new copper mines, caution should be taken to minimize the emission of sulphur dioxide.

[10] Kalipeni, *Population Growth*, 6; Muhamed Salih, "Introduction," in *Environmental Policies and Politics in Eastern and Southern Africa*, (ed.), Muhamed R. A. Salih and Shibru Tedla (New York: St. Martin's Press, 1991).

[11] Jeremiah Dibua, *Modernization and the Crisis of Development in Africa: The Nigerian Experience* (Burlington, VT: Ashgate, 2006), 249-274.

many parts of Africa."[12] As the previous Chapter showed, amidst such degradation, Africa's population continues to explode. One may agree with Böserup's hypothesis, but Africa's population growth is not matched by meaningful technological advancements or economic growth. Amidst extreme poverty, this growth has far-reaching implications for life as a whole.

Accordingly, G. Letamo and O. Totolo argue that the effects of land degradation are especially visible around big resettlements. Soil erosion, deforestations, desertification, and a massive influx of rural poor to urban slums are common across the continent. In the Gwembe Valley, for example, the Lusitu River which was a major source of water at the time of resettlement in 1958 is now buried in sand; and soil erosion keeps threatening roads and homes during the rainy seasons.

While the blame can be placed on the people, the developer of the Kariba Dam should shoulder much of the responsibility. Chenje confirms this argument when he associates much of contemporary ecological problems in the Zambezi Basin with development strategies of the 1950-1960 era. Such strategies, he argues, maximized exploitation of natural goods and ignored Earth's integrity. "As a result, no serious or effective measures were taken to control environmental degradation, including pollution."[13]

The same sorts of problems can be identified in connection with countless development projects that have been instituted on the continent. Maximization of production has become the norm for African economic growth while the consequences of such projects on the Earth and the poor are ignored. As repeatedly noted, generally African communities had special attachment to the land and have historically worked to protect it; but the coming of Western civilization, Christianity, and commerce led them into abandoning their traditional lifestyles. Whereas some parts of

---

[12] United Nations, *Land and Environmental Degradation and Desertification in Africa*, FAO Corporate Document, 2007. http://www.fao.org/docrep/x5318e/x5318e01.hlm. Accessed 10/10/2008.
[13] Chenje, *State of the Environment*, 194.

Africa were prone to droughts, the environment was not severely damaged. Brian Fagan explains,

> [Africans] maintained a detailed knowledge of grazing and water supplies over enormous areas, moved their herds constantly, and adjusted month to month to changing conditions. Their mobility, low population densities, and careful judgments gave them the ability to endure drought, the ravages of cattle disease, and constant uncertainties.[14]

This knowledge helped them to negotiate droughts and famines, which is not the case today.

Fagan follows Michael H. Grantz in arguing that uncontrolled population growth, environmental degradation and poor land management policies are responsible for sub-Saharan famines.[15] He rejects the hypothesis that the West African Sahel droughts are totally caused by lack of rainfall or climate change. While these factors play a role, rapid population growth and careless, naïve planning that pays little attention to the environmental history of the Sahelian regions or "simply ignore famines when they occur,"[16] are mostly to blame. Fagan is right: our governments have done a poor job of addressing drought related famines. From early missionary documents to scientific studies, Africa has proved to be a drought-prone continent. Sadly, our governments behave as if

---

[14] Brian Fagan, *Floods, Famines and Emperors: El Nino and the Fate of Civilization* (Basic Books, 1999, 2009), 266.

[15] According to Michael H. Grantz, drought follows the plow in that "with increasing pressure to cultivate marginal areas, drought episodes will become more prevalent. This can result from the fact that crops grown in the more reliably watered areas are not well suited to environmental conditions in the margins. Whereas climate often is blamed for crop failure, that failure may prove to be more to the result, for example, of poor land-management." Michael H. Grantz, "On the Interactions Between Climate and Society," *Population and Development Review* 16, Supplement: Resources, Environment, and Population: Present Knowledge, Future Options (1990), 188. See also "Drought Follows the Plow," *The World and I* (April 1988), 208-213.

[16] Brian Fagan, *Floods, Famines and Emperors*, 266. Fagan argument is that the 1968-73 and other related famines in the region that result in deaths of both animals and people are nothing new to the region. Governments ought to put in place measures to mitigate the effects since these droughts have a history.

environmental history does not matter.[17] African governments should take into consideration the continent's environmental and cultural history in the development of long-term food security policies.

Severine Deneulin and Masooda Bano, Jeffrey Haynes, and Jeremiah Dibua, among many scholars contend that appreciating the people's socio-cultural environment is crucial to meaningful development. Accordingly, Dibua sees the interaction between culture and technology in development. Because knowledge is the product of people's experiences within their local environment, he insists, traditional knowledge "constitutes the basis for the development of appropriate technology that is adaptable to the culture and ecology of the society while promoting sustainable technological development and industrialization."[18]

Is the economic and ecological crisis confronting Africa a result of developmental efforts that ignore local worldviews? Dibua thinks so. "The crisis of industrialization confronting African countries," he argues, "is largely a product of the denigration of indigenous technological knowledge and culture in favor of Western technology under the misguided belief that the associated technology transfer would promote African industrialization."[19]

It is tempting to conclude that the ecological and economic crisis facing Africa is largely due to misguided economic principles on which the continent's economic development policies are built. The sidelining of indigenous knowledge in the formulation of Africa's economic development programs and policies simply worsens the ecological crisis. Unless economic policies take into consideration the traditional heritage, we will exploit natural goods without remorse for Earth. Africa is our motherland and our fatherland; it is our spiritual and moral responsibility to guard

---

[17] The West African famine threatened over 23 million people with starvation in 2012. http://www.dailymail.co.uk/news/article-2133992/West-Africa-famine-threatening-kill-23million-starvation. Accessed 12/23/2012.
[18] Dibua, *Modernization and the Crisis*, 164-165.
[19] Ibid., 166.

Africa from both domestic and foreign exploitation. *Our children, grandchildren and future generations are more likely to forgive colonialists for exploiting Africa's natural goods than to forgive us for destroying our motherland and fatherland!*

## Migration: We Don't Want Strangers in our Land

Africa's double curse is that colonialism condemned her children to racial and economic humiliation, while corruption in post-independence Africa thrusts them into extreme poverty. To negotiate this double curse, most Africans are forced to migrate to urban areas hoping for a better life. As James Nash notes, however, across the globe, "that strategy is decreasingly feasible. Increasing numbers of environmental refugees are aggravating social and environmental problems elsewhere and adequate places to migrate are becoming increasingly rare."[20]

Migration is decreasingly feasible, not just in rural to urban and global South to North migration, but in rural to rural relocations. V. Dzingirai's study of the Zimbabwe's Bhinga Tonga of the Gwembe valley reveals that rural local communities view newcomers negatively. Newcomers, he observes, are viewed as dispossessing local communities of land, wildlife, and other natural goods.[21]

But, the struggles over limited resources should be discussed within the wider context of colonial land tenure acts. During this period, Africans were forced to settle in areas designated as "native" or "communal lands" while their "original" land was given to European farmers. In Kenya, the "Crown Lands Ordinance No. 27," section II of 1902 blatantly claimed all Kenyan land as "Crown land"—save the lands designated "native lands." The Governor had the power to administer land while the Commissioner divided it into farms not exceeding 7500 acres. At the time, only Europeans

---

[20] Ibid., 47.
[21] V. Dzingirai, *Stealing the Birthright, Migration Dynamics in the Zambezi Valley of Zimbabwe*, Institute of Natural resources, University of Natal, Pietmaritzburg, 2003. http://www.id21.org/id21ext/s10cvd1g1.html. Accessed 12/20/2008.

had access to such farms. Since Africans communally owned the land that was to be divided, the loss of land was a loss to the entire community culture.[22] As Gillian Solly observes,

> If an African is driven off the land under which his ancestors lived, he could not practice his religion and he was no longer a person at all. This is because land belonged to the family and not an individual and the family consisted not only of its living members but also of those who died and those who were yet unborn. If the individual therefore lost the land which was in his use, his ancestors and his unborn descendants would have lost it with him. He, the trustee during his lifetime for this sacred piece of soil, had committed the unforgivable sin against his father and forefathers just as much as against his children and his children's children.[23]

Africanists have confirmed Solly's observations. Generally, Africans understand land as held in trust on behalf of countless future generations. As the *lwiindi* revealed, the distribution of natural goods is conditioned on negotiating the needs of the living dead, the living, and "the living unborn."[24] Kwame Nkrumah fastidiously puts it as follows: "Earth belongs to the family of which many are dead, few are living, and countless members are unborn."[25] Because the circular time of past, present, and future meet in this life, land issues have moral and religious implications. To remove an African community culture (as was the case with the Gwembe Tonga) from the land is to destroy the entire community. As Chapter Two revealed, this belief was one of the many reasons

---

[22] Mbiyu Koinange, *Africa and the Future: Land Hunger in Kenya* (Nairobi: UDC Publication, 1952), 6-7.
[23] Gillian Solly, *Background to the Land Question*, Undated, Boston University African Studies Library, Kenya Collection, 1-2. The sacredness of land is equally found among Native Americans, who according to Hart, believe that land belongs to the entire nation. John Hart, *The Spirit of the Earth: A Theology of the Land* (Ramsey, New Jersey: Paulist Press, 1984), 43-45.
[24] By living unborn, I mean future generations. Since the African concept of time is circular, future generations are not abstract but living beings with rights to be protected and defended.
[25] Kwame Nkrumah, *Ghana* (Edinburgh: T Nelson and Sons Ltd, 1959), 10.

why the Gwembe Tonga resisted relocation from their ancestral lands.

The implicit and sometimes explicit belief in the power of ancestors to defend their descendants' land is founded on the sacredness of the land. A closer examination of African cosmologies reveals that nobody could exist without the land. Land was a communal trust to which every family and community culture were entitled. To possess *ubuntu* implied taking care of ancestral land and handing it over to future generations. To neglect ancestral lands was tantamount to obliteration of self and ultimately the entire community culture.

The value of land in African cosmologies can be illustrated by how communities dealt with conquered cultures. Historically, Africans conquered other cultures, but the sacred nature of the land stopped them from grabbing vanquished peoples' lands. This is because:

> they [Africans] feared the curses of those same spirits [of conquered peoples] far more than the spears of their living descendants and would not (in fact did not) drive their enemies off the land. They robbed, raided, set fire to villages, and did any other damage they could think of, but scarcely ever dared to march into an enemy's country and occupy it.[26]

The sacredness of land provided future security for many Africans until Europeans brought what Sallie McFague terms the "neo-classical" economic paradigm which does not respect nature "for itself." According to this paradigm, land is "just another form of property, of money."[27] But, Africans value land from the ecological economic perspective, in which, to borrow McFague's wording, land "is more like our "mother" than our property. It is the source of our being, the one from whom we can never be weaned, and the one that we must care for."[28] Mbiyu Koinange, thus regrets,

---

[26] Solly, "Background to the Land Question," 2,4-5.
[27] Sallie McFague, *Life Abundant: Rethinking Theology and Economy for a Planet in Peril* (Minneapolis: Fortress Press, 2000), 119.
[28] Ibid.

> African communal ownership had divided the land, with more or less justice, according to the needs of the people. But the Protectorate Government...divided the land according to another principle. Thus European settlers received the best land, but Africans were 'restricted' to inferior land.[29]

It is important, however, to assert that not all native reserves were inferior, as Koinange wants us to believe. Most native lands were fertile at the time of designation, but were stressed beyond their natural limits as populations grew. Rather than addressing land shortages, Europeans believed that land degradation in African villages could be solved through proper land husbandry and in some cases, industrial developments.

Unfortunately, industrial development did not do this. In most cases, it made the situation worse. Most people left native lands for urban areas due to over-crowdedness, work–related migration, and other reasons. However, they did not abandon their ancestral communities; hence, they kept their rural homes active while working in urban areas. Social problems created by this lifestyle not only led many men to have at least two wives, but also raised the population in rural and urban communities; thereby creating a two way crisis as land degradation and population growth occurred on both fronts: in urban and rural areas. Needless to say, Africans migrated (and still do) to urban areas as teenagers, and returned to their rural homes permanently after reaching the age of retirement. Negotiating a degraded environment after retiring from formal employment is even harder.[30]

Conversely, the restriction of people to "native reserves" had a negative impact on human community and the rest of the ecosphere. One would have hoped that with the advent of self-rule, land would be allocated equally; unfortunately this was not so. Many Africans are still landless while those who claim to hold

---

[29] Koinange, *Africa and the Future*, 6-7
[30] See James Ferguson, *Expectations of Modernity: Myths and Meanings of the Urban Life on the Zambian Copperbelt* (Berkeley & Los Angeles: University of California Press, 1999), 229-233.

unto traditional or ancestral lands exist on the margins of society. In most cases, they are displaced at will without compensation.

None of this is new. It is well documented that the arduous result of such displacements is extreme poverty and starvation. Aside from blaming rapid population growth for poverty in developing nations, the Report of the World Commission on Environment and Development (WCED) noted that:

> [the] growing demands for the commercial use of good land, often to grow crops for exports, have pushed many subsistence farmers onto poor land and robbed them of any hope of participating in their nations' economic lives. The same forces have meant that traditional shifting cultivators, who once cut forests, grew crops, and then gave the forest time to recover, now have neither enough land nor time to let forests re-establish. So forests are being destroyed, often only to create poor farmland that cannot support those who till it.[31]

It is ironic that African nationalistic movements employed the "land problem" as the organizing tool against colonialism, but ignored land ethics after they got into power. In fact, they simply continued with colonial land tenure policies that worsened the plight of the poor. For instance, in colonial times, land belonged to the Crown. In post-colonial Africa, however, it belonged to the State; cultural leaders played little role in its administration. In Zambia, every piece of land belonged to the state from 1964 to 1995, when some lands were returned to customary leaders or chiefs. Under this new land tenure, traditional leaders recommend land to be given to individuals or companies. Thereafter, such individuals apply for a title from the government.

Sadly, rural people do not usually understand the value of title deeds, and the process of obtaining title is extremely multifaceted and expensive—making it impossible for rural folks to have title to their residential, grazing and farming lands. While this land may remain within one's inheritance and is handed over from generation to generation for a while, it is easily lost without

---

[31] United Nations, *Our Common Future*.

compensation when a "developer" comes around. As was the case with the Tonga in colonial days, today, most Africans watch their ancestral lands taken over by "developers" without any legal protection or meaningful monetary compensation. In Zimbabwe, the recent discovery of diamonds in Marange and Chiadzwa area—which "some experts believe...is the largest diamond discovery in generations"—has led to forced removals of thousands of people in the area.[32] Zimbabwean authorities are quick to point to modern homes built for some displaced families and the economic benefits of this venture to the nation, but the eco-social impact of this resettlement on the people of Marange should not be ignored.

Already, the social impact is being felt. According to the Zimbabwe Environmental Law Association (ZELA), the relocation exercise "resulted in food insecurity, loss of common lands and resources, increased health risks, social disarticulation, and the disruption of formal educational activities."[33]

ZELA further expressed concern that even social services—boreholes, schools and healthcare are not enough to meet the needs of the resettled communities. Worse still, people were "being relocated" close to the city of Mutare, thereby forcing them to live an urban lifestyle as opposed to the traditional one. In terms of compensation, some communities did not receive meaningful monetary payment "except $1000 each family as what the government and mining companies called a disturbance allowance and groceries for one month."[34]

Aside from the various insults associated with resettlement, most resettled communities are not spiritually attached to the new land. In most cases, the new land becomes the symbol of ancestral

---

[32] Victoria Eastwood and Robyn Curnow, "Inside Zimbabwe's Controversial Marange Diamond Field," CNN, March 16, 2012. http://edition.cnn.com/2012/03/15/business/zimbabwe-marangediamondfield/index.html. Accessed 04/02/2012.
[33] Shamiso Mtisi, Mutuso Dhliwayo and Gilbert Makore, *Extractive Industries Policy and Legal Handbook: Case study of the Plight of Marange and Mutoko Mining Communities* (Harare, Zimbabwe Environmental Law Association, 2011), 40-41.
[34] Ibid., 42.

punishment as opposed to their blessings. Hence, traditional ecological injunctions that once safeguarded the land are hard to uphold in the new environment. This complex land issue provides a good illustration of why Africa needs an economic theory that is based on traditional values of interconnectedness of *ubuntu*.

## Limitless Growth on a Limited Planet

Guyanese historian and scholar, Walter Rodney, insisted that "Imperialism was in effect the extended capitalist system, which for many years embraced the whole world—one part being the exploiters and the other the exploited, one part being dominated and the other acting as overlords, one part making policy, and the other being dependent."[35]

No well-meaning African scholar can wholly deny the truth of Rodney's observations. When it comes to economics, Africa must dance to the tune of the Western world, and now China. As Michael Darkoh and Apollo Rwomire contend, Africa has been separated from its own social, economic, and political history, and forced to adapt to European capitalistic values. But, the imposition of foreign values on Africa has led to various socio-economic problems on the continent. In their words,

> Africa now has to cope with the unresolved clash of European and indigenous systems, as well as the legacy of its grossly unequal incorporation into an economic system created by and for the Western World....Whereas the Western world itself is slowly coming to grips with reconciling technology, development and environment in its realm, this is far from the case in Africa. Unfortunately for the African continent, the driving force for rapid development is powered by policies of exploitation of its forests, soils, minerals and other natural resources for quick gain, and in all too many instances, the culprits are the capitalist countries.[36]

---

[35] Walter Rodney, *How Europe Underdeveloped Africa* (Washington D.C: Howard University Press, 1982), 12.
[36] M.B.K. Darkoh, and A. Rwomire, (eds.), *Human Impact on Environment and Sustainable Development in Africa* (Hampshire: Aldershot, 2003), 7.

African countries can boast of political independence, but their natural goods are still colonized. In fact, the entire economic organization of the Western world is built around exploitation. For example, Africa's natural goods are exploited on the premise of "international investment." To make matters worse, the World Bank and the IMF encourage or require the exploitation of Africa's natural goods as the condition for aid. To these institutions, Africa's development depends on how the continent opens its natural goods to international exploiters in exchange for foreign currency. Amid ever increasing population pressures and limited economic growth, the poor and Earth suffer the most.

Across Africa, poverty is intensified by unequal distribution of the nation's wealth. Delfin S. Go and John Page observe that sub-Saharan Africa's average income per person was unchanged between independence and the turn of the $21^{st}$ century. Yet, Africa has experienced accelerated economic growth which has raised income and potential for human development since the mid 1990s. In line with their thesis that the $21^{st}$ Century may mark a turning point in Africa's economic performance due to good economic policies, they assert that there is need to develop institutional bases for sustaining this growth.[37]

Nonetheless, Africa's good economic performance can be deceptive. Economically, the continent's "GDP per capita is still 50% of the level of East Asia...and the growth rate is far short of the 7% per year needed if poverty is to be halved by 2015."[38] When poverty is further examined:

> [The continent's] mean income/expenditure of the poor—those earning less than one PPP dollar a day—is much lower than in East

---

[37] Jorger Arbache, Delfin S. Go and John Page, "Is Africa's Economy at a Turning Point?" in *Africa at a Turning Point? Growth, AID, and External Shocks*, (ed.), Delfin S. Go and John Page (Washington DC: The World Bank, 2008), 76.

[38] Ibid. Sub-Saharan Africa and South Asia are the two regions not expected to meet the MDGs. However, Mauritius has already met four, Botswana has met three and will possibly meet another one, and South Africa has met three. Another nine countries will meet two each. 23 will meet one. Ibid., 76-77.

> Asia or South Asia....Africa is far behind all other regions in terms of the UN human development index....It will also lag behind in most MDGs [Millennium Development Goals]...if current trends continue, it will not meet the 2015 target of reducing poverty. In 1990, 47% of Africans lived in poverty. In 2004, 41% did, and at the present trend, 37% will in 2015.[39]

It is clear that to address poverty, African governments should develop strategies of "delivering more and better services for human development."[40]

Regardless, Africa is registering economic growth at the expense of environmental degradation. Most economists share the assumption of limitless growth, hence their economic analyses ignore ecological wellbeing as an economic issue. Thus, the question whether Africa's economy is at the turning point is definitely irrelevant given the fact that economists gauge economic growth based on GDPs without addressing the grand economy of Earth. In fact, optimism brought about by current economic growth in Africa is based on the fallacy that Africa's natural goods can be exploited endlessly without damaging the economy of Earth.

It is one thing to speak about a "global village"; it is another to live in "a global metropolitan area," with an extremely rich minority and extremely poor majority. The WCED picked up this issue when it concluded that:

> Earth is one but the world is not. We all depend on one biosphere for sustaining our lives. Yet each community, each country, strives for survival and prosperity with little regard for its impact on others. Some consume Earth's resources at a rate that would leave little for future generations. Others, many more in number, consume far too little and live with the prospect of hunger, squalor, disease, and early death.[41]

This situation is arguably the biggest scandal of our time. Rather than accepting it as a norm, we must confront it with prophetic

---

[39] Ibid., 74-75.
[40] Ibid., 74.
[41] U.N, *Our Common Future*.

rage. Further, our careless exploitation of natural goods raises ethical and theological questions about human responsibility toward one another, God's creation and future generations of life.

## The Concept of Sustainable Development

The introduction of the concept of "sustainable development" as the viable economic path was an attempt to address the above dilemma. Proponents of sustainable development argue that development should improve the livelihoods of the majority of the world's population while maintaining human responsibility to future generations. They also realized that to be sensitive to the justifiable demands of future generations, we need an economic path that provides both economic growth and ecological wellbeing.

Although the Club of Rome—a network of thinkers concerned with the future of humanity and Earth—challenged the belief in endless growth with the document "Limits of Growth" in 1972,[42] it was WCED that defined sustainable development in 1983 as development that "meets the needs and aspirations of the present without compromising the ability to meet those of the future."[43] Whereas development as originally conceived implied endless economic progress and growth without concomitant moral obligations to humanity and God's Earth, the WCED defined development from an eco-social moral perspective.[44] "Sustainable development is the way in which economic growth must be fashioned and organized, not only taking into account the long term considerations but also the modulations in the Market economy, with limits, that make it socially and ethically

---

[42] The Club of Rome was founded in 1968 as a network of independent thinkers across disciplines—politics, business and science—concerned with the wellbeing of the world. Members share a common concern for the future of humanity and the Earth. http://www.clubofrome.org/?p=324. Accessed 05/05/2012.
[43] United Nations, *Our Common Future: The World Commission on Environment and Development* (Oxford/New York: Oxford University Press, 1987), 43.
[44] See Gilbert Rist, *History of Development: From Western Origins to Global Faith*, Third Edition (London: ZED Books, 2002); Hawken, *The Ecology of Commerce*, 105ff.

acceptable."[45] In line with the moral argument raised in Chapter One, the WCED advanced an argument that economic development ought to carry moral obligations. Thus,

> Sustainable development results from a unit of public or private actions which aim to satisfy the essential needs of populations and organize an economic growth which benefits the greater welfare of individuals and ensure social cohesions; which takes into account the challenges of good governance and cultural diversity whilst ensuring that the capacity of future generations to respond to their needs is not compromised.[46]

Aptly stated,

> Sustainable development is a process of change in which the exploitation of resources, the direction of investments, the orientation of technological development; and institutional change are all in harmony and enhance both current and future potential to meet human needs and aspirations.[47]

The above definition has influenced all Earth-related "summits." Today, African governments employ "sustainable development" as a "tag" word in their economic development policies. Ironically, the environment has continued to suffer amid the so-called sustainable development.[48] Clearly, the concept seems to promote

---

[45] The entire WCED document is reproduced in Rhazaoui Ahmed Grégoire and Luc-Joël Soraya Mellali (eds), *Africa and the Millennium Development Goals* (Paris: Economica, 2005), 182.
[46] Ibid.
[47] U.N., *Our Common Future*.
[48] The Rio Earth Summit accepted the notion of sustainable development and proposed the action plan called Agenda 21. The Kyoto Protocol of 1997 set some objectives for the reduction of greenhouse gases to protect the Earth. The 2002 World Summit on Sustainable Development (WSSD) in Johannesburg concluded that despite the fact that certain achievements have been registered, greater efforts were needed to realize Agenda 21. The WSSD plan of implementation incorporated the MDGs and recommended actions that promoted their realization. The United Nations Secretary General identified five key priority areas for action—water, energy, health, agriculture and biodiversity. Ines Havet and Luc-Joel Gregoire, "The Environmental Challenges for Africa and the Implementation of the Millennium Development Goals," in *Africa and The Millennium Development Goals*, ed., Ahmed Rhazaoui, Luc-Joel Gregoire, and Soraya Mellali (Paris: Economica, 2005), 180.

human responsibility to future generations on one hand, while advocating the instrumental value of natural goods on the other. However, it is incongruous to expect humanity to be mindful of future generations while we exploit natural goods endlessly. This is a fallacy which cannot be defended ecologically. The 2012 Global Environmental Outlook 5—released on the eve of Rio+20 raised this humbling reality. The document warned that the noble vision of providing all people with "food, safe drinking water, improved sanitation and modern sources of energy, all within the ecological limits of the planet" by 2050 is impossible without major changes in how contemporary business is done.[49] It warned that:

> continuing on the current trajectory would lead, by 2050, to major environmental damage, a serious loss of ecosystem services, depletion of natural resources and many people left without sustainable access to food, water or energy. As a consequence, most internationally agreed goals and targets would be missed, some by a wide margin, particularly those related to climate change, biodiversity, water and food security.[50]

The declining of natural goods across the globe is indicative of the fact that we are living beyond planetary means. As James Nash puts it, "The maximization of current benefits for a minority of the present generation is being archived by the reduction of potential benefits for future generations. If humans have responsibilities for future generations, economic systems that stress the virtues of sustainability and frugality are essential."[51]

Evidently, Africa's economic growth is based on the endless exploitation of natural goods for global markets as opposed to localized needs. In this case, any discussion of sustainable development should deal with the role the Global North and now China are playing in Africa's "economic" growth. There is a danger in ignoring the fact that for development to be realized across the

---

[49] UNEP, *Global Environmental Outlook 5*, June 6, 2012. http://www.unep.org/geo/pdfs/ geo5/GEO5_report_full_en.pdf.451. Accessed 06/06/201.
[50] Ibid.
[51] Nash, *Loving Nature*, 44.

globe, the global North and China should slow down their development rates and change their consumption patterns.[52] But, sustainable development ought to address massive corruption in many African states, where some political leaders accumulate wealth at the expense of their people. Nigeria, Zambia, Zimbabwe, and Libya, to mention but four, boast of abundant natural goods. Yet, the majority of these countries' citizens exist in perpetual poverty while politicians pocket much of the wealth.

## "Sustainable Development" or Sustainable Living?

Since colonial times, sub-Saharan Africa has been valued for its instrumental significance to the world economy—the "World Bank" of raw materials. Unfortunately, most of the deposits in this "bank" are nonrenewable. So amidst the uncontrolled exploitation of Africa's natural goods, Africa's economic growth is short-lived. But, as Economist David Korten argues, we need to rediscover "the truth that has defined the values of high functioning indigenous societies from the beginning of time: The living Earth is sacred, beyond price, and not for sale. Rather than seeking to suppress, dominate, and exploit it, we must align ourselves in integral partnership with its structure and dynamics."[53] As previous Chapters showed, traditional societies related to Earth as a sacred commons. In fact, it is humanity that is expected to align with the Earth's under-workings and not vice versa.

Korten's argument that the Wall Street global economy "centralizes power in anti-democratic/anti-market institutions that value only financial gain and deny responsibility for the social and environmental consequences of their actions," rings true across Africa. As was the case with the Kariba Dam, Korten argues, the current economy,

---

[52] United Nations, *Our Common Future*.
[53] David Korten, "In Partnership with the Biosphere, Reframing the Debate on Limits," Club of Rome blog, http://www.clubofrome.org/?p=2832. Accessed 4/5/2012.

> [S]trips people, communities and Main Street economies of the power and ability to engage in the locally adaptive self-organization required to steward and utilize local resources in response to changing local needs and circumstances. In its single-minded pursuit of financial gain for the world's ruling oligarchy, it self-organizes toward suicidal social and environmental system imbalance and collapse.[54]

This pursuit of endless profits is one of the moral scandals of our time. So what is the meaning of sustainable development in the globalized world, where economic and political power is still imprisoned in the hands of the few?

The concept of sustainable development, some scholars object, does not go far enough to address the problem at hand. They contend that the concept does not acknowledge nature's intrinsic value nor does it aggressively address the role of the Wall Street economy in the global economy. Leonardo Boff from South America and Larry Rasmussen from North America exemplify this sort of opposition. Independently, they argue that the concept of sustainable development is an extension of the ideology of 'limitless growth' which is putting our planet in jeopardy. Like Korten, they insist that the desire for unlimited growth means invention of destructive forces, and the death of God's Earth.[55]

Although the concept has gained ground in many circles, Boff contends that the idea never gets away from its economic origins of ever-increasing or limitless economic growth. Thus, it "is an oxymoron since it is built on the economic system that believes in limitless growth."[56] Boff's skepticism is varied. For instance, the WCED links sustainable development to "rapid economic growth in both industrial and developing countries."[57] But, it also antipates "a five-to tenfold increase in the world industrial output...by the

---

[54] Ibid.
[55] Leonardo Boff, *Cry of the Earth, Cry of the Poor* (Maryknoll: Orbis Books, 1995), 67; Larry L. Rasmussen, *Earth Community, Earth Ethics* (Maryknoll: Orbis Books, 1996), 117.
[56] Boff, *Cry of the Earth*, 67.
[57] UN., *Our Common Future*.

time the world population stabilizes [around 2050]."[58] As already noted, during this period, the world population will be above 10 billion. The population of India alone will be around 1.8 billion, making it the most populous nation on Earth. Kenya's population would have also risen from 41 million in 2011 to 160 million.[59] Confronted with these figures, the oxymoron of the doctrine of sustainable development is visibly apparent.

According to Rasmussen, the current economic system or the belief in the "Big economy," overlooks the working of the ecosphere, "the Great economy." He asserts that:

> Just as there can be no post-agricultural society, there can be no economic order that is not totally dependent upon the planet's ecosystems and the biosphere and geosphere as a whole. Economic production and consumption, as well as human reproduction, are unsustainable when they no longer fall within the borders of nature's regeneration. So the Bottom line below the Bottom line is that if we don't recognize that the laws of economics and the laws of ecology are finally the same laws, we are in doodoo. Eco/nomics is the only way possible.[60]

With this in mind, it is clear that the concept of sustainable development has done little to address the ecological crisis in the world and Africa in particular. This is because the notion of sustainable development has limitless economic growth as its goal.

Sadly, this global assumption is reflected in Africa's own economic development plans. Amidst the stress of poverty, governments are deceived into thinking that the overexploitation of natural goods will transform their nations into developed countries, which is not true. Neither should we think that the Earth has unlimited natural goods to meet all our wasteful lifestyles. We can only do so at the risk of ending this Earth as we know it.

---

[58] Rasmussen, *Earth Community*, 117.
[59] Kenya's population rose from 8.1 million in 1960 to 41.6 million in 2011. This is an increase of over 414 percent during the last 50 years.
[60] Rasmussen, *Earth Community*, 112.

Ironically, most African countries are parties to treaties or agreements regarding biodiversity, climate change, desertification, endangered species, hazardous wastes, ozone layer and wetlands protection. However, these countries, while pledging to uphold ecological sensitivity, continue to exploit natural goods without any apparent moral consideration for the poor, and worse still the ecosystems. Being aware of the dangers of ecological degradation and at the same time being unable to act fully to address them has been the experience of many countries. One would disagree with Aristotle--knowledge does not always lead to good judgment.

It is undeniable that the current economic system is responsible for extincting more nonhuman species than any other human economic system in history. Sadly, most of these species being extincted are not invisible to urban dwellers; they can be found in zoos and museums. But the truth is, human wellbeing does not depend on how much money or skyscrapers we construct. On the contrary, it depends on the ecological wellbeing of the entire Earth community. Maybe it is time to remind ourselves of one existential truth—*unlike biblical manna, our "daily bread" does not come from heaven or supermarkets, but from God's Earth.*

## An Ethic of Sustainable Living

All is not lost. An African belief in the sacredness of creation, the manifestation of ancestors and high gods in nature, coupled with the belief in the interconnectedness of the cosmos can aid Christian reflections and actions on the recurring ecological crisis. The natural world does not belong to us; it is a sacrament of divine mysteries. For this reason, Christian ethical teaching should instill spiritual values that heal and protect the Earth from vulture capitalism. It must also advocate an economic paradigm that accepts that we are connected to other species through the web of life. Here, how we relate to Earth is a spiritual and moral issue.

One way this can be done is through an ethic of "sustainable living" rather than "sustainable development." An ethic of sustainable living demands that humans examine their attitudes toward Earth's goods. Sustainable living seeks to meet the needs and not wants of human beings. It demands that we align ourselves to the ecological community and act to defend Earth's integrity. Any action that seeks to destroy life will be opposed and that which encourages the enhancement of life will be encouraged. Generally, indigenous peoples practiced this ethic and lived sustainably with the entire biota.

The economic pressures Africa faces have contributed to the abandonment of the ethic of sustainable living on which the ancestral phenomenon of *ubuntu* depends. As a result, people are failing to share their resources equally and this has led to food shortages across the continent. While traditional thought would attribute the current food shortages to the wrath of the ancestors against the living for violating the ethics of *ubuntu*, scholars attribute it to various secular factors. Of course, certain agriculture methods—slash and burn, overuse of pesticides, deforestation and the over-exploitation of marginal lands—accelerate environmental degradation. In this case, African governments should invest in agricultural research and production, and repeal land tenure laws that discriminate against the poor.

On the other hand, the global community is equally responsible for Africa's environmental degradation. For the most part, Western monetary authorities have pressured African countries to degrade their environment. Since Western governments' economic policies depress and destabilize world prices for poor countries' products, developing countries are forced to over-exploit natural goods to meet their budgets and in the context of the International Monetary Fund, access international loans.

Despite the over-exploitation of Africa's natural goods for centuries, the plight of the continent remains. Today, Africa can hardly provide safe drinking water for the majority of its current populations, and only a fraction of that population has access to proper sanitation. Further, Africa does not produce enough food to feed its population. This dire situation demands that we address the environmental challenges undermining food security. For how long will Africa depend on other nations to feed its population? Even if one can agree with the Neo-Böserupian assumption that development in agriculture coupled with sound government policies can address Africa's food shortages, the future of food security ought to be addressed in the context of consumption of available goods. Missiologically, it is not about *how many people or Christians will be in Africa in 2050,* but *what the continent can sustainably afford given the above exploitative realities.*

To ensure Africa's ecological integrity, ethicists and theologians need to inculcate the ethics of sustainable living in African Christianity. Centuries ago in distant Europe, St. Francis of Assisi demonstrated that poverty need not be an enemy of nature or of community wellbeing—where it is voluntary and its practitioners have the freedom to respect Earth, humanity and all creatures. However, in Africa, conditions in which families and communities are deprived of a sufficiency of needed natural goods demonstrate that involuntary poverty definitely increases pressure on poor people, and affects how they relate to the Earth Community.

The increasing population and poverty is forcing families to redefine the meaning of solidarity and the ethics of *ubuntu*. In the past, the concept of family carried a community focus and care of children was a community activity. Today, the community is not involved in the caring of children; resulting in a breakdown of traditional family networks that previously provided support to individuals in times of eco-social crisis. In past eras, one did not starve when his/her harvest failed; rather, the society provided for such a one from community goods, out of the ethics of *ubuntu*. With the growth of population, poverty and landlessness, such values are disintegrating. The good news is, Africa still possesses theological, ethical, and community consciousness that can re-activate the values of *ubuntu*. As Christianity makes its home in Africa, an understanding of Jesus as an ecological ancestor of all biota is long overdue. The next Chapter will focus on this Christological hypothesis.

# Chapter Seven
## The Challenge of Doing Ethics: Toward the Christology of Earth

### Doing Christian Ethics in Africa

The challenge of doing ethics in Africa is that some Western ethicists expect African Christian ethics to be in line with Western thought; but the worldviews that inform Western and African values are very different. While the center of Christianity has shifted to the global South, in reality, the global North remains the unspoken standard of doing Christian theology and ethics. For instance, while moral theologies from the non-Western worlds are qualified (Asian moral theology, Latin American moral theology, African moral theology, etc.), Western ethics still enjoys the normative position it held in the first half of the 20th century.

Jehu J. Hanciles has attempted to address this problem. In what he terms "Western intellectual hegemony," Hanciles argues that various reasons have led to this Third World intellectual dependence syndrome. As is the case with Western political and economic structures through which the West dominates the global South, Western intellectual journals, universities, and publishing houses overshadow non-Western ones. To some extent, Third World scholars only find credibility by belonging to Western academic organizations and publishing in Western journals. While accepting the power of globalization, he maintains that the escalating experience of interdependence encourages new hegemonic relationships. At the least, globalization works to the advantage of the global North and in most cases "worsen global inequalities and intensify exploitative structures."[1]

---

[1] Jehu J. Hanciles, "New Wine in Old Wineskins, Critical Reflections on Writing and Teaching a Global Christian History," *Missiology: An International Review* XXXIV, no.3 (July 2006), 374.

The normative status of Western intellectual ideologies, knowingly or unknowingly, promotes these exploitative structures. Non-Western intellectuals are viewed as consumers of Western-produced agendas; and scholars who explore indigenous ideologies are easily dismissed or simply ignored.

But the accountability of non-Western theological ethics to Western thought has seriously compromised the academic freedom of non-Western scholars to examine and affirm some aspects of their cultures that may contradict Western thought. In the case of an ancestor cult, until recently, only elements that corresponded with established Western Christological facets were analyzed for their theological significance. As this study has revealed, the role of ancestors as guardians of the land and rain-givers, and their nonhuman manifestations, were not given adequate theological attention. Likewise, the gender balancing roles of high gods and ancestors, the motherhood of God and the interconnectedness of all life were not sufficiently addressed.

The selective use of certain elements of the cult of ancestors has created what Matthew Schoffeleers called a "Christological crisis" among theologians. Schoffeleers notes:

> Africans find it difficult to integrate the person of Jesus Christ in their belief system, either because he is automatically associated with the West and the colonial past, or because his very essence is supposed to be incompatible with autochthonous [indigenous] religious conceptions.[2]

Although he is speaking about the title of Christ as a healer (*nganga*)—the title taken up by Buana Kibongi, Gabriel Setiloane, and Michael Kirwen—Schoffeleers' point needs emphasizing. Ethicists and theologians were uncomfortable with titles that contradict Western theology or Western-developed Christological titles. As the following discussion will reveal, despite the ancestor

---

[2] Matthew Schoffeleers, "Folk Christology in Africa: The Dialectics of the Nganga Paradigm," *Journal of Religion in Africa* 19, Fasc. 2 (Jun. 1989), 157. Also published in *Religion in Africa: Experience and Expression*, (ed.), Thomas D. Blakely, Walter E. A. van Beek and Dennis L. Thomson (London: James Currey, 1994), 73-88.

cult's ecological implications, African scholars only analyzed its anthropocentric elements in their theologizing.

## From Cult to Christology

The discussion on the *Iwiindi* revealed that the cult of ancestors has ecological connotations. However, it also exposed shortfalls of Christologies that present Jesus as an "ancestor" while ignoring the ecological role of the living dead. The following discussion is an attempt to develop a Christology of Jesus as the ecological ancestor, to which the biblical testimony also attests.

The Bible presents Jesus as the "origin" of creation and "the first born of all creation" (Col 1:17).[3] African cosmology, however, views the ancestors as the first persons to exist or simply the first born of the human lineage on Earth. Just as Jesus finds his source in God, ancestors originate from the Supreme Being. Because of their ontological position, however, ancestors are the guardians of the land. From this perspective, Jesus, our origin and ecological ancestor, is by default the Supreme guardian of the land.

In Chapter Two, we observed that the authority of ancestors has dominated anthropological literature. In theological literature, however, it is their functional roles that dominate the discourse. Ghanaian John S. Pobee, writing from an Akan perspective, views Jesus as *Nana*, "the Great and Greatest Ancestor."[4] As for Charles Nyamiti, who developed the ancestor Christology more than any theologian, Jesus should be viewed as our brother-Ancestor.[5] François Kabasélé adds that Christ is an elder brother-ancestor.[6] For Bénézet Bujo of the Congo, however, Christ is the proto-ancestor, healer and master of initiation.[7] These Christological

---

[3] All biblical quotations are from the New International Version.
[4] John Pobee, *Toward an African Theology* (Nashville: Abingdon, 1979), 94.
[5] Charles Nyamiti, *Christ As Our Ancestor: Christologies from an African Perspective*, (Gweru: Mambo Press, 1984).
[6] Robert J. Schreiter (ed.), *Faces of Jesus in Africa* (Maryknoll, New York: Obis Books, 2001).
[7] Bénézet Bujo, *African Theology in Its Social Context* (Maryknoll, New York: Orbis Book, 1992).

titles are indicative of the multi-functional roles ancestors play in African cosmologies. Hence, the preceding Christologies were born out of a desire to make Christ relevant to Africans.

Susan Smith argues that biblical writers constantly negotiated the positive dialectical relationship between the gospel and culture in how they presented their messages. Early Church history, she asserts, is a narrative of primitive Christian communities' responses to the challenge of the gospel. Thus, the four Gospels "are wonderfully crafted texts that point to the different authors' judicious awareness of and reliance on Hebrew and Greco-Roman literary traditions, and responsiveness to the reality of their respective communities' contexts."[8]

Smith points out that the act of enculturation belongs primarily to the local community, which she argues is the primary agent of inculturation or contextualization. Since the local community is connected to other communities of faith, there is mutual and dialectical relationship between the local and the global. This interaction is fundamental to enculturation.[9]

The dialectical and mutual interaction of the local and the global communities is significant to develop any given Christology. Sadly, only non-Western Christological titles are subjected to these interactions. Western titles usually escape such scrutiny. As Smith observes above, however, each gospel writer intended to make it clear that Jesus is the Son of God. Nonetheless, how each writer communicated this theological conviction depended on the socio-cultural context of the author and his audience. This observation suggests that the number of Christologies found in Africa today is not a crisis *per se,* as Schoffeleers suggests. Rather, it is an attempt to incarnate Jesus into the different eco-social and cultural contexts of God's people.

While the incarnation of Jesus has been understood as justifying the sacredness of humanity, in reality, it makes all creation a

---

[8] Susan Smith, "Gospel and Culture," *Missiology: An International Review* XXXIV, no.3 (July 2006), 347.
[9] Ibid., 344.

sacrament. The assurance of salvation in the world to come should be balanced with an invitation to inherit the Kingdom of God in this world (Luke 17:21). More still, the concept of salvation as an escape from this corrupt Earth is foreign to Africans. As repeatedly stated, Africans understand salvation as earthly rather than heavenly. They do not conceive the end of Earth as leading to the destruction of sinners and the rapture of the righteous. Neither do they expect Armageddon through which this Earth ends up in flames as the righteous are miraculously rescued while sinners and innocent animals are roasted alive. Instead, the living and their ancestors will continuously co-exist in everlasting harmony on Earth. Thus, the restoration of Earth to its original state with abundant water, animals, trees and other biota, and fertile lands is what constitutes African eschatology. Further, God and ancestors are the very forces behind the restoration of Earth's capacity to provide abundant life. In sum, African eschatology upholds the restoration of Earth, and never its destruction (Rev 21-22).

## Christ the Ecological Ancestor: A Biblical Perspective

The ecological role of the ancestor cult has not received serious attention in Christian theology. This oversight does not negate the value of an ancestor Christology at all. According to Donald J. Goergen, the value of ancestor Christology lies in the fact that it "is both thoroughly African and also thoroughly Christian."[10] While he argues that globalization will reduce the influence of the ancestor cult, he insists that the concept *"inculturates Jesus within African cultures. It inserts Jesus into African soil. It incarnates Jesus as God's Word in an African context. It is an African Jesus. Jesus is our ancestor, an ancestor of all Africans, the proto-ancestor of us all, the new Adam, our new ancestral origin."*[11]

---

[10] Donald J. Goergen, "The Quest for the Christ of Africa." http://www.sedos/org/english/goergen/htm. Accessed 01/20/2009.
[11] Ibid.

Goergen is right. Jesus is the ultimate ancestor to all human races across the globe. However, Jesus is equally the ecological ancestor to rats, bugs, donkeys, lambs, ants, and ultimately the entire creation. However, the assumption that globalization will reduce the influence of the ancestor cult is farfetched. As this study has shown, the cult continues to resurface in the face of globalization.

It is important to note that traditions pertaining to ancestors vary from community to community. Nonetheless, all African cultures agree that ancestors are always physically dead members of one's family, clan, or community culture who are concerned with the eco-social wellbeing of their descendants. In this case, rather than debating the historical and traditional differences of the cult across the continent, this Chapter will explore the ecological role of ancestors in African cosmologies. In line with Mutukudzi, amidst the mounting crisis, we need to bring ancestors back to Earth. For Christians, however, it demands expanding the redemptive activities of Jesus to all creation. Yet to develop the Christology of an ecological ancestor, it is necessary to develop a biblical basis for this argument.[12]

The biblical world held ancestors in great esteem. To them, ancestors were the source of life and identity. While God was held as the source of the nation, Abraham and Sarah, Isaac and Rachel, and Jacob, Rebecca and Leah were the founders of the nation. The call of Abraham and Sarah was vital to Israel's self-understanding (Gen 12:1-3). Abraham and Sarah's obedience to God not only served as the foundation for the unique relationship Israel enjoyed with Yahweh, but also set the standard for Israel's obedience. Israel, like Abraham and Sarah, was expected to be faithful to Yahweh's demands. Even when the Hebrews were in bondage in

---

[12] Many Africanists argue that their societies hold many things in common with the biblical world. Polygamy, drinking of ritual beers, belief in witchcraft, honoring of ancestors, dreams, and sacrifices are among some shared elements. While these similarities are issues that demand research from African scholars, I limit my discussion to the topic of ancestors.

Egypt, God identified the Godself to Moses as the God of Abraham, Isaac, and Jacob (Ex 3:1-15). In short, Israel's identity and religion was planted in the cult of ancestors.

Furthermore, the Israel of the living was directly linked to that of "the living dead" through the Abrahamic covenant. The rite of "circumcision" which was laid on the nation of Israel should be viewed as an ancestral ritual through which Israel is reminded of her historical relationship with Abraham and Yahweh.

Like Africans, the Jewish society viewed their ancestors as the living dead. They never conceived Abraham, Isaac, and Jacob as dead, but alive. Based on Abraham's cultic immortality, Jesus spoke of the biblical God as the God of the living (Mk 12:27). Yet the God of Abraham could also be said to be the God of Moses, Miriam, Joshua, Ruth, David, Esther and many more. Each generation had its own names, which it considered to be the archetype and epitome of obedience to Yahweh, but Abraham, Isaac, and Jacob remained the *basangu* or the vital link to Yahweh's covenant.

Biblical genealogies were meant to link past, present, and future generations. If we accept that much of the Hebrew Bible was written during the exile, then it makes sense to argue that such genealogies were transmitted verbally, just as Africans have done over the centuries. Interestingly, even Jesus is presented according to the above understanding. Matthew begins his account with the words, "An account of the genealogy of Jesus the Messiah, the son of David, the son of Abraham"(Mt 1:1). Luke addresses this when he speaks about the ministry of Jesus. "Now Jesus himself was about thirty years old when he began his ministry. He was the son, so it was thought, of Joseph, son of Helli...son of Judah, son of Jacob, Son of Isaac, son of Abraham...son of Adam, son of God."(Lk 3:23-38). To Mark, however, Jesus was the son of God; John does not present the genealogy, but provides a prologue which locates Jesus in God. In sum, Matthew and Luke provide the human ancestry of Jesus, while Mark and John provide his divine origin.

The Jews took their ancestry very seriously. Raymond Brown, one of the most respected New Testament scholars, observes that genealogies tended to serve many purposes. In various ways, they established one's identity for survival purposes.[13] (For example, Paul used his ancestry to argue against those who were doubtful of his Jewish ancestry, and used his Roman citizenship to gain release from prison). Ancestry also established one's identity in regard to certain offices. For one to be a king in ancient Israel, such a one was expected to have descended from royal ancestry of David. Priests, too, were expected to trace their ancestry to Aaron before they could be admitted into Temple services.[14] In fact, these perspectives guided the gospel writers when they addressed the pedigree of Jesus.

As already observed, in the Ancient Near East, a person was a person through his ancestry; and forgetting one's ancestry had negative repercussions. For instance, Paul boasted of his zeal to keep the traditions of his ancestors (Gal. 1:14). When his authority was disputed, he wrote, "if anyone else has reason to be confident in the flesh, I have more: circumcised on the eighth day, a member of the people of Israel, of the tribe of Benjamin, a Hebrew of Hebrews" (Phil. 3:4-6). Paul did not end by citing Israel (Abraham, Isaac, and Jacob), but mentioned the tribe of Benjamin and finally made an individual case for his parents, "a Hebrew of Hebrews."

By arguing from his Jewish ancestry, Paul linked himself to Abraham, Isaac, and Jacob, and ultimately to God. This example demonstrates how Jews understood themselves. As children of Abraham through their ancestry, they had the inherent right to the natural goods of the land that God gave to their ancestors. Through the ritual of circumcision, a male Jew inherited the life of Abraham and became a friend of God after the pattern of Abraham, his first ancestor.

---

[13] Raymond Brown observes that Mathew identified Jesus as son of David and Abraham as illustrated through his ancestors to provide Jesus' identity in a mixed community of Jews and Gentiles. Raymond Brown, *The Birth of the Messiah* (Garden City: Doubleday, 1977), 64-66.

[14] Ibid.

From an African perspective therefore, an argument can be made that the biblical phrase "son of" should not be taken as referring to living parents alone, but the "living dead." This is why the Jews can claim to be the children of Abraham. Likewise, the fourth commandment to honor one's parents is not limited to the living (Ex 20:12), but includes the living dead. This standpoint explains why the existence of Jesus "before Abraham" was viewed as blasphemy by his fellow Jews (Jn 8:58).

Honoring the traditions of ancestors was also behind Jesus' discourse with the Samaritan woman. As among Africans, the ancient Near East viewed ancestral shrines (*malende*) as sacred places where one communed with the divine and ancestral powers. In the story of the Samaritan woman, St. John alerts us to the cultic controversy between the Jews and the Samaritans. The Woman told Jesus, "Our ancestors worshiped on this mountain, but you say that the place where people must worship is in Jerusalem." Jesus replied, "Woman, believe me, the hour is coming when you will worship [God] neither on this mountain nor in Jerusalem" (Jn 4:20ff).

As a Jew, Jesus could have contended for the superiority of the Jewish ancestors in the divine covenant over the Samaritans. However, as the Christ (*logos*) and the origin of all creation, he was equally an Origin-Ancestor to Samaritans. By declaring that "the hour is coming when you will worship [God] neither on this mountain nor in Jerusalem," Jesus makes Jewish and Samaritan, and by extension African ancestors, subordinate to his reign. This is because his incarnation inaugurated a new age of divine favor. In this age, all people are brought together in one ancestor, Jesus Christ who is both God and ecological ancestor of all biota.

In African perspective, the *malende* at which Samaritans approached God was on Mount Gerizim, whereas the Jews did so at the temple in Jerusalem. Jesus, however, did not promote one place over the other. Neither did he denounce such historical shrines. Rather, he declared that the time had come to relate to the Creator after the order of the Spirit. Unlike the old order which separated people into camps based on their ancestor cults and sacred spaces, the Spirit brings about new relationships among God's creation and demands a new way of relating to God. Samaritans and Jews are challenged to abandon their traditional manner of worship at their ancestral shrines (*malende*) and to accept the code that Jesus the Christ instituted. Under this new code, every space on Earth becomes the Spirit's sacramental shrine (*malende*) from which God can be experienced, worshipped and adored. In this sense, the authority of Christ obliterates that of Abraham, Isaac, and Jacob and, by extension, African ancestors.

It is now God's son who takes over the authority to direct and intercede for rain on behalf of God's creation. And, this new order brings about a new era in which Jews, Samaritans, Europeans, Africans, nonhumans and humans can worship together. All this is possible through one ecological Ancestor *par excellence*, Jesus Christ, who existed long before Abraham, African ancestors, and every ancestor in creation history. Therefore, Jesus is the origin of all creation and the sole ecological ancestor of all biota.

To some extent, the dispute between Jesus and the Jewish authorities in the New Testament illustrates this theological fact. Like African theologians, the Jewish theologians tended to limit the understanding of ancestorship to humanity and saw Abraham as their supreme ancestor, whose authority was unquestionable. They claimed to be the descendants of Abraham and rightly so. However, Jesus declared himself to be above Abraham and by extension the origin of every ancestor. Thus, "before Abraham was born, I am!" (John 8:59). While most scholars tend to understand this verse as referring to the divinity of Christ, this verse is vital to an ancestor Christology of Earth. Anthropologically, it does not make sense to argue that Jesus is an African or Jewish Ancestor. But as the origin of all biota, the "I AM" is the life and the ancestor of the entire cosmos.[15]

---

[15] The question of the salvation of ancestors is thereby resolved. If Abraham was justified based on his relationship with the I AM, there is enough room to argue that before our African ancestors were even born, Jesus existed. In this case, they saw the day

The interpretation of Christ as "our" ancestor is problematic and might even be viewed as heretical if by "our" we exclude nonhumans. As the Origin-Ancestor of all ancestors, Jesus is not just the ecological ancestor of all creation, but *the abundant life*. The gospel of John testifies to this ecological ancestorhood of Christ when it states that "through him, all things were made and without him, nothing made was made" (Jn 1:3). It is to this reality that the Nicene Creed points when it affirms that Jesus is the only Son of God and "through him all things were made."[16] Although the creed limits redemption to humanity, it is time to advocate an inclusive and ecological creed that accepts Christ as both the guardian and the origin of all life. Christ as "the first born of all creation," then, becomes the brother and the origin of every ancestor in creation history. This interpretation has ethical and theological implications for human–nature relations—we are created for communion with nature and not dominion.

## Celebrating Life: Rejecting Dominion

The Christian concept of dominion has received different interpretations at different times in Church history—ranging from unlimited domination to stewardship of Earth. Mostly, the socio-cultural and economic historical contexts have affected how people have understood this concept. However, the recurring ecological crisis demands the re-examination of the doctrine of dominion. Our failure to discern, honor and respect ecological relationships can lead to a one-sided interpretation of the doctrine of dominion. It can also promote the irresponsible idealism that we have a divine mandate to abuse Earth. As article 17 of the Dominican Bishops' Conference observed,

---

of the Lord and rejoiced. However, like the Jews, many theologians are likely to question when and how Jesus met our ancestors. His answer remains the same, before your "ancestor was born, I AM."

[16] The Episcopal Church, *Book of Common Prayer* (New York: Church Publishing Incorporated, 1979), 362.

> Human beings are born, grow, and develop within a system that is complex, closed, and interrelated. Nature is home in which they live. They depend on her for their existence and the quality of their lives. In turn, nature depends on human beings who with their intelligence and capacity (both scientific and technical) must preserve, defend, better, and perfect it. In this system of many and varied interrelated levels, the breakdown of or interference with one of these has a negative repercussion on all.[17]

Subsequently, Christian Creation theology is founded on God's creative love for all creatures. Genesis 3 makes it clear that human betrayal of God's trust upset sound relationships among all creatures. It is time to realize that the bleeding Earth is crying for help and only a theology of creation that is non-anthropocentric and self-limiting in consumption can address Earth's wounds. We must accept that the Creator declared creation *"very good"* and that our activities are compromising the sacramental web of life. Earth is the mother of all life and how we relate to creation is full of moral and theological implications. Being servants of God, caring for Earth is our sacred duty.

Furthermore, the oneness of creation has implications for Christian ecological ethics. As observed in Chapter Five, the future of Earth depends on our attitudes toward the natural world. Corporate systemic attitudes that exploit the Earth for profits and individual attitudes that encourage materialism are slowly driving us to our own demise. Mutukudzi's assertion is worth repeating: *By destroying Earth, we are spitting into the well from which we all drink.* Our strength is only maintained by the knots of life that connect us to each other, and make us one Earth family. Attitudes that separate the rich from the poor, the global North from the global South, men from women, people of color from whites, and humans from nonhumans weaken God's Family.

---

[17] The Dominican Episcopal Conference, "Pastoral Letter On the relationship of Human Beings to Nature, article 17," in *And God Saw that It Was Good, Catholic Theology and the Environment,* (eds.), Drew Christiansen and Walter Grazer (Washington DC, United States Catholic Conference, 1996), 262.

The above observation suggests that human freedom is directly linked to Earth's liberation. Africa's freedom will not be complete without the full liberation of Earth, Earth's biota, and Earth's poor. The prophet Isaiah was right when he proclaimed God's salvation as the restoration of all creation. God's intention is to create new heavens and the new Earth in which all creatures will live in perfect harmony. In the new Earth, the weeping of Earth and the poor will be heard no more (Is 65:20; Rev 21:1-4). There, every creature will have equal access to Mother Earth's goods (Is 65:21-24).

It is clear that God desires harmony between humanity and nonhumans. Just as humans will come to live as one, God will enable humans to relate to nonhumans in perfect shalom. Again, the prophet Isaiah asserts,

> Wolves will live with lambs. Leopards will lie down with goats. Calves, young lions, and year-old lambs will be together, and little children will lead them. The cow will feed with the bear, their young will lie down together, and the lion will eat straw like the ox. The infant will play near the hole of the cobra, and the young child put his hand into the viper's nest (Is. 11:6-9; cf. Is. 65: 25).

Paul concurs with Isaiah's prophetic eschatology. To him, the fullness of time will involve "the summing up of all things in Christ, things in the heavens and things on the earth" (Eph. 1:10). As long as enmity between created beings persists, we cannot speak about the reign of God being established on Earth. The fear of creation that has sometimes led to the destruction of nonhumans will be replaced with the fellowship of all creatures. Against this background, poverty, landlessness, corruption, uneven distribution of natural goods, and overpopulation are all sinful acts.

Sadly, these oppressive attitudes are religiously conditioned. As already established, some missionary teachings presented Earth as existing solely for human use. Such religious teachings somehow changed people's attitudes toward the once sacred Earth in Africa. However, since the spiritual, the natural, and the human worlds are interconnected, such a paradigm did not distance from Earth those Africans who retained this cosmology, if only surreptitiously under colonial rule. As a result, while Earth is understood and treated as a commodity by some, many Africans still associate sacredness with certain aspects of the natural world.

If the Bible does not sanction the destruction of God's creation, then our attitude toward Earth's natural goods should be informed and directed by this ecological consciousness. The appropriation of Earth's natural goods by less than 20 percent of the world's population, the violations of poor people's rights, unfair trade between the global North and South, increasing poverty, the destruction of rainforests, and unprecedented corruption in post-colonial Africa are among the many issues that Christian ecological ethics ought to address. By ignoring them, we sin against God, ancestors, future generations of life, and God's Earth.

Moreover, Christ the supreme guardian of the land demands that we examine our attitudes toward Earth. The theological notion of resident aliens, which can sometimes negate Earth as our home in favor of another world to come, demands revisiting. If we view ourselves as strangers on Earth, then destroying Earth simply accelerates our arrival to our heavenly city. As immigrants going to our heavenly city, we care less for Earth. However, by virtue of Christ's relationship with Earth, this Earth is our sacramental home. It is therefore our religious and moral duty to guard God's Earth.

This understanding is equally found in traditional religions, where Earth is considered our home forever. We have no other home to which we migrate; Earth is our permanent home. Accepting Earth as our permanent home has practical implications for our relationships; human to human, and nature to human. For instance, rather than promising the poor a better world to come, Christianity must be willing to address socio-political and economic injustices that have reduced the majority to abject poverty. Acknowledgement, in practice as well as in theory, of Earth's status as our home, is also fundamental to meeting the Millennium Development Goals. This requires that ethicists and theologians engage economic and political issues from the perspective of Earth. It involves a learning process based on critical scrutiny of long-held assumptions about Earth. As long as God's Earth is viewed as our property, the crisis will persist.

## Respecting Life

The origin-ancestorship of Christ demands that Christianity re-examines its attitude toward nonhumans and the Earth as a whole. If Christ is the ancestor of every creature, then, the doctrine of dominion which some theologians have employed to justify human exploitation of nature cannot be defended theologically. Albert Schweitzer's 1936 article, "The Ethics of Reverence for Life," for example, rejected the doctrine of dominion. He insisted that humanity is just one among the many creatures of God in the cosmos. Like Francis of Assisi, Schweitzer advocated biota egalitarianism whereby:

> [humanity reverences] every form of life, seeking as far as possible to refrain from destroying any life, regardless of its particular type. -- We happen to believe that man's life is more important than any other form of which we know. But we cannot prove any such comparison of value from what we know of the world's development.[18]

Schweitzer further points to the interconnectedness of life as being at the center of this ethic. As humans, he argues, "we are directly connected to other forms of life and are born of other lives; we possess the capacities to bring still other lives into existence."[19] Schweitzer's point is that humanity cannot live in isolation from other creatures; thus, mutual interdependence is the law of nature.

Subsequently, Sallie McFague categorically defends the sacredness of all life. She warns that since our life is directly linked to other beings in the ecosphere,

---

[18] Albert Schweitzer, "The Ethics of Reverence for Life." http://www1.chapman.edu/scheitzer/sch/reading4/html. Accessed 07/16/08. Originally published in *Christendom* 1 (1936), 225-39.
[19] Ibid., 10.

> By destroying the health of nature, we are undermining our own. The ecological model does not support either/or thinking: *either* my good or yours, *either* our good or nature's. The good life for nature—a resilient, complex nature—is what we must have, for our good life rests on our caring for nature's well-being.[20]

Not all ecologists would accept this. In fact, the late James Nash objects that "biota egalitarianism" is a moral absurdity and an antihuman ideology. Arguing against Albert Schweitzer, Nash posits that biota egalitarianism fails to appreciate "the unique capacities of humans to experience and create moral, spiritual, intellectual and aesthetic good. The value-creating and value-experiencing capacities of humans are morally relevant differences between us and all other species, and justify differential and preferential treatment in conflict situations."[21]

In contrast, John Hart promotes biota egalitarianism. According to Hart, humanity is "one part of a dynamic biotic community living in egalitarian relationships in ecological systems."[22] Giving an example of how salmon is honored by the Wanapum Indians in the U.S. Northwest, Hart argues that "Salmon and all creatures are good, and their natural rights, based on their intrinsic value, are egalitarian rights."[23] All creatures, he argues, have complementary capacities. However, humans have moral agency; thus, *responsible predators*—with a moral regard for the well-being of all biota.[24]

Hart's observation shares something in common with how Africans understand their role on Earth. As previous Chapters have shown, the preferential treatment of humans over nature was not always accepted in traditional Africa. In some cases, certain creatures occupied (and still do) superior positions.

---

[20] Sallie McFague, *Life Abundant: Rethinking Theology and Economy for a Planet in Peril* (Minneapolis: Fortress Press, 2000), 117-8.
[21] James Nash, *Loving Nature: Ecological Integrity and Christian Responsibility* (Nashville: Abingdon Press, 1991), 149.
[22] John Hart, *Sacramental Commons: Christian Ecological Ethics* (Lanham, Maryland: Rowman and Littlefield, 2006), 70.
[23] Ibid., 111.
[24] Ibid., 128.

The extincting of nonhuman species is compromising Earth's vital force in which we experience life. On this basis, the reverence for life should become a Christian duty. After all, Christian love demands that we love God with all our hearts and our neighbors as ourselves (Deut 6:5; Mk 12:30). Since love should be ecological in its expression, humanity has much to learn from St. Francis of Assisi, Schweitzer, African and other traditional peoples' attitudes toward creation. Nature to Francis was one big family, with the same origin in God.[25] Again in Africa, conversion to ecological consciousness means returning to traditional worldviews.

## The *Telos* of Creation

Since most African Christians are likely to hold the Bible as the supreme source of morality, it is important to address the biblical concept of creation. Biblically, Earth exists through and for the Creator God, who created heavens and Earth (Gen. 1:1ff). The creation of Earth is fundamental to life. In fact, the first human being was created from *adamah*, the Hebrew for clay (Gen. 2:9). This theological understanding suggests the sound relationship between humanity and Earth, which is reiterated in the story of the Fall: "For Earth you are, and to Earth you will return" (Gen. 3:19). Not only are humans Earth but they, like any other part of creation, belong to the Creator God (Ps 24:1-2).

The belief that Earth came into being by God's own love and care is, in fact, a biblical given. Biblical writers were careful not to treat Earth or humanity as above God. Doing so would be considered idolatry. Neither did they present Earth as something outside God's realm. Earth is God's—thus, Yahweh's covenant is not just with humans; it is with Earth and all biota. In this covenant, God promises never to destroy Earth again (Gen 9:11-13). In other

---

[25] St. Francis, "Little Flowers of St. Francis," in *St. Francis of Assisi: Writings and Early Biographies, English Omnibus of the Sources for the Life of St. Francis*, (ed.), Marion A. Habig (London: SPCK, 1973), 1348-1351.

words, the Creator cares for every creature, big and small (Ps 89:11 cf.1 Cor 10:26).

The Old Testament conviction that Earth is the Lord's is carried over into the New Testament, where the supremacy of Christ is linked to creation (Jn 1:1-5; Col 1:15-20).In these texts, Jesus is ecologically connected to every creature. Unlike an African ancestor, Jesus is the source of creation visible and invisible. That said, Christ becomes the ecological ancestor and a relative to all biota. It is through him, in him, and for him that all creation exists. Thus, the interconnectedness of creation is based on the power of Christ, who is both the Creator and the Supreme vital force behind creation. Like an African ancestor, Christ is that vital force that connects Earth to the Creator and vice versa.

The *telos* (goal) of creation is also hereby pronounced. Whereas, outside Christian thought (and sometimes, unfortunately, within Christian thinking) it is assumed that creation exists exclusively for humanity, in the New Testament, the natural world exists for Christ who is the Creator, ecological Ancestor and the *telos* of creation. This observation finds expression in other biblical books as well. Writing to the Romans, Paul asserts, "For from Him and through Him and to Him are all things" (Rom. 11:36). This biblical conviction is important to develop a Christology of Earth. Christ is not only the origin of life; he is the life (cf. Jn 1:4). Here, the belief that Earth exists solely for its instrumental value, fails to address the ecological importance of creation to Christ. Just as humans exist to worship God, every creature exists to worship its Creator. Psalm 148 invites the entire Earth community to praise the Creator (Ps 148:1-11; Ps 150:6). Despite our attempts to limit worship to humanity, the Bible teaches that worship is a cosmic act in which the entire Earth community partakes. Because of this reality, many saints and mystics have seen creation as a companion to worship. Theologically therefore, destroying nature is a crime against the Creator, whose praise we diminish.

In distant Europe, St. Francis of Assisi invited animals and birds to praise their Creator after the pattern of Psalm 148. In the

"Canticle of Brother Sun," also known as *Laudes Creaturarum* (Praise of the Creatures)—composed around 1225, when his health was at its worst—St. Francis illustrates the ecological praise rendered to the Creator. Isaiah equally invites mountains and trees to shout for joy before the Creator (Is 44:23; cf. 49:13; 55:12). Isaac Watts expressed this in a Christmas carol:

> Joy to the world! the Lord is come:
> Let earth receive her King;
> Let every heart prepare him room,
> And heaven and nature sing
> ............................
> Joy to the world! the Savior reigns;
> Let us our songs employ,
> While fields and floods, rocks, hills and plains
> Repeat the sounding joy.

Surely, from the divine perspective, all Creation exists to worship the Creator.

## Natural Rights to Life

In Chapter Three, we noted that the acceptance of human interconnectedness to the natural world through totems (*mukowa/mutupo*) confirms that nonhumans are an extension of our common life. Africans expressed this belief through traditional rituals and ceremonies. Unfortunately, such ceremonies are not only threatened by poverty, but are slowly being lost to globalization. Today, it is the perspective that nature is a reservoir of raw materials that seems to control how we relate to Earth. According to this view, we are the only species with unchallenged natural rights to Earth's goods and life.

Nicholas Wolterstorff's definition of justice is a perfect example. A community "is just insofar as its members—both individual members and its institutional and communal members—enjoy those goods to which they have a right. To fail to enjoy one's right is to be wronged."[26] Here justice is inherent in natural rights and to be denied these rights is to be wronged.

While philosophers have viewed natural rights as a product of the Enlightenment, Wolterstorff contends otherwise. He notes that the fact that the 12$^{th}$ Century canon lawyers appealed to "natural human rights" suggests the Bible as the source of our conception of these rights. To him, human rights can hardly be defended from a secular position since "there is no adequate secular grounding for human rights, and unlikely there ever will be one; the only adequate grounding is the theistic grounding which holds that each and every human being bears the image of God and is equally loved by God."[27] Thus, we seek social justice because we believe that "each and every human being, no matter what she has done, no matter what capacities she has or lacks, possesses a dignity that must never be violated."[28] Defending the wronged ought to be paramount to Christian ethics and spirituality.

From this perspective, it is understandable that human beings have natural rights to be protected. However, grounding these natural rights in God implies extending them to the entire cosmos. After all, creation reveals the Creator; for God and not humanity, is the source of nature's inherent value and natural rights. The instrumental value we attach to nature cannot be held as the defining factor of nature's worth since the natural world was declared "very good" long before humanity set sight on it (Gen 1:11,13,19). As God's people, we ought to be humble enough to accept that we are part of the whole and not that "whole."

Ultimate humility should inform our attitudes toward the territorial rights of nonhuman beings. Understandably, the issue of space puts humanity and other species in moral conflict. Who counts, snakes or humans? Should we stop building a dam simply because it is a home to an endemic species? Since we are the

---

[26] Nicholas Wolterstorff, "How Social Justice Got Me and Why It Never Left," *Journal of the American Academy of Religion* 76, no.3 (September 2008), 669.
[27] Ibid., 673.
[28] Ibid., 679.

decision makers, we usually side with our own kin; leading to untold violations of territorial rights of nonhumans across the world. But as moral beings, we have a distinct responsibility to respect other species' places, something that other species can hardly do for themselves. Some species are endemic, hence displacing them is forcing them into extinction.

Ethically, biodiversity is another biotic condition that we should hand over to future generations. In order to do this, the ethical conviction that Earth species have natural rights to space and life should be brought into theological and ethical discourse. African and Christian traditions are agreed that every creature was given space on Earth. In the Bible, God's garden was a gift to all creatures (Gen 1-3). Since the restoration of creation is central to the theology of redemption, securing other species' space is a theological and moral imperative of our time. We should work out means of living within the limits of Earth; thereby limiting the displacement of nonhuman species from their habitats.

But, there is another moral reason why we should protect biodiversity. Earth and all her species belong to our ancestor and the Creator God. Our God and our ancestors (who in essence are the guardians of natural goods) are provoked when species are forced into extinction. Traditionally, biodiversity represents their presence and blessings, while extinction point to their banishment. Since God and ancestors manifest in the natural world, extinction of species robs them of physical bodies.

Finally, the concept of totems makes biodiversity important to African worldviews. If my father's rat totem is extincted, I will grow up without knowing who I am, to whom I am related, and how I am related to the natural world. Although this might sound silly to the Western mind, in Africa, who I am is linked to, and rooted in a particular species or element of the natural world. It is for this reason that Christianity should develop theologies that encourage frugality and replenishing of Earth's renewable goods.

## Replenishing the Earth

Understanding Christ as the Origin and Ecological Ancestor of every creature has implications for how we relate to Earth. Since all creatures trace their ancestry to Christ, they are ontologically related to each other and ultimately to God. As a result, we all have a moral responsibility not only to acknowledge our evil acts toward nature, but also to repair the damage we have caused to our nonhuman brothers and sisters. Sin is not just limited to human actions against fellow humans, but extends to how we behave toward nonhumans, too. *Ubuntu* cannot be limited to humans either. Ecologically, our relationship with God should inform our relationships with one another, the natural world, and ultimately with Jesus Christ.

Amidst the unfolding crisis, Christianity ought to develop a theological rationale for Earthcare. In fact, we should urgently develop an ethic of replenishing Earth through tree planting, and restocking of other natural goods. This is even more urgent when we take into consideration the issues of overpopulation, lucrative timber trade, firewood, and the clearing of rainforests for cash crops. Since forests are the only source of livelihood to forest peoples, "[d]eforestation means lost lives and livelihoods."[29]

But, deforestation also means lost lives of millions of nonhumans species—most of which are yet to be known. Michael Northcott estimates that the extinction rate over the many millennia of Earth's existence did not exceed one species per year.[30] Today, however, habitat loss alone is "creating a mass extinction on a scale comparable to those that ended the geologic

---

[29] Gary Gardner, "The Challenge for Johannesburg: Creating a More Secure World," in *State of the World*, The World Watch Institute (New York: Norton Books, 2002), 9.
[30] Michael Northcott, *The Environment and Christian Ethics* (Cambridge: Cambridge University Press, 1996), 25; Leonardo Boff, *Cry of Earth, Cry of the Poor* (Maryknoll, New York: Obis Books, 2003).

eras."[31] Ironically, habitat loss is something we can address by halting deforestation and encouraging tree planting.

In Africa, however, the ethic of replenishing Earth is not a very common virtue.[32] Traditionally, Africans understood that natural goods came from the world of ancestors. As the *lwiindi* revealed, for Africans, drought, famines, floods, and other natural disasters are under the control of ancestors and the Supreme Being.

This understanding influence how the disappearance of natural goods is perceived. The assumption is that if we follow the rulings of the ancestors and the High God, these natural goods would be readily available. Extinctions of wildlife, fish and other natural goods, then, are interpreted as punishment for our moral lapses.

Of course, ancestors have all the reasons to punish us for not protecting the natural world. Nevertheless, it is our responsibility to right the wrongs. Our ancestors and Christ our ecological ancestor will not resolve the recurring crisis. We are the causers and the solution to this crisis. So by defining the crisis as human caused, Christianity can inculcate the ethics of replenishing Earth as an applied biblical mandate to "serve" and "guard" the Earth (Gen 1.15). When people are conscious of the extinction of natural goods due to overpopulation and over-exploitation, the value of replenishing the Earth becomes our religious duty.

Indeed, African ethics is open to other ethical systems. Here, we should employ diverse theological and scientific outlooks in our endeavor to heal the bleeding Earth. Although God is the owner of creation, science can aid our understanding of what types of trees or fish stocks to grow in specific environments. However, to solely push the scientific agenda over the African traditional heritage will not attract positive responses from many Africans who respect the

---

[31] Richard P. Cincotta and Robert Engleman, *Nature's Place: Human Population and the Future of Biological Diversity* (Washington, DC: Population Action International, 2003), 8.
[32] I am aware that some communities in West Africa have systematically increased the tree cover around their villages over the past century, as shown by old and recent photographs. James C. McCann, *Green Land, Brown Land, Black Land: An Environmental History of Africa 1800-1990* (Portsmouth: Heinemann Educational Books, 1999), 60-63.

ancestral world more than post-colonial political authorities. As long as environmental policies continue to lack spiritual sanctions, attempts to heal the Earth will be achieved with great difficulties. For this reason, social and ecological ethics in post-independence Africa should call on the authority of ancestors as Mutukudzi did on one hand, and employ scientific knowledge on the other hand. Integration rather than separation is the only viable way to deal with the life threatening environmental crises.

That the Bantu did not have an active ethic of replenishing Earth does not mean that they were ignorant about the matter. Most African cultures throughout history domesticated animals, planted fruit trees, maintained sacred groves, and tended precious gardens. That they knew the importance of saving for future use suggests that the ethic was present, if perhaps unspoken. If we are to develop an ethic of replenishing renewable goods among Africans, we should capitalize on this heritage. Tree planting, restocking of wildlife and fish are excellent examples here.

**Spitting Into the Well from Which We Drink**

The modern age promoted the belief that Earth exists solely for human use. Sadly, this perspective highly influenced missionary activities in Africa. Since the gospel of plenty was indicative of Christian civilization, missionaries assumed that non-Westerners would one day live and consume at the same levels as Westerners. But this "good news" has led to severe ecological degradation. According to Jonathan Bonk, missiologists are slowly realizing:

> that strategies (Western mission theories) for saving the world have been framed within a theological cocoon that prevented them from adequately understanding the end result of their civilization's notions of progress, development, and the social-material destiny of humankind. The planet is simply too small to accommodate large numbers of human beings who think and live as we do.[33]

---

[33] Jonathan Bonk, "Mission and the Groaning of Creation," *International Bulletin of Missionary Research* 32, no.4 (Oct. 2008), 170.

Ronald J. Sider makes a similar observation. He argues that advertisements are behind materialism in the global North. To him, materialism "is the god of...North America and the adman is its prophet."[34] Like Bonk, Sider notes that the world does not have limitless resources to sustain lavish lifestyles. Rather, human beings need to share Earth's goods equitably.

The commercialization of Earth's natural goods has caused a great deal of suffering to the economically challenged. Originally, Africans had unlimited access to the beauty of creation, today, nature has become a luxury to which only the rich are entitled. Despite being direct victims of the dam, for example, the people of chief Chipepo and Simaamba have little access to the Kariba dam.[35]

The privatization of natural goods is not just limited to waterfront areas. Across Africa, Western Safari operators control access to most game parks. While the intention is to protect wildlife from poachers, natural goods are sacramental commons to which all people should have access regardless of their ability to pay. Ethically, commercial interests should always be balanced with community interests, which is not the case in Africa today.

The transformation of existing economic principles may take many years, but acknowledging human responsibility to the natural world and to future generations demands speedy response. To use Charles Lagus's phrase, the "White Man's disease" of exploiting nature is in Africa to stay. However, it is time to heal Africa from this illness. The therapy demands accepting human responsibility to the natural world and future generations as a spiritual, social, and scientific necessity. *Ignoring this therapy is spitting into the well and bringing ourselves closer to self-annihilation.* That said, the triumph of Western civilization over African religious thought should be challenged by an ecological consciousness informed by *ubuntu*, which alerts us to the interconnectedness of the ecosphere.

---

[34] Ronald J. Sider, *Rich Christians in an Age of Hunger* (Dallas: Word Publishing, 1990), 28.
[35] Interview with Chief Chipepo, Lusaka, October 2006; Interview, Chief Simaamba, Lusaka, October, 2006.

# Chapter Eight
## Christian Ethics of *Ubuntu*

Christianity, informed directly or indirectly by African traditions, is among the fastest growing religions in the world today. As indicated throughout this study, since the mounting ecological crisis has religious ramifications, Christianity should work to address the crisis significantly and forcefully. African traditional religious teachings, integrated with Christian ethical teachings, can approach the crisis with complementary views on the value of creation via the divine perspectives expressed in their respective traditions. While both African and Christian ethics were said to be deeply anthropocentric, critical examinations of both religious worldviews have uncovered complementary emphases on human responsibility toward planet Earth and future generations. Most significantly, both religious cosmologies view Earth as the universe of intimately related beings.

This study has argued that to fault Christianity as primarily responsible for the current crisis, as some critics have done, is not entirely accurate. Certainly, Western-controlled development of a type of "civilization" distinct from traditional African cultural and religious worldviews, encouraged the exploitation of the natural world. However, the Bible and the Christian heritages have proved over time the ecological sensitivity of Christianity. In fact, the major teachings and representatives of Christianity illustrate ambivalent ecological premises in Christian traditions. Saint Francis of Assisi and many Desert Fathers and Mother Ascetics alike, lived in harmony with nature. Aside from the fact that these Christians understood themselves as sacramentally connected to the natural world, in an African context, they would recognize that rats, crocodiles, trees, gazelles, and lions are all symbols of divine revelation and presence, just as wolves, snakes, and deer are in other geographic areas and bioregions.

Similarly, biblical teachings and ideas developed during the past half-century by Christian ethicists and theologians cited throughout this work, have affirmed the intrinsic value of creation and human responsibility to the Creator, Creation, and future generations of life. Such examples illustrate how Christianity has much to learn from African traditional religions, and contemporary Christian teachings on human-nature relationships. Denouncing Christianity in the continent where it's growing rapidly will not help to mitigate the consequences of the ecological crisis. Rather, attempts to integrate Christian and African traditional religious teachings on the meanings of "nature" and "natural" in the cosmos can lead to positive ecological actions.

By advocating for Christian teaching, one should not ignore some actions by those early missionaries who destroyed sacred groves and considered nature-related rituals idolatrous. However, African religions hold the world as interconnected, the very views once held by Christian saints and early missionaries to Africa like Albert Schweitzer, and now, Marthinus Daneel.

The interconnectedness of nature is the foundation of traditions that attributed sacredness to or, better, acknowledged sacredness in the natural world. Ancestors, gods, and other spirits reveal themselves in nature—sacred groves, rivers, and animals. Unlike in Christianity, where humanity claims to be the sole *Imago Dei* based on its intellectual and moral faculties, Africans perceived humanity as one of the many images of God. Just as diviners and *n'ganga* (spiritual healers) can become avenues through which humanity encounters the Supreme Being and ancestors, a python or a cow can equally be that medium.

This study has considered how the destruction of these creatures was viewed as an affront on our ancestors and the Supreme Being. It has argued that this understanding directed the active interaction between ancestors, the living, and God's Earth. In fact, Africans express and celebrate this interaction through rituals, totems, taboos, and many eco-social sanctions.

In times of crisis, Africans would consult the diviners and elders, who in turn would consult the ancestors and, in extreme cases, the Supreme Being. Usually, the forthcoming answer was associated with the natural world. An explanation could be, for example, that somebody annoyed the ancestors by polluting the land through social inflictions. This pollution could be in the form of murder, cutting a sacred tree or even killing a sacred animal. In traditional societies, some of which still survive today, the relationship is only restored by killing the persons responsible for such acts. Harsh as this sounds, the goal was to uphold human interconnectedness to the natural world while maintaining a favorable relationship with ancestors and the Supreme Being. In this regard, *ubuntu* is closely associated with the ethics of ecological interconnectedness.

The spiritual significance of nature in African cosmology is experienced at two levels. First, every creature possesses a vital force which, as we already observed, is the knot that binds nonhumans and humans together. Therefore, human behavior toward nature is of spiritual importance to the community; to possess *ubuntu* includes living in harmony with the rest of creation. For this reason, a person who possesses *ubuntu* respects nonhumans' natural rights out of respect for the Creator Spirit and the ancestors.

Second, Africans respect the natural world for its spiritual overtones. In addition to taboos associated with the forests, rivers and mountains, the natural world is an avenue through which we ultimately understand our own world. This revelatory quality does not come from creation in itself. Rather, the Creator Spirit and ancestors confer it. Sacred mountains, rivers, trees, snakes, and many other creatures are respected by virtue of their association with the spirit world. In a sense, the natural world is the emissary of God to human mind.

The interconnectedness and sacredness of the universe provide a foundation for Christian ecological ethics. Earth is part of the complex sacred whole in which every creature has an equal claim. Similarly, the universe is sacred by virtue of its origin. To destroy the Earth is to commit sacrilege against the Creator who conferred Mother Earth with sacred worth. As God's and Earth's children, we ought to love and respect God's Earth as the mother of all life. This understanding finds support in Christianity and African traditional religions. Christianity teaches that creation originates from God. So since the Spirit is present in the cosmos, the cosmos is another form of divine revelation. It is on these two assumptions that the doctrine of natural revelation affirms nature's sacramental value.

The sacramental value of Earth is similarly complemented by the belief that land is a generational heritage and our common home. Like the body of Christ in the Holy Eucharist, which is given for all people, Earth's natural goods are sacred commons and must be enjoyed equally: Not only by humans, but by all living creatures. Therefore, the destruction of habitats for Earth's species ought to prompt prophetic outrage from African traditionalists and Christians alike since both religious heritages acknowledge that Earth is a God-provided home to all creatures.

On the economic front, this study has argued that Western export-driven capitalist economies and the continent's exploding demographic growth are putting extreme pressure on Africa's natural goods and subsequently degrading the land. It argues that Western driven economic paradigms do not pay attention to the ecological integrity of the land. Neither do they take into consideration the plight of the poor. Amid corruption in post-independence Africa, these economic policies deceive us into believing that we have a livable future without Earth.

But Christianity and traditional religions understand that such a belief is invalid; our future, and that of Africa, depends on how we act today to save our planet. The concept that Africans can act as if there is no future misleads on all fronts. Although Mbiti denies the importance of an indefinite future in African traditional life, Africans have understood the meaning of the "future" and planned for it. They understood that what we do today has significant and, perhaps, severe implications for tomorrow. Such an understanding explains why so many Africans refused to part with the land even when they had the freedom to do so. Theologians and ethicists should therefore re-examine some ecological themes already present in African religions to integrate them into the global ecological discourse. As this study has revealed, the ancestor cult, the *Iwiindi*, and other rituals can be instrumental to Earth healing.

This book has particularly considered the case of the Kariba Dam. To many Europeans, the construction of the dam was purely an economic issue. But for Africans, the entire project was a threat to the interconnected universe. Aside from opposing it for its social impacts, many Africans resisted the dam because they saw it as an attack on the very center of their being; the Supreme Being and the ancestors.

The sacrifice and appeasements that followed the construction of the dam illustrate how many Africans relate to civilization. To them, life cannot be separated into spheres—secular and spiritual—as the Western intellectual world tends to do. Within an African world life, however, social, economic, political, and now ecological issues are equally spiritual. In this case, presenting these issues as solely secular is missing the point. The ongoing ecological crisis should be presented as an eco-ethical spiritual issue that threatens the interconnectedness of God's Earth.

As the Kariba case demonstrated, the significance of the belief that *Nyami-Nyami* and other *basangu* spirits would destroy the dam is that it provided the Tonga people with spiritual reasons for resisting resettlement. Existentially, faithfulness to the ruling of ancestors was more important than economic development. The so-called "developmental" issues, then, have significant spiritual implications to Africans.

Further, our realization that life is interconnected ought to direct Christian ecological actions. Ecological ethics should alert all disciplines of human knowledge to the environmental predicament facing the continent and propose lasting solutions to it. This study has attempted to make such an inter-disciplinary contribution. Since the ecological crisis knows no boundaries, it is proper to conclude that the African concept of interconnectedness serves as a point of contact between African Christian ecological ethics and the rest of the world. Marthinus Daneel and African Earthkeepers, and the late 2004 Nobel Peace Prize Winner Wangari Maathai, highlighted and capitalized on this relationship in their Earth-healing initiatives.

African and Christian values are profoundly compatible when it comes to the human-nature relationship. This is not to say that these religions are fully ecological in their outlook or practice. Rather, in light of our current ecological consciousness, these religions possess strong ecological insights and themes necessary for healing the bleeding Earth. Thus, appreciating local people's heritages is critical to doing global environmental ethics.

Again, the false belief that Earth exists solely for its instrumental value is a form of idolatry, deserves reaffirming. We must recognize instead that Earth is a sacramental commons, with its own intrinsic value. It is also our obligation to conserve and care for this Earth out of our moral responsibility to future generations of life. As people of faith, we ought to uphold an *"eco-humano-relational* ethic" about, and exist in a "relational community" with, nonhumans in the sacred universe of life. Because Earth is a sacred trust entrusted to us by God and our ancestors, we are responsible for our planet's wellbeing. Neglecting this role is an abomination to God and our ancestors. Our love for God, Jesus Christ, ancestors and our moral responsibility to future generations of life should also inform our relationships with the Earth's Community. Loving nature means accepting that we are part of the Earth's family, and share a common origin in Christ.

The theologies of inculturation, contextualization, liberation and adaptation that characterize theology in Africa can, and should engage the ongoing crisis as a matter of urgency. The biblical mandate to love God and our neighbors as ourselves should now extend to God's Earth. This understanding should be concretized in various Earthkeeping projects—recycling, reforestation, limiting consumption, and cleaning the waters around us, on which all life depends. In the same way, this understanding entails standing up for the natural rights of all biota and the world's poor.

Further, ecological ethics should take the Earth's family as a whole, rather than humanity alone, as an ethical starting point.

God did not create humanity in isolation from nonhumans. Rather, God created the entire Earth family, proclaiming all creation "very good" (Gen 1:31).

The current destruction of Earth due to human-related activities demands immediate ethicizing at all levels, and in all places and institutions. For ethicists, this entails employing both Western and African heritages in our ethical analysis. The ethical concept of interconnectedness illustrated by the ethics of *ubuntu* should be emphasized and extended to our dealings with Earth community.

While the forces of Christianity, civilization, and commerce still influence and inform Christian Ethics, in this study, we have explored how traditional ecological themes and insights can enhance Earth-healing actions and responsibilities. The concept of time, totems, and ethics related to *ubuntu* and sacred groves are among the many insights that offer particularly good examples of such contributions. The ethical ideal of *ubuntu* demands living in harmonious relationships with nature. Since the ecological crisis threatens this harmony, the ethics of *ubuntu*, considered here at length, should determine our relationships with the natural world.

Christian ethics of *ubuntu* also suggest that every creature has sacred value before God. The manifestation of God, ancestors, and other spirits in nature does not only suggest that Earth is sacred; it also reminds us of the interconnectedness of the universe. Equally important is the Christian doctrine of natural revelation, which confirms the sacredness of nature. Therefore, humanity ought to relate to nature from a sacramental perspective; our redemption will not be complete unless Earth is so liberated. Paul makes this clear when he observes:

> The creation waits in eager expectation for the [children] of God to be revealed. For the creation was subjected to frustration, not by its own choice, but by the will of the one who subjected it, in hope that the creation itself will be liberated from its bondage to decay and brought into the glorious freedom of the children of God. We know that the whole creation has been groaning as in the pains of childbirth right up to the present time (Rom 8: 19-22).

Biblical witness that creation is in God's redemptive plan is consistently clear. Therefore, the liberation of Earth and all biota from current exploitation should also characterize the ethics of *ubuntu* in Africa and elsewhere.

This study has further considered how an ecological nature of African communities is behind the respect accorded to ancestors as guardians of the land. In fact, territorial and ancestor cults function as insurances for community ecological wellbeing; they enforce directives with regard to a community's use of natural goods. In African worldviews, scarcities of food, and drought and other natural disasters, are attributed to human failure to live in harmony with the environment. This was illustrated in this study by recounting some elements of Chief Simaamba's *Iwiindi*. Such cultic observations enjoin ecological injunctions and influence the production and the distribution of natural goods. These ecological dimensions are readily present across Africa, and ethicists should explore them for good ecological practices.

Indeed, Africa faces problems of ecological devastation evident from rapid population growth, migration, poverty, deforestation, and ever increasing corruption and bad governance. Regardless of these sad developments, African Christianity is growing rapidly; thereby presenting opportunities for positive ecological actions and contributions. Christianity should capitalize on its numbers and influence to transform peoples' views about Earth; it must also inculcate Earthkeeping spirituality in its adherents by utilizing the African heritage in dialogue with representatives of the Western heritage. The ethics of interconnectedness, found in both Christianity and African religions, could be useful to this task.

Cognizant of the impact of overpopulation on the environment, Africans must reject the hypothesis that abundant life means having unlimited number of children. Retaining this understanding and practice will undermined ecological initiatives on the continent. Because ancestors are vital to addressing population growth, it is time African elders were alerted to the negative effects of this growth on the biota, the land, and our communities.

Together, ancestors and elders can be called on to recognize that land is limited, and overpopulation will lead to land-related conflicts and extreme poverty among their descendants.

Finally, ancestors are crucial to upholding ecological injunctions. This study has considered how an identification of Jesus with ancestors has ecological implications. Since Jesus is the Origin and an ecological ancestor of all biota, his "vital force" is inherently active and present in every existing creature. Ignoring the current environmental predicament while species are extincted and Earth dies, means disregarding the ethical sanctions of Christ, who is the Origin, the Ecological Ancestor, and the Life of all creation. Jesus, our ancestors and our future descendants, however, demand more from us: *ubuntu* rather than indifference and exploitation should characterize global human ecological consciousness and conduct.

# Afterword

Dr. Kapya J. Kaoma invites us to rethink our social, economic and theological assumptions about God's Earth and our fellow human beings. Planted in both African and Christian traditions, *God's Family, God's Earth* alerts us to a vital existential reality—the future of our race and planet Earth depends on our willingness to become Earthkeepers. Kaoma's work is of singular importance for various reasons:

First, a comprehensive theological study on the environment from the perspective of African realities, philosophy and religions, has long been overdue. Kaoma's work therefore represents a landmark in that he boldly and with great enthusiasm selects and addresses major ecological issues worthy of consideration.

Second, the author's narratives on African cosmologies and related religious subjects are sufficiently and carefully located within the orbit of the publications of prominent African theologians, such as John Mbiti, Bénézet Bujo, Charles Nyamiti, Okot p'Bitek and others to enhance the further development of insights and stimulate discourse at the core of African theology and related disciplines.

Third, the author explores the cosmology of the Simaamba Tonga in the Kariba region of the Gwembe Valley, and the centrality of their relatedness to the ancestors, who are the guardians of the land. Likewise, the Tonga people's religiously defined opposition to the building of the Kariba dam is masterfully woven into the text as an illustration of a crucial dimension to the development of Christian ecological ethics. From a carefully crafted vignette of fieldwork among the Tonga, Kaoma arrives at the conclusion that "the ancestor cult is in fact the cult of Earth since it seeks to uphold the ecological balance of the ecosphere."

Fourth, it is the centerpiece of Kaoma's treatise; the development of an authentic African Christian vision and spirituality of *ubuntu*. Derived from a well-known Bantu term, *ubuntu* signifies "to be fully human." In the context of Earth-Ethics, it means active and respectful interconnectedness of humans with the entire Earth-community, starting with the Supreme Being, the ancestors, and the entire creation. In African Christian terms, the values of interconnectedness expressed in the spirituality of *ubuntu*, according to the author, inevitably calls for a Christology of the Earth—presenting Jesus as the ecological ancestor of all creation.

This book breathes the spirit of a prophet! In so far as it celebrates, by implication, the sacrificial lives of thousands of African Earthkeepers who have already enacted their own brand of *ubuntu*—through the planting of millions of trees in Kenya and Zimbabwe—it rekindles the flames of engagement in the struggle for the liberation and salvation of God's creation throughout Africa and the entire world.

Professor Marthinus Louis Daneel
Boston University
Author of *African Earthkeepers* Vols. 1 & 2
Founder of Zimbabwean Institute of Religious Research and Ecological Conservation

# BIBLIOGRAPHY

Abimbola, Wande. "Ifa: A West African Cosmological System." In *Religion in Africa: Experience and Expression*, ed. Thomas D. Blakely, Walter E. A. van Beek and Dennis L. Thomson, 101-166. London: James Currey, 1994.

Addai, Isaac. "Does Religion Matter in Contraceptive Use among Ghanaian Women?" *Review of Religious Research* 40, no.3 (Mar., 1999): 259-277.

Adongo, Philip B., James F. Phillips and Fred N Binka. "The Influence of Traditional Religion on Fertility Regulation among the Kassena-Nankana of Northern Ghana." *Studies in Family Planning* 29, no.1 (Mar.,1998): 23-40.

Alam, Shahid M. "Anatomy of Corruption: An Approach to the Political Economy of Underdevelopment." *American Journal of Economics and Sociology* 48, no.4 (Oct., 1989): 441-456.

Amadi, Elechi. *Ethics in Nigerian Culture*. Ibadan: Heinemann Educational Books, 1982.

Amadiume, Ifi. *Reinventing Africa: Matriarch, Religion and Culture*. New York: ZED Books, 1997.

Appiah-Kubi, Kofi and Sergio Torres, eds. *African Theology En Route*. Maryknoll, New York: Orbis Books, 1979.

Azfar, Omar, Young Lee and Anand Swamy. "The Causes and Consequences of Corruption." *Annals of the American Academy of Political and Social Science* 573 (Jan., 2001): 42-56.

Barclay, William. *The Gospel of Matthew*. Louisville: Westminster John Knox Press, 1975.

Barker, Drucilla K. and Susan F. Feiner. *Liberating Economics, Feminist Perspective on Families, Work, and Globalization*. Michigan: University of Michigan, 2006.

Bartley III., W.W. "The Reduction of Morality to Religion." *The Journal of Philosophy* 67, no.20 (Oct.22, 1970): 755-767.

Battle, Michael. *Reconciliation: The Ubuntu Theology of Desmond Tutu*. Cleveland, Ohio: The Pilgrim Press, 1997.

Baudin, R.P. *Fetishism and Fetish Worshipers*. Translated by M. McMahon. New York: Benziger Brothers, 1885.

Baur, John. *2000 years of Christianity in Africa: An African History, 1962-1992*. Nairobi: Pauline Publication, 1994.

Bediako, Kwame. *African Christianity: Renewal of a Non-Western Religion*. Maryknoll, New York: Obis Books, 1995.

_____. *Jesus and the Gospel in Africa: History and Experience*. Maryknoll, New York: Orbis, 2004.

Benedict XVI, Pope. "The Human Family, a Community of Peace." http://www.vatican.va/holy_father/benedict_xvi/12/19/2007. Accessed 01/04/2009.

Berkes, Frikret, Mina Kislalioglu, Carl Folke, and Madhav Gadgil. "Exploring the Basic Ecological Unit: Ecosystem-Like Concepts in Traditional Societies." *Ecosystems* 1, no.5 (Sept-Oct. 1998): 409-415.

Blakely, Thomas D., Walter, van Beek A. and Dennis, Thomson L., eds. *Religion in Africa: Experience and Expression*. London: James Currey, 1994.

Boff, Leonardo. *Cry of the Earth, Cry of the Poor*. Maryknoll, New York: Orbis Books, 1995.

_____. *Ecology and Liberation: A New Paradigm*. Maryknoll, New York: Orbis Books, 1995.

_____. *Jesus Christ Liberator: A Critical Christology for our Time*. Maryknoll, New York: Orbis Books, 1978.

Boff, Leonardo and Elizondo Virgil, eds. *Ecology and Poverty*. Maryknoll, New York: Orbis Books, Concillium, 1995.

Bongmba, Elias K. "Reflections on Thabo Mbeki's African Renaissance." *Journal of Southern African Studies* 30, no.2 (June 2004): 291-316.

Bonk, Jonathan. "Mission and the Groaning of Creation." *International Bulletin of Missionary Research* 32, no.4 (Oct. 2008): 169-170.

Bookchin, Murray. "The Population Myth—I." *Green Perspective: Newsletter of the Green Program Project*, A Left Green Publication no.8, July, 1988. http://dwardmac.pitzer.edu/anarchist_archives/bookchin/gp/perspectives8.html. Accessed 01/16/2009.

Booth Jr., Newell S. "Time and Change in African Traditional Thought." *Journal of Religion in Africa* VII, no.2 (1975): 81-91.

Bosch, David J. *Transforming Mission: Paradigm Shifts in Theology of Mission*. Maryknoll: Orbis Books, 1999.

_____. "Currents and Crosscurrents in South African Theology." *Journal of Religion in Africa* 6, no.1 (1974): 1-22.

Boserup, Ester. *The Conditions of Agricultural Growth: The Economics of Agrarian Change under Population Pressure*. Chicago: Aldine, 1965.

Brian, James L. "Ancestors as Elders in Africa: Further Thoughts." *Africa: Journal of the International African Institute* 43, no.2 (Apr.,1973): 122-133.

Brown, Lee M. "Understanding and Ontology in Traditional African Thought." *African Philosophy* (Feb., 2004): 158-193.

Brown, Lester R. "Feeding Six Billion." *World Watch* (Sept./Oct. 1989): 32-40.

Brown, Raymond. *The Birth of the Messiah*. Garden City: Doubleday, 1977.

Bujo, Bénézet. *African Theology in Its Social Context*. Maryknoll, New York: Orbis Book, 1992.

_____. *The Ethical Dimension of Community: The African Model and the Dialogue between North and South*. Translated from German by Cecilia Namulondo. Nairobi: Paulines Publications Africa, 1998.

_____. *African Christian Morality at the Age of Inculturation*. Nairobi: St. Paul, 1990.

Caldwell, John C, Pat Caldwell, and Pat Quiggin. "The Social Context of AIDS in sub-SaharanSub-Saharan Africa." *Population and Development Review* 15, no.2 (Jun., 1989): 185-234.

Caldwell, John C. and Pat Caldwell. "The Cultural Context of High Fertility in Sub-Saharansub-Saharan Africa." *Population and Development Review* 13, no.3 (Sep., 1987): 409-437.

_____. "The Role of Marital Sexual Abstinence in Determining Fertility: A Study of the Yoruba in Nigeria." *Population Studies* 31, no.2 (Jul., 1977): 193-217.

Chadwick, Owen. *The Mackenzie's Grave*. London: Hodder & Stoughton, 1959.

Chenje, Munyarazi. *State of the Environment 2000: Zambezi Basin*. Maseru: Lesotho, 2000.

Childster, David. *Savage Systems: Colonialism and Comparative Religion in Southern Africa*. Charlottesville: University of Virginia Press, 1996.

Chinyanta, M and J. C Chiwale. *Mutomboko Ceremony and the Lunda-Kazembe Dynasty*. Lusaka: Kenneth Kaunda Foundation, 1989.

Christ, Carol P. *Laughter of Aphrodite: Reflection on a Journey to the Goddess*. San Francisco: Harper & Row, 1987.

Christiansen, Drew and Grazer Walter, eds. *And God Saw that it was Good: Catholic Theology and the Environment*. Washington, DC: United States Catholic Conference, 1996.

Cincotta, Richard P. and Robert Engleman. *Nature's Place: Human Population and the Future of Biological Diversity*. Washington, DC: Population Action International, 2003.

Clausen, A.W. *Population Growth and Economic and Social Development: Addresses by A.W. Clausen, President, The World Bank and International Finance Corporation*. Washington, D.C.: The World Bank, 1984.

Clements, Frank. *Kariba: The Struggle with the River God*. London: Methuen, 1959.

Cliggett, Lisa. *Grains from Grass: Aging, Gender, and Famine in Rural Africa*. Ithaca: Cornell University Press, 2005.

Colson, Elizabeth. *The Plateau Tonga of Northern Rhodesia: Social and Religious Studies*. Manchester: Manchester University Press, 1962.

_____. "Converts and Tradition: The Impact of Christianity on Valley Tonga Religion." *Southwestern Journal of Anthropology* 26, no.2 (Summer, 1970): 143-156.

_____. "Rain Shrines of the Plateau Tonga of Northern Rhodesia." *Africa: Journal of the International African Institute* 18, no.4 (Oct., 1948): 272-283.

_____. "The Father as Witch." *Africa: Journal of the International African Institute* 70, no.3 (2000): 333-358.

_____. *Social Organization of the Gwembe Tonga*. Manchester: Manchester University Press, 1960.
_____. *The Social Consequences of Resettlement: The Impact of the Kariba Resettlement upon the Gwembe Tonga*. Manchester: Manchester University Press, 1971.
_____. *Tonga Religious Life in the Twentieth Century*. Lusaka: Bookworld Publishers, 2006.
_____. "A Continuing Dialogue, Prophets and Local Shrines among the Tonga of Zambia." In *Regional Cults*, ed. Werbner, Richard P., 119-137. London: Academic Press, 1977.
Colson, Elizabeth and Scudder Thayer. *For Prayer and Profit*. Stanford: Stanford University Press, 1988.
Colson, Elizabeth and Max Gluckman, eds. *Seven Tribes of British Central Africa*. Manchester: Manchester University Press, 1959.
Comaroff, Jean. *Body of Power, Spirit of Resistance: The Culture and History of a South African People*. Chicago: University of Chicago Press, 1985.
Comaroff, Jean and John Comaroff. "Christianity and Colonialism in South Africa." *American Ethnologist* 13, no.1 (Feb., 1986): 1-22.
_____. *Of Revelation and Revolution: Christianity, Colonialism and Consciousness in Southern Africa*, vol. 1. Chicago: Chicago University Press, 1997.
Cooper, John M. "The Relations between Religion and Morality in Primitive Culture." *Primitive Man* 4, no.3 (July, 1931): 33-48.
Dafni, Amots. "Why are Rags Tied to the Sacred Trees of the Holy Land?" *Economic Botany* 56, no.4 (Winter, 2002): 315-327.
Daly, Mary. *Beyond God the Father*. Boston: Beacon Press, 1985.
Daneel, Marthinus L. *African Earthkeepers: Wholistic Interfaith Mission*. Maryknoll: Orbis Books, 2001.
_____. *The God of the Matopo Hills: An Essay on the Mwari Cult in Rhodesia*. The Hague, Paris: Mouton, 1970.
_____. *African Initiated Churches in Southern Africa: Protest Movements or Mission Churches?* A.H. no.33. Boston: Boston University African Studies Center, 2000.
_____. *African Earthkeepers: Interfaith Mission in Earth Care*, vol. 1. Pretoria: UNISA Press, 1998.
_____. *African Earthkeepers: Environmental Mission and Liberation in Christian Perspective* Vol.2. Pretoria: UNISA Press, 2000.
Danquah, J.B. *Akan Doctrine of God*. London: Frank Cass, 1968.
Darkoh, M.B.K, and A. Rwomire, eds. *Human Impact on Environment and Sustainable Development in Africa*. Hampshire: Aldershot, 2003.
Darr, Richard S. *Protestant Missions and Earthkeeping in Southern Africa, 1817-2000*. Th.D. diss, Boston University, 2005.

Deneulin, Severine and Masooda Bano. *Religion in Development: Rewriting the Secular Script*. London: ZED Books, 2009.
Devall, Bill and George Sessions. *Deep Ecology*. Salt Lake City: G.M. Smith, 1985.
DeWitt, Calvin and Ghillean T. Prance, eds. *Missionary Earthkeeping*. Macon: Mercer University Press, 1992.
Dibua, Jeremiah. *Modernization and the Crisis of Development in Africa: The Nigerian Experience*. Burlington, VT: Ashgate, 2006.
Dickson, Kwesi and Paul Ellingworth, eds. *Biblical Revelation and African Beliefs*. London: Lutherworth Press, 1969.
Dickson, Kwesi. *Theology in Africa*. Maryknoll, New York: Orbis Books, 1984.
Driberg, J.H. "The Secular Aspect of Ancestor-Worship in Africa." *Journal of the Royal African Society* 35, no.138 (Jan., 1936): 1-21. http://www.jstor.org/stable/716389. Accessed 05/04/2009.
Duff, Alexander. *Missions as the Chief End of the Christian Church*. Edinburgh: John Johnstone, 1840.
Dyson, Tim. "Population Growth and Food Production: Recent Global and Regional Trends." *Population and Development Review* 20, no.2 (Jun., 1994): 397-411.
Dzingirai, V. "Stealing the Birthright, Migration Dynamics in the Zambezi Valley of Zimbabwe." *Institute of Natural Resources*, University of Natal, 2003.
Earth Charter Initiative. *The Earth Charter*. http://www.earthcharterinaction.org/content/pages/The-Earth-Charter.html. Accessed 06/06/09.
Earthy, E. Dora. "The VaNdau of Sofala." *Journal of the International African Institute* 4, no.2 (Apr., 1931): 222-230.
Effa, Allen. "The Greening of Mission." *International Bulletin of Missionary Research* 32, no.4 (2008): 171- 174.
Ela, Jean-Marc. *African Cry*. Translated from French by Robert R. Barr. Maryknoll, New York : Orbis Books, 1986.
_____. *My Faith as an African*. Translated from French by P. John Brown and Susan Perry. Maryknoll, New York: Orbis Books, 1988.
Energy, Environment and Development Programme. "Illegal-Logging Info." London: Chatham House. http://www.illegallogging.info/sub_approach.php?approach_id=15&subApproach_id=55. Accessed 07/13/2008.
Ezekwonna, Chukwuagozie Ferdinand. *African Communitarian Ethic: The Basis for the Moral Conscience and Autonomy of the Individual: Igbo Culture as a Case Study*. Bern, New York: Peter Lang, 2005.
Fagan, Brian. "Drought Follows the Plow." *The World and I* (April 1988): 208-213.
Fardon, Richard. *Between God, the Dead and the Wild: The Chamba Interpretation of Religion and Ritual*. Washington: Smithsonian Institution Press, 1990.

Ferguson, James. *Expectations of Modernity: Myths and Meanings of the Urban Life on the Zambian Copperbelt*. Berkeley & Los Angeles: University of California Press, 1999.

Fields, Karen E. *Revival and Rebellion in Colonial Central Africa*. Princeton, NJ: Princeton University Press, 1985.

Fletcher, Richard. *The Barbarian Conversion: From Paganism to Christianity*. New York: H. Holt and Co., 1998.

Fortes, Meyer. "The Authority of Ancestors." *Man, New Series* 16, no.2 (Jun., 1981): 300-302.

_____. "Pietas in Ancestor Worship." *The Henry Myers Lecture*, 1960. http://era.anthropology.ac.uk/Ancestors/fortes1.html. Accessed 02/06/2009.

Fox, Matthew. *Creation Spirituality: Liberating Gifts for the Peoples of the Earth*. San Francisco: HarperSanFrancisco, 1991.

_____. *The Coming of the Cosmic Christ: the Healing of Mother Earth and the Birth of a Global Renaissance*. San Francisco: Harper & Row, 1988.

_____. *Natural Grace: Dialogues on Creation, Darkness, and the Soul in Spirituality and Science*. New York: Image Books/Doubleday, 1997.

Francis, Saint. *The Little Flowers of St. Francis*. Translated by W. Heywood. London: Methuen and Co.1906.

_____. *The Writings of Saint Francis of Assisi*. Translated by Paschal Robinson. Philadelphia: The Dolphin Press, 1905.

Gardner, Gary. "The Challenge for Johannesburg: Creating a More Secure World." In *State of the World: A World Watch Institute Report on Progress Toward a Sustainable Society*, ed. Flavin Christopher, Hilary French and Gary Gardner, 3-23. New York: W. W. Norton and Company, 2002.

Gibbons, Major A.H. *Africa from South to North through Marotseland*, vol. 1. London: John Lane, 1904.

Gitau, Samson K. *The Environment Crisis: A Challenge for African Christianity*. Nairobi: Acton Publishers, 2000.

Glazier, Jack. "Mbeere Ancestors and the Domestication of Death." *Man, New Series* 19, no.1 (Mar., 1984): 133-147.

Go, Delfin S. and Page John., eds. *Africa at a Turning Point? Growth, AID, and External Shocks*. Washington DC: The World Bank, 2008.

Goergen, Donald. J. "The Quest for the Christ of Africa." *The Journal of the Faculty of Theology Catholic University of Eastern Africa* 17, no.1 (March 2001): 5-51.

Goldenberg, Naomi. *Changing of Gods: Feminism and the End of the Traditional Religions*. Boston: Beacon Press, 1979.

Gonzalez, Andrew and Chaneton Enrique J. "Heterotrophy Species Extinction, Abundance and Biomass Dynamics in an Experimentally Fragmented Microecosystem." *Journal of Animal Ecology* 71 (2002): 594-602.

Goodwin, Harvey. *Memoir of Bishop Mackenzie*. Cambridge: Bell & Co., 1864.
Gore, Al. *Earth in Balance: Ecology and the Human Spirit*. New York: Plume, 1993.
Gray, Richard. "Christianity, Colonialism, and Communications in Sub-Saharansub-Saharan Africa." *Journal of Black Studies* 13, no.1 (Sep., 1982): 59-72.
Graybill, Lyn S. "Pardon, Punishment and Amnesia: Three African Post-Conflict Methods." *Third World Quarterly* 25, no.6 (2004): 1117-1130.
Gregson, Simon, Zhuwau Tom, Anderson M.Roy and Chandiwana K. Stephen. "Apostles and Zionists: The Influence of Religion on Demographic Change in Rural Zimbabwe." *Population Studies* 53, no.2 (Jul., 1999): 179-193.
Grenz, Stanley J. *A Primer on Postmodernism*. Grand Rapids, Michigan: William B. Eerdmans Publishing Company, 1996.
Grottanelli, Vinigi L. "Gods and Morality in Nzema Polytheism." *Ethnology* 8, no.4 (Oct.,1969): 370-405.
Gumbo, Mufuranhunzi (Daneel, I. M). *The Guerrilla Snuff*. Harare: Baobab Books, 1995.
Gunther, John. *Inside Africa*. New York: Harper, 1953.
Habig, Marion A. ed. *St. Francis of Assisi: Writings and Early Biographies, English Omnibus of the Sources for the Life of St. Francis*. London: SPCK, 1973.
Hanciles, Jehu J. "New Wine in Old Wineskins, Critical Reflections on Writing and Teaching a Global Christian History." *Missiology: An International Review* XXXIV, no.3 (July 2006): 361-382.
Harden, Blaine. *Africa: Dispatches from a Fragile Continent*. New York: W.W. Norton & Co., 1990.
Hart, John. *The Spirit of the Earth: A Theology of the Land*. Ramsey, New Jersey: Paulist Press, 1984.
_____. *Sacramental Commons: Christian Ecological Ethics*. Lanham: Rowman and Little Publishers, 2006.
_____. *What Are They Saying about Environmental Theology*. New York: Paulist Press, 2004.
Hawken, Paul. *The Ecology of Commerce: A Declaration of Sustainability*. New York, New York: Harper Business, 1993.
Haynes, Jeffrey. *Religion and Development: Conflict or Cooperation*. Palgrave: Macmillan, 2007.
Heusch, Luc de. "Myths and Epic in Central Africa." In *Religion in Africa: Experience and Expression*, ed. Thomas D., Blakely, Walter van Beek and, Dennis L. Thomson, 229-238. London: James Currey, 1994.
Hinde, Robert A. "Law and the Sources of Morality." *Philosophical Transactions: Biological Sciences* 359, no.1451 (Nov. 29, 2004): 1685-1695.

Holden, John, Peacock James, and Williams, Trevor. *Genes, Crops and the Environment*. Cambridge: Cambridge University Press, 1993.
Hudson, John. *A Time to Mourn*. Lusaka: Bookworld Publishers, 1999.
Husted, Bryan W. and Instituto Tecnologico y de Estudios. "Wealth, Culture and Corruption." *Journal of International Business Studies* 30, no.2 (2$^{nd}$ Qtr., 1999): 339-359.
Idowu, Bolaji. *Olodumare: God in Yoruba Belief*. London: Longmans, 1963.
_____. *African Traditional Religion: A Definition*. London: SCM Press, 1973.
Iloanusi, Obiakoizu A. *Myths of the Creation of Man and the Origin of Death in Africa*. New York: Peter Lang, 1984.
Isichei, Elizabeth. *A History of Christianity*. Grand Rapids: William B. Eeerdmans Publishing, 1995.
Jahn, Janheinz. *Muntu: An Outline of the New African Culture*. Translated by Marjorie Grene. New York: Grove Press Inc. 1961.
Jean, Tim. *Livingstone*. New York: G.P. Putnam's Sons, 1973.
Jenkins, Phillip. *The Next Christendom: The Coming of Global Christianity*. Oxford: Oxford University Press, 2002.
Johnson, Elizabeth. "Heaven and Earth are Filled with Your Glory: Atheism and Ecological Spirituality." In *Finding God in all Things*, ed. Michael J. Himes and Stephen J. Pope, 84-101. New York: The Crossroad Publishing Company, 1996.
_____. "Losing and Finding Creation in Christian Tradition." In *Christianity and Ecology: Seeking the Well-Being of Earth and Humans*, ed. D. T. Hessel and R.R. Ruether, 3-22. Cambridge: Harvard University Press, 2000.
Kabasele, Francois. "Christ as Ancestor and Elder Brother," In *Faces of Jesus in Africa*, ed. Robert. J. Schreiter, 103-15. Maryknoll, New York: Orbis Book, 1998.
Kahl, Colin H. "Population Growth, Environmental Degradation, and State-Sponsored Violence: The Case of Kenya, 1991-93." *International Security* 23, no.2 (Autumn, 1998): 80-119.
Kaler, Amy. "The Moral Lens of Population Control: Condoms and Controversies in Southern Malawi." *Studies in Family Planning* 35, no.2 (Jun., 2004): 105-115.
Kalinga, Owen J.M. "Trade, the Kyungus, and the Emergence of the Ngonde Kingdom of Malawi." *International Journal of African Studies* 12, no.1 (1979): 17-39.
Kalipeni, Ezekiel. *Population Growth and Environmental Degradation in Southern Africa*. Boulder: Lynne Rienner Publishers, 1994.
Kalu, Ogbu U. "Religion and Social Control in Igboland." In *Religious Plurality in Africa: Essays in Honor of John Mbiti*, ed. Jacob K. Olupona and Sulayman Nyang S., 109-131. Berlin: Mouton de Gruyter, 1993.

Kaoma, John. "God, Humanity and Nature." *Listening: Journal of Religion and Culture* 35, no.3 (Fall, 2000): 222-238.

Kaoma, John Kapya. "Missio Dei or missio Creator Dei: Witnessing to Christ in the Face of the Occurring Ecological Crisis." In *Mission Today and Tomorrow*, ed. Kirsteen Kim, Andrew Anderson, 296-303. Oxford: Regnum Books, 2011.

_____. "The Fifth Mark of Mission: To Strive to Safeguard the Integrity of Creation and Sustain and Renew the Life of the Earth." In *Life-Widening Mission: Global Anglican Perspectives*, ed., Cathy Ross, 75-92. Oxford: Regnum Books, 2012.

_____. "Earthkeeping as a Dimension of Christian Mission: David Livingstone's attitude Toward Life: A Challenge to Earthkeeping Missions." In *Tracing Contours: Reflecting on World Mission and Christianity*, ed. Rodney L. Petersen and Marian Gh. Simion, 74-76. Newton Center: Boston Theological Institute, 2010.

_____. "Witnessing for Christ Today: Christian Mission Beyond Edinburgh 2010." In *2010 Boston: The Changing Contours of World Christianity*, ed., Todd M. Johnson and others, 267-272. Eugene: Pickwick Publication, 2012.

_____. *Ubuntu, Jesus, and Earth: Integrating African Religion and Christianity in Ecological Ethics*. Th.D Dissertation: Boston University, 2010.

Kenyatta, Jomo. *Facing Mount Kenya: The Tribal life of the Gikuyu*. London: Secker and Arburg, 1938.

Kibougi, Buana R. "Priesthood." In *Biblical Revelation and African Beliefs*, ed. Dickson Kwesi and Paul Ellingworth, 47-56. London: Lutterworth Press , 1969.

Kirkpatrick, Sale. *Dwellers on the Land: the Bioregional Vision*. Georgia: University of Georgia Press, 2000.

Kirwen, Michael C. *The Missionary and the Diviner: Contending Theologies of Christian and African Religions*. Maryknoll, New York: Orbis Books, 1987.

Koinange, Mbiyu. *Africa and the Future: Land Hunger in Kenya*. Nairobi: UDC Publication, 1952.

Kopytoff, Igor. "Ancestors as Elders in Africa." *Journal of the International African Institute* 41, no.2 (Apr., 1971): 129-142.

Korten, David. "The Great Turning: From Empire to Earth Community," *Yes! Magazine* (Summer 2006): 12-18.

_____. *When Corporations Rule the World*, San Francisco: Berrett-Koeher Publishers, 2001.

_____. "In Partnership with the Biosphere, Reframing the Debate on Limits." *Club of Rome Blog*. http://www.clubofrome.org/?p=2832. Accessed 4/5/2012.

Kudadjie, J.N. "Does Religion Determine Morality in African Societies? A View Point." In *Religion in a Pluralistic Society: Essays presented to Prof. C.G.*

Baeta, ed. Pobee, John S., 60-77. Leiden: E.J. Brill, 1976. Originally published in *The Ghana Bulletin of Theology* 4, no.5 (Dec 1973): 30-49.

Lagus, Charles. *Operation Noah*. London: William Kimberly and Co., 1959.

Lancaster, C.S. and Pohorilenko, A. "Ingombe Ilede and the Zimbabwe Culture." *The International Journal of African Historical Studies* 10, no.1 (1977): 1-30.

Lancaster, Chet S. "Ethnic Identity, History, and 'Tribe' in the Zambezi Valley." *American Ethnologist* 1, no.4 (Nov 1974): 707-730.

Lippmann, Walter. *A Preface to Morality*. New York: Macmillan, 1929.

Lipton, Michael. *New Strategies and Successful examples for Sustainable Development in the Third World, Testimony presented at a hearing on "Sustainable development and economic growth in the Third World" held by the Joint Economic Committee of the U.S. Congress, Subcommittee on Technology and National Security, June 20, 1989*. Washington, DC: International Food Policy Research Institute, no.170, 1989.

Livingstone, David and Charles Livingstone. *The Expedition to the Zambesi and Its Tributaries*. Reprinted. New York: Harper & Bros., 2001.

Lovin, Robin W. and Reynolds E. Frank. "Ethical Naturalism and Indigenous Cultures." *Journal of Religious Ethics* 20 (Fall 1992): 267-413.

MacAlphine, Alexr G. "Tonga Religious Belief and Customs." *Journal of the Royal African Society* 6, no.24 (Jul., 1907): 375-384.

Mackenzie, Rob. *David Livingstone: The truth Behind the Legend*. Chinhoyi: Fig Tree Publications, 1993.

Macrae, F.B. "Notes on Part of the Gwembe Valley in Northern Rhodesia." *The Geographical Journal* 91, no.5 (May, 1938): 446-449.

Madziyire, Salathiel K. "Heathen Practices in the Urban and Rural Parts of Marandellas Area and their Effects upon Christianity." In *Themes in the Christian History of Central Africa*, ed. T. O. Ranger and John Weller, 76-82. London: Richard Clay, 1975.

Magesa, Laurenti. *African Religion: The Moral Traditions of Abundant Life*. Maryknoll, New York: Orbis Books, 1997.

_____. "Christ the Liberator and Africa Today." In *Faces of Jesus in Africa*, ed. Robert J. Schreiter, 151-163. Maryknoll, New York: Obis Books, 2001.

Maguire, Daniel and Larry Rasmussen, eds. *Ethics for a Small Planet*. New York: State University of New York Press, 1998.

Makwasha, Gift. *The Repression, Resistance, and Revival of the Ancestor Cult in the Shona Churches of Zimbabwe: A Study in the Persistence of a Traditional Religious Belief*. Lewiston, N.Y: Edwin Mellen Press, 2010.

Mama, Amina. "Is it Ethical to Study Africa? Preliminary Thoughts on Scholarship and Freedom." *African Studies Review: The African Studies Association* 50, No.1 (April 2007): 1-26.

Margolis, Sarah Pasque. "Population Policy, Research and the Cairo Plan of Action: New Directions for the Sahel." *International Family Planning Perspective* 23, no.2 (June, 1997): 86-89.

Marshall, Katherine and Marisa Bronwyn Van Saanen. *Development and Faith: Where Mind, Heart, and Soul Work Together.* Washington, DC: The World Bank. 2007.

Mather, Charles. "Shrines and the Domestication of Landscape." *Journal of Anthropological Research* 59, no.1 (Spring, 2003): 23-45.

Mathus, Thomas R. *An Essay on the Principle of Population: A View of its Past and Present Effects on Human Happiness; with an Inquiry into Our Prospects, Respecting the Future Removal or Mitigation of the Evils which it Occasions.* [Book on Line] London: John Murray, 1826. http://www.econlib.org/library/Malthus/malPlong.html. Accessed 10/10/09.

Matthews, Tim. "Notes on the Precolonial History of the Tonga, with Emphasis on the Upper River Gwembe and Victoria Falls Area." In *The Tonga-Speaking Peoples of Zambia and Zimbabwe,* ed. Chet Lancaster and Kenneth P. Vickery, 13-33. New York: University Press of America, 2007.

Mazzucato, Valentina and David Niemeijer. "Population Growth and the Environment in Africa: Local Institutions, the Missing Link." *Economic Geography* 78, no.2 (Apr., 2002): 171-193.

Mbeki, Thabo. "Address of the President of South Africa, Thabo Mbeki, on the occasion of the Heritage Day celebrations, Taung, North West Province." http://www.info.gov.za/speeches/2005/05092612151004.htm. Accessed. 11/27/10.

_____. "The African Renaissance, South Africa and the World." 9 April 1998. http://www.unu.edu/unupress/mbeki. html. Accessed 11/27/08.

Mbiti, John S., ed. *African and Asian Contributions to Contemporary Theology.* Bossey: World Council of Churches, 1977.

Mbiti, John S. *African Religion and Philosophy.* London: Heinemann, 1969.

_____. *Concepts of God in Africa.* London: Praeger Publishers, 1970.

_____. *New Testament Eschatology in an African Background: A Study of the Encounter between New Testament Theology and African Traditional Concepts.* London: Oxford University Press, 1971.

McCann, James C. *Green Land, Brown Land, Black Land: An Environmental History of Africa 1800-1990.* Portsmouth: Heinemann Educational Books, 1999.

McCall, John C. "Rethinking Ancestors in Africa." *Africa: Journal of the International African Institute* 65, no.2 (1995): 256-270.

McFague, Sallie. *The Body of God: An Ecological Theology.* Minneapolis: Fortress Press, 1993.

_____. *Life Abundant: Rethinking Theology and Economy for a Planet in Peril.* Minneapolis: Fortress Press, 2000.

McQuillan, Kevin. "When Does Religion Influence Fertility?" *Population and Development Review* 30, no.1 (Mar., 2004): 25-56.
Mitchell, Robert C. *African Primal Religions*. Niles: Argus Communications, 1977.
Montinola, Gabriella R. and Robert Jackman W. "Sources of Corruption: A Cross-Country Study." *British Journal of Political Science* 32, no.1 (Jan., 2002): 147-170.
Moorman, John R.H. *St. Francis of Assisi*. London: SPCK, 1963.
Mpanya, Mutombo. "The Environmental Impacts of a Church Project." In *Missionary Earthkeeping*, ed. DeWitt, Calvin and Ghillean T. Prance, 91-109. Macon: Mercer University Press, 1992.
Mtisi, Shamiso, Mutuso Dhliwayo and Gilbert Makore. *Extractive Industries Policy and Legal Handbook: Case study of the Plight of Marange and Mutoko Mining Communities*. Harare: Zimbabwe Environmental Law Association, 2011.
Mugambi, J.N.K., and A. Nasimiyu-Wasike, eds. *Moral and Ethical Issues in African Christianity: Exploratory Essays in Moral Theology*. Nairobi: Acton Publishers, 1999.
Mugambi, J.N.K. "Christological Paradigms in African Christianity." In *Jesus in African Christianity: Experimentation and Diversity in African Christology*, ed. J.N.K Mugambi and Laurenti Magesa, 136-161. Nairobi: Initiatives Ltd., 1989.
Maake, N.P. "Multi-Cultural Relations in a Post-Apartheid South Africa." *African Affairs* 91, no.365 (Oct.,1992): 583-604.
Muzorewa, Gwinyai H. "Christ as Our Ancestor: Christology from an African Perspective." *Africa Theological Journal* 17, no.2 (1988): 255-64.
_____. *The Origins and Development of African Theology*. New York: Orbis Books, 1985.
Mnyandu, Michael. "Umuntu as the Basis of Authentic Humanity." In *Perspectives on Ubuntu: A Tribute to Fedsem*, ed. M.G Khabela and Z.C. Mzoneli. Alice: Lovedale Press, 1998. Also published as "Ubuntu as the Basis of Authentic Humanity: An African Perspective." *Journal of Constructive Theology* 3, no.1 (1997): 77-91.
Næss, Arne. "The Shallow and the Deep, Long Range Ecology Movement: A Summary." [Originally published in *Inquiry* 16). In *The Deep Ecology Movement: An Introductory Anthology*, ed. Alan Drengson and Yuichi Inoue, 3-9. Berkeley, CA: North Atlantic Books, 1995.
Nash, James. *Loving Nature: Ecological Integrity and Christian Responsibility*. Nashville: Abingdon Press, 1991.
Newman, Jay. "Two Theories of Civilization." *Philosophy* 54, no.210 (Oct.,1979): 473-483.
Nkemnkia, Nkafu Martin. *African Vitalogy: A Step Forward in African Thinking*. Nairobi: Paulines Publications, 1999.

Nkrumah, Kwame. *Ghana*. Edinburgh: T Nelson and Sons Ltd, 1959.
Northern Rhodesia. *Report of the Commission appointed to Inquire into the Circumstances leading up to and surrounding the recent Deaths and Injuries caused by the use of Firearms in the Gwembe District and Matters Relating Thereto*. Lusaka: Government Printers, 1958.
Northcott, Michael. *The Environment and Christian Ethics*. Cambridge: Cambridge University Press, 1996.
Ntarangwi, Mwenda, ed. *Jesus and Ubuntu: Exploring the Social Impact of Christianity in Africa*. New Jersey: Africa World Press, 2011.
Nyamiti, Charles. "The Church as Christ's Ancestral Mediation: An Essay on African Ecclesiology." In *The Church in African Christianity*, ed. J.N.K. Mugambi and Magesa L., 129-177. Nairobi: African Initiatives, 1990.
_____. *Christ as our Ancestor: Christology from an African Perspective*. Gweru: Mambo Press, 1984.
_____. *The Scope of African Theology*. Kampala: Gaba Publications, 1973.
Nyajeka, Tumani M. "Shona Women and the Mutupo Principle." In *Women Healing Earth: Third World Women on Ecology, Feminism, and Religion*, ed. Rosemary R. Ruether, 135-142. Maryknoll, New York: Orbis Books. 1996.
O'Brien, Dan and Carolyn, O'Brien. "Religious and Group Identity of the Tonga: An Examination of the Lwiindi Festival." In *The Tonga-Speaking People of Zambia and Zimbabwe*, ed. Lancaster Chet and Kenneth P. Vickerly, 63-81. New York: University Press of America, 2007.
_____. "The Monze Rain Festival: The History of Change in a Religious Cult in Zambia." *The International Journal of African Historical Studies* 29, no. 3 (1997): 519-541.
O'Brien, Dan. "Chief of Rain—Chief of Ruling: A Reinterpretation of Pre-Colonial Tonga (Zambia) social and Political Structure." *Africa: Journal of the International African Institute* 53, no.4 (1983): 23-42.
O'Neill, William R. "African Moral Theology." *Theological Studies* 62 (2001): 122-139.
Obiakoizu, Iloanusi A. *Myths of the Creation of Man and the Origin of Death in Africa*. New York: Peter Lang, 1984.
Oduyoye, Amba Mercy. *Beads and Strands, Reflections of an African Woman on Christianity in Africa*. Maryknoll, New York: Orbis, 2004.
_____. *Hearing and Knowing: Theological Reflections on Christianity in Africa*. Maryknoll, New York: Orbis Books, 1986.
Oelschlaeger, Max. *Caring for Creation: An Ecumenical Approach to the Environmental Crisis*. New Haven: Yale University Press, 1994.
Okafor, Stephen O. "Bantu Philosophy: Placide Tempels Revisited." *Journal of Religion in Africa* 13 (1982): 83-100.

Olupona, Jacob. "Comments on the Encyclopedia of Religion and Nature." *Journal of the American Academy of Religion* 77, no.1 (March, 2009): 60-65.

Olupona, Jacob K. and Sulayman Nyang S., eds. *Religious Plurality in Africa: Essays in Honor of John Mbiti*. Berlin: Mouton de Gruyter, 1993.

Onwubiko, Oliver A. *African Thought, Religion and Culture*. Enugu: SNAAP Press, 1991.

Oruka, Odera H., ed. *Philosophy, Humanity, and Ecology*. Nairobi, Kenya: ACTS Press, 1994.

Osoba, S. O. "Corruption in Nigeria: Historical Perspectives." *Review of African Political Economy* 23, no.69 (Sep., 1996): 371-386.

p'Bitek, Okot. *African Religions in Western Scholarship*. Kampala: East African Literature Bureau, 1970.

Parrinder, Geoffrey E. *Religion in Africa*. New York: Praeger Books, 1969.

Enslin, Penny and Kai Horsthemke. "Can Ubuntu provide a Model for Citizenship Education in African Democracies?," *Comparative Education* 40, no.4, Special Issue (Nov.2004): 545-558.

Pfleiderer, Otto. "Is Morality without Religion Possible and Desirable." *The Philosophical Review* 5, no.5 (Sept.): 449- 472.

Phillipson, W. and Brian M. Fagan. "The Date of the Ingombe Ilede Burials." *Journal of African History* (1969): 199-204.

Phiri, D.D. *Malawian to Remember John Chilembwe*. Lilongwe: Longman, 1976.

Plato. *The Last Days of Socrates*. Translated and with an introduction by Hugh Tredennick. Harmondsworth, Middlesex: Penguin Books, 1954.

Pobee, John S. *Toward an African Theology*. Nashville: Parthenon Press, 1979.

_____. *Skenosis: Christian Faith in an African Context*. Gweru: Mambo Press, 1992.

Poewe, Karla O. "Matriliny in the Throes of Change Kinship, Descent and Marriage in Luapula, Zambia." *Africa: Journal of the International African Institute* 48, no.3 (1978): 205-218.

Pope-Levison, Priscilla and John Levison R. *Jesus in the Global Contexts*. Louisville: Westminster/John Knox Press, 1992.

Porter, Andrew. "'Commerce and Christianity': The Rise and Fall of a Nineteenth-Century Missionary Slogan." *The Historical Journal* 28, no.3 (Sep., 1985): 597-621.

Rahnema, Majid and Victoria Bawtree, eds. *The Post-Development Reader*. London: Zed Books, 1997.

Ramitsindela, Maano. *Transfrontier Conservation in Africa: At the Confluence of Capital, Politics and Nature*. Oxfordshire: Cabi, 2007.

Ranger, Terence O. "Territorial Cults in the History of Central Africa." *The Journal of African History* 14, no.4 (1973): 581-597.

_____. *Voices from the Rocks: Nature, Culture and History in the Matopos Hills of Zimbabwe*. Indiana: Indiana University Press, 1999.
Ranger, Terence O. and John Weller, eds. *Themes in the Christian History of Central Africa*. London: Richard Clay, 1975.
Ranger, Terrance O. and I.N. Kimambo, eds. *Religious Symbols in East and Central Africa: Historical Study of African Religion*. Los Angeles: University of California Press, 1972.
Ransford, Oliver. *Livingstone's Lakes: The Dream of Nyasa*. London: John Murray, 1966.
Rasmussen, Larry. *Earth Community, Earth Ethics*. Maryknoll, New York: Orbis Books, 1996.
Reefe, Thomas Q. "Traditions of Genesis and the Luba Diaspora." *History in Africa* 4 (1977): 183-206.
Reid, George W. "Missionaries and West African Nationalism." *Phylon* 39, no.3 (3$^{rd}$ Qtr., 1978): 225-233.
Renner Michael. *The Anatomy of Resource Wars* (New York: World Watch Paper 162, October 2002.
Rhazaoui, Ahmed, Grégoire Luc-Joël, and Mellali Soraya, eds. *Africa and the Millennium Development Goals*. Paris: Economica, 2005.
Rist, Gilbert. *History of Development: From Western Origins to Global Faith*. Third Edition. London: ZED Books, 2002.
Robert, Dana L. *Christian Mission: How Christianity Became a World Religion*. Chichester, West Sussex: Wiley-Blackwell, 2009.
_____. "Historical Trends in Mission and Earth Care."*International Bulletin of Missionary Research* 35, no.3 (July 2011): 123-128.
Robertson, Govan William. "Kasembe and the Bemba (Awemba) Nation." *Journal of the Royal African Society* 3, no.10 (Jan., 1904): 183-193.
Rochelle, Gabriel C. "Aphophatic Preaching and the Postmodern Mind." *St. Vladimir's Theological Quarterly* 50, no.4 (2006): 397-419.
Rodney, Walter. *How Europe Underdeveloped Africa*. Washington D.C.: Howard University Press, 1982.
Roman Catholic Bishops of New Mexico. "NMCCB Statement on the Environment: Partnership for the Future." http://www.archdiocesesantafe.org/Environment.html. Accessed 10/01/2008.
Rosman, Abraham and Rubel, G. Paula. *The Tapestry of Culture: An introduction to Cultural Anthropology*. New York: Random House, 1985.
Rotberg, Robert I., ed. *"Strike a blow and Die:" A Narrative of Race Relations in Colonial Africa by George S. Mwase*. Cambridge: Harvard University Press, 1967.
_____. *Rebellion in Black Africa*. Oxford: Oxford University Press, 1971.

_____. *The Rise of Nationalism in Central Africa: The Making of Malawi and Zambia 1873-1964*. Cambridge: Harvard University Press, 1965.
Rouch, Catherine M. *Mother/Nature: Popular Culture and Environmental Ethics*. Bloomington: Indiana University Press, 2003.
Rowley, Henry. *The Story of the Universities' Mission to Central Africa: from its Commencement, under Bishop Mackenzie, To its Withdrawal from Zambesi*. Saunders: Otley and Co., 1867.
Ruether, Rosemary R., ed. *Women Healing the Earth*. New York: Orbis Books, 1996.
_____. *Gaia and God: An Ecofeminist Theology of Earth Healing*. New York: HarperCollins, 1992.
_____. *Introducing Redemption in Christian Feminism*. Sheffield: Sheffield Academic Press, 1998.
Sands, Kathleen M. *Escape from Paradise: Evil and Tragedy in Feminist Theology*. Minneapolis: Fortress Press, 1994.
Sachs, Wolfgang. *The Development Dictionary*. London: Zed Books, 1991.
Samkange, S. and T.M. Samkange. *Hunhuism or Ubuntuism: A Zimbabwe Indigenous Political Philosophy*. Salisbury: Graham Publishing, 1980.
Sanneh, Lamin. *Whose Religion is Christianity? The Gospel Beyond the West*. Grand Rapids: Eerdmans Publishing, 2003.
Santmire, Paul H. *Ritualizing Nature: Renewing Christian Liturgy in a Time of Crisis*. Minneapolis: Fortress Press, 2008.
_____. *The Travail of Nature: The Ambiguous Ecological Promise of Christian Theology*. Philadelphia: Fortress Press, 1985.
_____. *Nature Reborn: The Ecological and Cosmic Promise of Christian Theology*. Minneapolis: Asgusburg Press, 2000.
Schoffeeleers, Matthew J. and Wim van Binsbergen, eds. *Theoretical Exploration of African Religion*. London: KPI, 1985.
Schoffeeleers, Mathew J., ed. *Guardians of the Land: Essays on Central African Territorial Cults*. Gwelo: Mambo Press, 1978.
_____. "Folk Christology in Africa: The Dialectics of the Nganga Paradigm." *Journal of Religion in Africa* 19, no.2 (Jun., 1989): 157-183.
Schreiter, Robert J., ed. *Faces of Jesus in Africa*. Maryknoll, New York: Obis Books, 2001.
Schwarz, Hans. *Creation*. Grand Rapids: Eerdman Publishing House, 2002.
Schweitzer, Albert. "The Ethics of Reverence for Life."Originally published in Christendom 1, (1936): 225-39. http://www1.chapman.edu/scheitzer/sch/reading4/html. Accessed 07/16/08.
Scudder, Thayer. "The Human Ecology of Big Projects: River Basin Development and Resettlement." *Annual Review of Anthropology* 2 (1973): 45-55.

_____. *A History of Development in the Twentieth Century: the Zambian Portion of the Middle Zambezi Valley and the Lake Kariba Basin.* New York: Clark University, 1985.

_____. *The Ecology of the Gwembe Tonga.* Manchester: Manchester University Press, 1962.

_____. *The Future of Large Dams: Dealing with Social, Environmental, Institutional, and Political Costs.* London: Earthscan, 2005.

Sempebwa, Joshua W. *African Traditional Moral Norms and their Implications for Christianity.* Steyler: Verlag, 1983.

Setiloane, Gabriel M. *African Theology: An Introduction.* Johannesburg: Skotaville Publishers, 1986.

_____. *The Image of God among the Sotho-Tswana.* Rotterdam: A.A. Balkema, 1976.

Shoko, Tabona. *Karanga Indigenous Religion in Zimbabwe: Health and Wellbeing.* Surrey: Ashgate Publishing, 2007.

Shailer, Mathews. "The Religious Basis of Ethics." *Journal of Religion* 10, no.2 (April. 1930): 222-231.

Sheridan, Michael J. and Celia Nyamweru. *African Sacred Groves: Ecological Dynamics and Social Change.* Oxford: James Curry, 2008.

Shorter, Aylward. *Toward a Theology of Inculturation.* New York: Orbis Books, 1989.

Siamwiza, Bennett S. "Famine and Hunger in the History of the Gwembe Valley, Zambia, c. 1850-1958." In *The Tonga Speaking Peoples of Zambia and Zimbabwe,* ed. Lancaster, Chet and Kenneth P. Vickery, 237-261. New York: University Press of America, 2007.

Sider, Ronald J. *Rich Christians in an Age of Hunger.* Dallas: Word Publishing, 1990.

Sindima, Harvey J. *Religious and Political Ethics in Africa: A Moral Inquiry.* Westport: Greenwood Press, 1998.

Skinner, Curtis. "Population Myth and the Third World." *Social Policy* (Summer 1988): 57-62.

Smith, O.B. and S. Koala, "Desertification: Myths and Realities," in *Human Impact on Environment and Sustainable Development in Africa,* ed. Darkoh, M.B.K, and A. Rwomire, 183-198. Hampshire, Aldershot: Ashgate, 2003.

Smith, Susan. "Gospel and Culture." *Missiology: An International Review* XXXIV, no.3 (July 2006): 338-348.

Smith, Edwin W and Murray Andrew Dale. *The Ila-Speaking Peoples of Northern Rhodesia.* London: Macmillan, 1920.

Smith, Edwin W. "La Philosophie Bantoue." *Journal of the International African Institute* 16, no.3 (July., 1946): 199-203.

_____. *African Ideas of God: A Symposium.* London: Morrison and Gibbs, 1950.

Solly, Gillian. "Background to the Land Question [in Kenya]." Boston University African Studies Centre: Kenya Collections. Undated.
Speckman, McGlory T. "Beyond the Debate: An Agenda for Biblical Studies in the New South Africa." *Religion and Theology* 3, no.2 (1996): 135-51.
Stanley, Brian. "Commerce and Christianity: Providence Theory, the Missionary Movement, and the Imperialism of Free Trade, 1842-1860." *The Historical Journal* 26, no.1 (Mar., 1983): 71-94.
Stanley, Brian. *Christian Missions and the Enlightenment.* Surrey: Curzon Press, 2001.
Sundermeier, Theo. *The Individual and Community in African Traditional Religions.* Hamburg: LIT, 1998.
Sung, Jong You and Sanjeev Khagram. "A Comparative Study of Inequality and Corruption." *American Sociological Review* 70, no.1 (Feb., 2005): 136-157.
Szeftel, Morris. "Between Governance and Underdevelopment: Accumulation and Africa's Catastrophic Corruption." *Review of African Political Economy* 27, no.84 (Jun., 2002): 287-306.
Tempels, Placide. *Bantu Philosophy.* Translated by A. Rubbens. Paris: Presence Africaine, 1952.
The Episcopal Church. *Book of Common Prayer.* New York: Church Publishing Incorporated, 1979.
The World Bank. *Toward Environmentally Sustainable Development in Sub-Saharan Africa: A World Bank Agenda.* Washington D.C: World Bank, 1996.
The World Watch Institute. *The State of the World 2000.* New York: Norton Books, 2000.
Tevera, Daniel and Sam Moyo., eds. *Environmental Security in Southern Africa.* Harare: Sapes Books, 2000.
Theo, D.D. and H.N. Chabwela. "Environmental Conservation and Planning in Zambia." In *Environmental Policies and Politics in Eastern and Southern Africa,* ed. Salih Mohamed M.A, and Shibru Tedla, 162-180. New York: St. Martin's Press, 1999.
Thomson, Elisabeth. *Our Gods Never Helped Us Again: The Tonga People Describe Resettlement and its Aftermath.* Lusaka: Panos Southern Africa, 2005.
Timamy, Khalil M.H. "African Leaders and Corruption." *Review of African Political Economy* 32, no.104/105 (Jun.-Sep., 2005): 383-393.
Torrend, J. *Specimens of Bantu Folk-Lore from Northern Rhodesia.* London: Kegan Paul, Trench & Trubner, 1921.
Tutu, Desmond. *God Has a Dream: A Vision of Hope for Our Time.* New York: Doubleday, 2004.
_____. *No future Without Forgiveness.* New York: Doubleday, 1999.

Ukaegbu, Alfred O. "The Role of Traditional Marriage Habits in Population Growth: The Case of Rural Eastern Nigeria." *Journal of African International Institute* 46, no.4 (1976): 390-398.

United Nations. *Our Common Future: Report of the World Commission on Environment and Development.* http://www.un-documents.net/ocf-01.htm. Accessed 07/05/2008.

United Nations. *United Nations Convention Against Corruption.* http://www.unodc.org/unodc/en/treaties/CAC/signatories.html. Accessed 04/07/2009.

United Nations. *Global Environmental Outlook 5,* June 6, 2012. http://www.unep.org/geo/pdfs/geo5/RS_Africa_en.pdf. Accessed 06/06/2012.

Vail, Leroy. "Ecology and History: The Example of Eastern Zambia." *Journal of Southern African Studies* 3, no.2 (Apr., 1977): 129-155.

Walls, Andrew. "The Legacy of David Livingstone." *International Bulletin of Missionary* Research 11, no.3 (July,1987): 125-129.

_____. *The Cross-Cultural Process in Christian History: Studies in the Transmission and Appropriation of Faith.* Maryknoll, New York: Orbis Books, 2002.

Werbner, Richard P. "'Totemism' in History: The Ritual Passage of West African Strangers." *Man: New Series* 14, no.4 (Dec., 1979): 663-683.

White, Lynn, Jr. "The Historical Roots of Our Ecologic Crisis." *Science, New Series* 155, no.3767 (Mar. 10, 1967): 1203-1207.

White, Landeg. *Magomero, Portrait of an African Village.* Cambridge: Cambridge University Press, 1987.

Willoughby, W.C. *The Soul of the Bantu: A Sympathetic Study of the Magico-Religious Practices and Beliefs of the Bantu Tribes of Africa.* London: Student Christian Movement, 1928.

Wilson, Godfrey. "An African Morality." *Journal of the International Institute* 9, no.1 (Jan., 1936): 75-99.

Wolf, James B. "Commerce, Christianity, and the Creation of the Stevenson Road." *African Historical Studies* 4, no.2 (1971): 363-371.

Wolterstorff, Nicholas. "How Social Justice Got me and Why it never Left." *Journal of the American Academy of Religion* 76, no.3 (Sept. 2008): 664-679.

Wringley, Christopher. "The River-God and the Historians: Myth in the Shire Valley and Elsewhere." *The Journal of African History* 29, no.3 (1988): 367–383.

Wuthnow, Robert. *Boundless Faith: The Global Outreach of American Churches.* Berkeley: University of California Press, 2009.

Zahan, Dominique. *The Religion, Spirituality, and Thought of Traditional Africa.* Translated by Kate Ezra Martin and Lawrence M. Martin. Chicago: The University of Chicago Press, 1970.

# Index

Abundant life 7n, 22, 26, 47, 59, 63n, 65f, 90, 95, 130f, 175, 181, 203

African Christianity 19n, 25, 28, 171, 205

African cosmologies 1, 19, 29, 52, 63, 67f, 70, 79, 81, 156, 207

African morality 7, 22, 62f, 83, 87f, 88n, 89, 92ff, 113f, 119, 130, 147, 188

African worldviews xii, 1, 7, 9, 20, 50, 65, 70, 87, 92, 102, 192, 205

Animals, xiii 4, 8, 10, 14, 25, 29, 36, 43, 53, 58f, 62, 66f, 70, 72, 75, 97ff, 101f, 120, 131, 175, 194, 199f

Bankrupt 5f, 109

Basangu, 4, 21f, 36f, 40, 42, 44f, 47, 50, 56, 178, 202

Biodiversity 100, 148n, 163n, 165, 169, 192

Biota 9, 14, 22, 28, 102, 170f, 176, 180ff, 184, 186fff, 203, 205

Chewa 54, 72

Christ 13f, 16, 18f, 26, 28, 100, 173fff, 179fffff, 188, 192f, 206

Churches, 6, 24n, 61, 64n, 94, 111, 137

Civilization 2, 5, 60, 62, 80n, 92f, 119, 121, 150, 195fff, 202, 204

Colonialism 21, 27, 36f, 40, 55, 62, 94,

Affiliation 75, 116

African Earthkeepers 10, 19, 25, 58n, 202, 208

African traditional religion 7n, 11, 27, 51n, 73n, 93, 127, 139, 199ff,

African Union xi, 116f, 119,

Ancestors 1, 3, 4, 8ffff, 19ffff, 29ffff, 140, 170

Ancestral spirits 50, 140f

Bantu 8f, 18, 31, 37, 49, 52, 63fff, 69f, 73ff, 91, 96ff, 101f, 104, 106, 108f, 195, 207

Bemba 64, 69, 74f, 79, 82f, 96, 101f, 108, 13f

Biosphere 120, 144, 162, 166n, 168

Capitalism 3, 12, 113, 146, 169

Children of 66, 179f, 204

Christology 14, 16, 18, 26, 28, 54, 171, 172n, 173fff, 181, 189

Akan 85ffff, 173

Climate change xi, 1, 28n, 29, 124, 125, 128, 152, 165, 169

Colonization 2, 60, 62

226

110, 116, 153, 157
Commerce 2f, 60, 92, 94f, 119, 151, 163n, 204
Conflicts 126, 147, 206

Consciousness 8, 13, 29, 70, 76, 79, 109, 171, 185, 188, 197, 203, 206
Contextualization 16, 175, 203

Cosmic 6n, 100, 101, 189

Cosmology 17, 21, 37f, 48, 52, 55, 93, 109, 185, 200, 207
Cosmovision 131, 136
Creator 9ff, 16, 62, 65, 67, 98, 101, 130n, 181, 183, 188ffff, 199ff
Deforestation 1, 31, 58, 100, 103, 126, 131, 148, 150, 170, 193f, 205
Demographic growth 12, 121, 124, 136, 142, 146, 201
Devastation 6, 204
Domination 27, 130, 182

Duty 53, 65, 68f, 79, 115, 183, 185, 188, 194
Earth priest 20f, 36, 40, 57f

Ecological integrity 6n, 118, 171, 201

Economic development 23, 126, 128, 134, 136, 142, 152, 163, 167, 201
 Economic theory 3, 160

Ecosphere 31, 54, 74, 108, 157, 168,

Communalism 112

Consumption 24, 75, 103, 126ff, 147,166, 168, 171, 183, 203
Conservation 3n, 6, 57, 59, 119, 123

Corruption 23ff, 70, 80n, 103, 111f, 114ff, 125, 133, 146, 153, 165, 183f, 200
Cosmologies 1, 5, 9n, 19, 29, 52, 63, 67f, 70, 79, 81, 156ff, 175ff, 196
Cosmos 73, 87, 104, 107, 130, 169, 174, 181, 186, 191, 199, 201
Covenant 14, 16, 76, 176f, 188

Customs 7, 38, 45n, 57, 61, 64, 78f, 87fff, 95, 103
Deity 17, 38, 49n, 88

Desertification 126, 131, 148f, 151, 169
Diviners 38, 82, 88, 99, 199
Drought 18, 22, 37, 40, 56, 93, 122, 148ff, 152, 194, 205
Earth charter 120f, 127

Ecological ancestor 12f, 26, 28, 70, 173, 176f,180ff, 189ff, 193f, 206
Ecological wellbeing 22, 26, 29, 44, 118, 162f, 169
Economic growth 23f, 151, 161ff, 165ff

Eco-social 55, 63, 103ff, 110f, 117, 125, 159, 163. 171, 175, 177, 199
Ecosystems 13, 24, 102, 108, 125, 144,

186, 197, 207
Egalitarianism 9, 14, 186f

Enlightenment 3, 60, 83, 92, 94, 191

Erosion 23, 126, 147ff, 155
Eschatology 78n, 79, 140, 176, 184

Ethnic 33n, 34, 126

Family 15, 20f, 30, 38, 47, 51, 72, 105ff, 113, 116, 120, 126, 130, 133f, 136f, 139, 141, 143, 158, 170, 176, 181, 202f
Fertility 15, 21, 35, 54, 93, 132, 136fff, 142f
Generations 4, 12, 17, 23f, 53, 54n, 70, 80f, 82, 110, 120, 123, 135, 140, 143, 154ff, 159, 161ffff, 178, 185, 192, 196fff, 203
Global North 24, 126f, 146f, 165f, 172, 183f, 196
Global warming, 128n, 131

Government 2, 23, 27, 60f, 109, 115, 118, 136f, 142, 148,150f, 159ff, 163, 167, 169f,
Gwembe 4n, 12, 15n, 18,20fffff, 33f, 34n, 55n, 66, 94, 121f, 151, 154f
Harmony 8f, 22, 62f, 72, 84, 86, 89, 106, 111, 127, 164, 176, 184, 198, 200, 205
High gods 81, 141, 169, 173

168ff
Elders 23, 29f, 41f, 44, 47f, 52, 54, 64, 93, 113, 133, 199, 205
Environment 3, 5f, 18, 19n, 28f, 56, 67, 108n, 111, 114, 117, 119, 122, 125, 135, 146, 148, 151, 157, 160, 205, 207
Europeans 39, 55, 92, 156f, 181, 202
Extinction 99f, 120, 124, 126, 132, 140, 146, 191ff
Family planning 126, 130, 133f, 136f, 139, 141f
Firstborn of 12, 173, 181

Gaia 15, 124n, 133n

Global 11, 13, 24, 29f, 103, 105f, 112, 114, 120, 122, 126, 133, 154, 165ff, 170, 175, 201, 203

Global South 24, 48n, 126f, 146, 154, 172, 183

Governance 19, 23, 36, 103, 111f, 116f, 164,
Guardians 17, 18n, 21, 26, 32, 38, 52, 56, 63, 66, 70, 173f, 192, 205, 207

Habitat 4, 31, 122, 192, 194, 201

Heritage 1, 10f, 13, 25, 95, 116, 152, 195, 198, 201, 204f

Homophobia 112

Idolatry 13, 187, 201
Imperialism, 60n, 159
Indigenous 88n, 102, 107n, 113, 125, 153, 160, 166, 170, 173
Integration 193

Islam 114, 130, 139

Kariba dam 3, 20, 22f, 32, 39f, 121, 157, 167, 202
Landscape 5, 57, 148

Limitless 159, 161, 166f, 195

Lozi 39, 54n, 72, 73n
Lwiindi 12, 20f, 28, 32f, 36ffff, 45ff, 50, 52ffff, 64, 93, 155, 174, 194, 202, 205
Malende 18, 22, 33, 37fff, 46, 56ff, 70, 180
Migration 126, 134n, 148, 153, 157, 205
Missionaries 6f, 51n, 60ff, 91f, 95, 195, 199


Morality 7, 22f, 32, 52, 60ffffff, 83fffff, 113, 199, 130, 147, 188
Motherland 25 152f
Mutupo 19, 73f, 189
Native Americans 13, 154n



Natural resources 2, 119, 135, 146,

IMF 159
Incarnation 16, 174, 179
Industrialization 124, 152

Interdependence 16, 72, 88, 105, 109, 113, 172, 186

Justice 6, 14, 63, 70, 90, 103, 110, 115, 120, 157, 190ff

Lands 5, 23, 27, 32, 131, 135, 147f, 154, 156, 158ff, 170, 176
Liberation 16, 19, 25n, 27, 68n, 184, 204, 205, 208
Living dead 7, 11, 54, 64, 70, 79, 91, 141, 154, 174, 178, 180
Lusitu 18n, 32, 40, 58, 122, 151
Malawi 34, 45, 72, 135


Malthusian 123, 125


Mission 2, 6, 7n, 10n, 60, 92, 93, 195

Moral 10, 23, 32, 37, 45f, 50, 53, 57, 60, 62fff, 83ffffffffffff, 109f, 119, 121, 141, 154, 162f, 167, 169ff, 185, 185, 187, 191ff, 194, 199, 203
Mother 15, 46, 51, 69, 71, 75, 123, 127, 156, 183f, 198, 200
Mukowa 73ff, 89, 190
Myths 7, 64, 71f, 73n, 75, 78, 89
Natural goods 2, 10, 23fff, 56, 66, 95, 110, 117ff, 124ff, 135, 144, 164ff153ff, 165f, 168, 179, 184, 192f, 205
Norms 46, 54, 62, 64, 69, 79, 83, 86,

229

160, 165
Ntu 96fffff, 108
Nyami-Nyami 5, 35, 38f, 202

Operation Noah 4, 22

Overpopulation 22, 58, 122ff, 134, 147, 184, 194f, 205f
Planet 1, 3, 7, 15, 108, 123f, 148, 159, 165, 167, 195, 201

Pollution 1, 103, 110, 124, 150f, 200
Population 23, 25, 36, 58, 70, 118, 140, 150, 156f, 167, 169f, 187, 192f

Population growth 1, 23, 70, 119, 121fff, 127, 130fffffff, 141f, 144, 150, 155f, 205,
Post-independence 18, 27, 110, 154, 195f, 201

Procreation 23, 69, 127, 130, 140, 142

Progress 60, 78, 80, 91f, 121, 136, 162, 195
Resettlement 4n, 18, 20, 35, 39, 40, 56, 121f, 151, 159, 202
Responsibility 1, 4, 12, 24, 57, 60, 70, 79, 107, 110, 113n, 120, 127, 150, 152, 162, 164f, 191f, 195fff
Rituals 7, 20f, 28, 35, 39, 50, 61f, 64, 73n, 78, 93, 190, 199, 202
Sacred groves 18, 20, 22, 39, 57f, 70,

92, 138f, 142

Ontology 22,31, 50, 52, 62, 66ff, 109, 133, 141
Origin 9, 12, 21, 26f, 33f, 40, 36, 50, 66f, 72, 85f, 89f, 94, 97, 103, 106, 130, 167, 174, 178, 178, 186, 188ff,193, 196, 200ff, 206
Philosophy 8f, 17, 66, 71, 96fff, 105, 108, 111, 113, 207
Policies 3, 10, 29, 110, 126, 128, 133, 135f, 139, 141, 144, 152f, 158, 160f, 164, 171, 195, 201
Political life 19, 115
Poor 3, 6, 19, 23f, 31, 57, 105, 109ff, 116f, 128, 130, 134f, 145ff, 157, 161, 168f, 194, 200, 202
Post-colonial 5, 114, 144, 158, 185

Poverty 12, 58f, 70, 105, 110, 122, 126f, 129fff, 147, 151, 160, 166, 168, 171, 184f, 190, 205f
Production 121, 122f, 132ffff, 151, 168, 170, 205
Relational 8, 13, 203

Replenishing 25, 192ff

Rights 10, 22, 66, 68, 70, 76, 80, 103, 107, 114, 120f, 136, 139, 185, 190ffff

Sacramental Commons 11, 13, 26f, 196, 203
Sacred places 7, 70, 180

195, 199f, 204
Sanctions 53, 58, 87, 88, 90f, 131, 195, 199, 206
Settlers 27, 91f, 122, 157
Shona 19, 21, 32ff, 40, 54, 70, 74f, 96, 108, 113
Snakes 10, 58f, 75, 98f, 191, 198, 200
Soils 35, 120, 122, 148, 160
South Africa 29, 103ff, 112, 114, 126n, 150
Species 14, 25, 29, 74, 99f, 107, 110, 120, 125, 126, 131, 147, 167, 169, 187ff, 190f, 205
Supernatural 10, 86, 89

Sustainable development 23f, 119, 131, 132n, 134n, 145, 147n, 159n, 163ffffff
Symbol 15, 61, 64, 66, 73, 75, 159, 198
Theologizing 17, 27, 174

Time 3, 13, 16, 21, 28f, 33, 40, 42, 52, 57f, 72, 76ffffffffff, 91, 93, 97

Totems 7, 73ff, 190, 192, 199, 204
Traditional religions 11, 27, 73n, 93, 100, 127, 130, 185 199, 201
United Nations 29, 114f, 121, 149

Value 2, 8, 10f, 17, 22, 62, 69, 73, 75,

Sasa 43n, 46n, 58n, 77f, 81f, 134

Sexuality 139, 143
Shrine 42, 45, 56f, 180f

Socio-economic 19, 23, 26, 40, 108, 115, 132, 156
Solidarity 67, 86, 89f, 113, 171
Southern Africa 3, 18n, 30, 94, 109, 111, 150
Sub-Saharan Africa 24, 61, 109, 112, 125, 136, 137n, 139, 161, 166

Supreme Being 8, 18, 23, 26, 37, 64, 66, 71f, 76, 82, 86, 102, 106, 140, 173, 194, 199f, 202, 207
Sustainable living 24, 166, 169ff


Territorial cults 18, 32n
Theology 6n, 11, 13f, 15n, 16f, 19, 27, 53, 68, 70f, 88, 104, 108, 172f, 176, 183, 192, 203, 207
Tonga 4f, 12, 18, 20ff, 29, 32ffffffff, 42fffff, 54fffff, 66, 74, 82,153ff, 196, 202
Traditional beliefs 1, 15, 92f, 132
Traditional rituals 7, 28, 39, 190

Universe 1, 9n, 10, 16, 20, 22, 26f, 47, 52, 62, 68, 71, 73f, 87, 89, 97f, 101f, 106f, 113, 120, 126, 130, 198, 200, 202ff
Vital force 8f, 37, 63, 67, 69, 71, 97,

95, 97f, 108, 112, 139, 144, 155, 157, 164, 175, 185, 188, 190, 193, 197f, 203

World Bank 24, 26n, 117, 129, 131n, 135, 160, 165

Zambia 20f, 32, 34, 40, 58, 75, 99, 115, 121, 130, 137, 147, 158, 166

106, 143, 187ff, 200, 206

Zamani 77ffffff, 134

Zimbabwe 10, 18n, 20f, 25, 34, 40, 58f, 70, 80, 110, 113, 115, 117, 154, 159, 166, 208

# Index of Names

Addai, Isaac. 133, 209
Appiah-Kubi, Kofi. 16n, 209
Bartley III., W.W. 85, 209
Baur, John. 16, 209
Benedict XVI, Pope. 14, 209
Bonk, Jonathan. 195, 196n, 210
Binka, Fred,. 133, 209
Bookchin, Murray. 145, 207
Böserup, Ester .123ff, 151,210
Brown, Lester R. 122, 210
Bujo, Bénézet. 65n, 173, 210
Caldwell, Pat. 137n, 141, 211
Christ, Carol P. 14, 15n, 211
Cincotta, Richard P. 193n, 211
Clements, Frank. 5, 38, 40n, 211
Colson, Elizabeth. 4, 17, 5n, 20f, 32f, 37n, 43n, 46n, 55ff, 74, 212
Daneel, Marthinus L. 6, 10n, 58, 64n, 198, 201, 212
Darkoh, M. B. K. 132n, 147n, 159, 213
Deneulin, Severine. 3n, 127n, 152, 212
Dibua, Jeremiah. 149n, 152, 213.
Driberg, J. H. 48, 51, 213
Dzingirai, V. 153, 213

Adongo, Philip B. 134n, 209
Aquinas, Thomas. 99
Battle, Michael. 104, 209
Bediako, Kwame. 18ff, 209
Berkes, Frikret. 102n, 108n, 210
Boff, Leonardo. 19, 25, 68, 130, 166
Bongmba, Elias K. 95, 96n, 112n, 207
Booth, Newell Jr. S. 76n, 82, 207
Brown, Lee M. 46, 122, 210
Brown, Raymond. 179, 210
Caldwell, John C. 137n, 141n, 211
Chenje, Munyarazi. 148n, 211
Christiansen I.S.J, Drew. 182n, 211
Clausen, A. W. 131n, 132n, 135f, 211
Cliggett, Lisa. 5, 38, 211
Comaroff, Jean. 61, 212
Danquah, J. B. 89,212
David Niemeijer. 124, 216
DeWitt, Calvin 6n, 93n, 210, 217
Dickson, Kwesi. 17, 213,
Dyson, Tim. 122, 123n, 210
Earthy, Dora E. 75n, 213

232

Elizondo, Virgil. 110, 207
Ellingworth, Paul. 17n, 217
Enslin, Penny. 112, 219
Fagan, Brian. 94n, 152, 215, 222
Fox, Matthew. 5n, 214
Gardner, Gary. 193, 214
Ghillean, Prance T. 6n, 93n, 210, 220
Glazier, Jack. 214
Goergen, Donald. J. 18n, 175f
Gray, Richard. 212
Grégoire Luc-Joël, 163f
Gunther, John. 96, 215.
Habig, Marion A. 12, 188n, 215
Hart, John. 2n, 6, 8, 10n, 13, 26n, 120, 187, 215
Haynes, Jeffrey. 3n, 152, 215
Holden, John. 124, 125n, 216
Janheinz Jahn. 97, 216
Kabasele, Francois. 18, 217.
Kalu, Ogbu U. 62, 64, 73, 90, 191, 217
Kenyatta, Jomo. 50, 217
Kirwen, Michael C. 173, 217
Koinange, Mbiyu. 156n, 156ff, 217
Korten, David. 1n, 149n, 166ff, 217
Lagus, Charles. 4, 196, 218
Levison, John R. 219
Lipton, Michael. 134n, 218

Lovin, Robin W. 88n, 92n, 215
MacAlphine, Alexr G. 45, 218
Macrae, F. B. 33f, 218
Maguire, Daniel. 53, 218
Mather, Charles. 219
Makwasha, Gift. 59, 94, 218
Margolis, Sarah Pasque. 141, 219
Marshall, Katherine. 26n, 219
Matthews, Tim. 34n, 37, 219
Mazzucato, Valentina 124, 219

Mbiti, John S. 1, 7n, 8n, 17, 76, 214,

Parrinder, Geoffrey E  70, 73, 222
Engleman, Robert. 194, 211
Ezekwonna, Ferdinand C. 12n, 213
Fortes, Meyer. 48, 50, 214
Francis, Saint. 12, 197
Gibbons, Major A. H. 37f, 211
Gitau, Samson K. 19, 214
Go Delfin S. 160, 214
Goldenberg, Naomi. 15, 214
Grazer Walter. 182n, 208
Grenz, Stanley J. 83n, 212
Hanciles, Jehu J. 172, 215
Harden, Blaine. 116, 117n, 215
Hawken, Paul. 3, 163n, 215

Hinde, Robert A. 85, 216
Horsthemke, Kai. 112, 222
Idowu, Bolaji. 48n, 51, 86n, 88ff, 216
Kalipeni, Ezekiel. 121, 150n, 216
Kaoma, John Kapya. 7n, 73n, 217
Kibougi, Buana R. 214
Kofi, Annan. 115
Kopytoff, Igor. 49ff, 214
Kudadjie, J. N. 86, 87n, 90, 218
Lancaster, Chet S. 21n, 33, 34, 95n, 222
Lippmann, Walter. 84, 218
Livingstone, David, and Charles Livingstone. 7, 54, 60, 214f, 218
Maake, N. P. 112, 220
Mackenzie, Rob. 218
Magesa, Laurenti. 7, 19n, 63, 218
Makore, Gilbert. 159n, 220
Malthus, Thomas R. 123ff. 219
Mama, Amina. 64n, 219
Marisa, Bronwyn Van Saanen. 26n, 219
Masooda Bano. 3n, 127n, 153, 213
Max Gluckman. 48n, 212
Mbeki, Thabo. 96n, 112n, 113, 114n, 207

McCall, John C. 53n, 219

233

219
McCann, James C. 193n, 219
Mellali, Soraya. 163n, 164n, 220
Mnyandu, M. 98f, 220
Montinola, Gabriella R. 217
Mpanya, Mutombo. 6, 93, 217
Mugambi J.N.K. 220
Murray, Andrew Dale. 15n, 223
Muzorewa, Gwinyai H. 220
Nash, James. 6, 145, 153, 164, 186, 217n
Nkemnkia, Nkafu Martin. 69, 71, 218
Northcott, Michael. 193

Ntarangwi Mwenda. 111
Nyajeka, Tumani M. 19n, 74n,
Nyamweru, Celia. 57
O'Brien, Carolyn. 20n, 218
Obiakoizu, Iloanusi 213, 218

Oelschlaeger, Max. 221
Olupona, Jacob K. 7n, 62n, 102, 217, 222
p'Bitek, Okot. 92, 222
Peacock James. 125, 216
Pobee, John S. 16n, 17, 87n, 174, 217, 222
Pohorilenko, A. 95n, 218
Porter, Andrew. 2n, 118, 222
Rahnema, Majid 11n, 222
Ranger, Terrance O. 18, 223

Reefe, Thomas Q. 32n, 223
Rhazaoui, Ahmed, 16n ff, 223
Robert, Dana L. 223
Rochelle, Gabriel C. 51n, 83, 98n, 223
Rosman, Abraham. 223

McCullum, Hugh. 126n
McFague, Sallie. 2, 3n, 9, 14, 107, 155, 186,220
McQuillan, Kevin. 139, 220
Moorman, John R. H. 220
Mtisi, Shamiso. 158n, 220
Mugabe, Robert. 58, 117, 118
Mutuso, Dhliwayo. 158n, 217
Næss, Arne. 217
Nasimiyu-Wasike. A. 217

Nkrumah, Kwame. 155
Northern Rhodesia. 15n, 33n, 39n, 40, 46n, 74n, 208, 215, 218

Nyamiti, Charles. 10, 66, 173, 218
O'Brien, Dan. 20n, 37n, 40, 218
O'Neill, William R. 66, 218
Oduyoye, Amba Mercy. 16, 24, 25n, 221

Okafor, Stephen O. 9, 222.
Osoba, S. O. 116, 222

Page, John. 116, 161, 214
Pfleiderer, Otto. 83n, 222
Poewe, O. Karla. 74n, 222

Pope-Levison, Priscilla. 222
Quiggin, Pat. 141, 142n, 208
Ramitsindela, Maano. 3n, 220
Rasmussen, Larry. 53n, 144n, 167, 218, 223

Reid, George W. 61, 223
Rist, Gilbert. 11n, 163, 223
Robertson, Govan William. 32, 223
Rodney, Walter. 160, 223
Rotberg, Robert I. 224

Roach, Catherine M. 15n, 224
Rubel, Paula G. 223
Rwomire, A. 132n, 148, 160, 213, 225
Samkange, Marie Tommie. 107n, 113, 224
Sands, Kathleen M. 15n, 224
Sanneh, Lamin. 224
Schoffeleers, Mathew J. 17ff, 32, 173, 175, 224
Schwarz, Hans. 14, 224
Scudder, Thayer. 4ff, 17, 20n, 21, 212, 225
Sergio, Torres. 16n, 209
Shailer, Mathews. 87, 225
Shoko, Tabona. 225
Siamwiza, Bennett S 225
Sindima, Harvey J. 19n, 225
Smith, Edwin W. 8, 9n, 15, 94n, 226
Solly, Gillian 155, 156n, 226
Stanley, Brian. 60, 226
Sundermeier, Theo. 73, 226
Feiner, Susan F. 209
Tempels, Placide. 1, 8, 9n, 52, 63n, 226
Thabo, Mbeki. 96n, 112n, 113, 207, 216
Thomson, Elisabeth. 18n, 226
Tutu, Desmond. 104 fff, 205, 227
Walls, Andrew. 227
Werbner, Richard P. 209, 227
White, Lynn, Jr. 1, 2n, 227
Willoughby, W. C. 227
Wim van, Binsbergen. 112, 227
Wolterstorff, Nicholas. 24, 191, 227
Wuthnow, Robert. 24, 228

Rowley, Henry. 224
Ruether, R. Radford. 13, 15,19n, 74n, 124, 133, 224
Sachs, Wolfgang. 11n, 224
Samkange, Stanlake. 107n, 113, 224

Sanjeev, Khagram. 114, 115n, 226
Santmire, Paul H. 6, 14, 100ff, 224
Schreiter, Robert J. 18n, 174n, 216, 224

Schweitzer, Albert. 7, 186f, 199, 225
Sempebwa, Joshua W. 225

Setiloane, Gabriel M. 51, 98n, 172, 225
Sheridan, Michael J. 57, 225
Shorter, Aylward. 225
Sider, Ronald J. 196, 225
Skinner, Curtis. 146, 225
Smith, Susan. 174, 206, 225
Speckman, McGlory T. 226
Sulayman, Nyang S. 7n, 62n, 217
Sung, Jong You. 114, 115n, 116, 226
Szeftel, Morris. 114, 115n, 117n, 226
Tevera, Daniel. 226

Theo, D. D. 226

Timamy, Khalil M. H 223
Ukaegbu, Alfred O. 139, 141n, 227
Weller John.. 218, 223
White, Landeg. 227
Williams, Trevor. 125n, 216
Wilson, Godfrey. 87, 88n, 227
Wolf, James B. 227
Wrigley, Christopher. 72n, 227
Zahan, Dominique. 80, 82, 138n, 142, 143n, 228

www.ingramcontent.com/pod-product-compliance
Lightning Source LLC
Chambersburg PA
CBHW021941290426
44108CB00012B/927